W9-BSW-340

Ajax

Your visual blueprint™ for creating rich Internet applications

by Steven Holzner, Ph.D.

WILEY

Wiley Publishing, Inc.

Ajax: Your visual blueprint™ for creating rich Internet applications

Published by
Wiley Publishing, Inc.
111 River Street
Hoboken, NJ 07030-5774

Published simultaneously in Canada

Copyright © 2006 by Wiley Publishing, Inc., Indianapolis, Indiana

No part of this publication may be reproduced, stored in a retrieval system or transmitted in any form or by any means, electronic, mechanical, photocopying, recording, scanning or otherwise, except as permitted under Sections 107 or 108 of the 1976 United States Copyright Act, without either the prior written permission of the Publisher, or authorization through payment of the appropriate per-copy fee to the Copyright Clearance Center, 222 Rosewood Drive, Danvers, MA 01923, (978) 750-8400, fax (978) 646-8600. Requests to the Publisher for permission should be addressed to the Legal Department, Wiley Publishing, Inc., 10475 Crosspoint Blvd., Indianapolis, IN 46256, (317) 572-3447, fax (317) 572-4355, or online: www.wiley.com/go/permissions.

Library of Congress Control Number: 2006925875

ISBN-13: 978-0-470-04306-6

ISBN-10: 0-470-04306-7

Manufactured in the United States of America

10 9 8 7 6 5 4 3 2 1

1D/RR/QX/QW/IN

Trademark Acknowledgments

Wiley, the Wiley Publishing logo, Visual, the Visual logo, Simplified, Master VISUALLY, Teach Yourself VISUALLY, Visual Blueprint, Read Less - Learn More and related trade dress are trademarks or registered trademarks of John Wiley & Sons, Inc. and/or its affiliates. All other trademarks are the property of their respective owners. Wiley Publishing, Inc. is not associated with any product or vendor mentioned in this book.

LIMIT OF LIABILITY/DISCLAIMER OF WARRANTY: THE PUBLISHER AND THE AUTHOR MAKE NO REPRESENTATIONS OR WARRANTIES WITH RESPECT TO THE ACCURACY OR COMPLETENESS OF THE CONTENTS OF THIS WORK AND SPECIFICALLY DISCLAIM ALL WARRANTIES, INCLUDING WITHOUT LIMITATION WARRANTIES OF FITNESS FOR A PARTICULAR PURPOSE. NO WARRANTY MAY BE CREATED OR EXTENDED BY SALES OR PROMOTIONAL MATERIALS. THE ADVICE AND STRATEGIES CONTAINED HEREIN MAY NOT BE SUITABLE FOR EVERY SITUATION. THIS WORK IS SOLD WITH THE UNDERSTANDING THAT THE PUBLISHER IS NOT ENGAGED IN RENDERING LEGAL, ACCOUNTING, OR OTHER PROFESSIONAL SERVICES. IF PROFESSIONAL ASSISTANCE IS REQUIRED, THE SERVICES OF A COMPETENT PROFESSIONAL PERSON SHOULD BE SOUGHT. NEITHER THE PUBLISHER NOR THE AUTHOR SHALL BE LIABLE FOR DAMAGES ARISING HEREFROM. THE FACT THAT AN ORGANIZATION OR WEBSITE IS REFERRED TO IN THIS WORK AS A CITATION AND/OR A POTENTIAL SOURCE OF FURTHER INFORMATION DOES NOT MEAN THAT THE AUTHOR OR THE PUBLISHER ENDORSES THE INFORMATION THE ORGANIZATION OR WEBSITE MAY PROVIDE OR RECOMMENDATIONS IT MAY MAKE. FURTHER, READERS SHOULD BE AWARE THAT INTERNET WEBSITES LISTED IN THIS WORK MAY HAVE CHANGED OR DISAPPEARED BETWEEN WHEN THIS WORK WAS WRITTEN AND WHEN IT IS READ.

FOR PURPOSES OF ILLUSTRATING THE CONCEPTS AND TECHNIQUES DESCRIBED IN THIS BOOK, THE AUTHOR HAS CREATED VARIOUS NAMES, COMPANY NAMES, MAILING, E-MAIL AND INTERNET ADDRESSES, PHONE AND FAX NUMBERS AND SIMILAR INFORMATION, ALL OF WHICH ARE FICTITIOUS. ANY RESEMBLANCE OF THESE FICTITIOUS NAMES, ADDRESSES, PHONE AND FAX NUMBERS AND SIMILAR INFORMATION TO ANY ACTUAL PERSON, COMPANY AND/OR ORGANIZATION IS UNINTENTIONAL AND PURELY COINCIDENTAL.

Contact Us

For general information on our other products and services, please contact our Customer Care Department within the U.S. at 800-762-2974, outside the U.S. at 317-572-3993 or fax 317-572-4002.

For technical support, please visit www.wiley.com/techsupport.

Evidence suggests that Leonardo da Vinci may have had a hand in the design of this jewel set in France's Loire Valley. Begun in 1519 by Francis I, the Château de Chambord served as an opulent summer retreat for royalty until revolutionaries looted it in 1793, leaving it largely unfurnished to this day. Identifying characteristics of this 440-room estate include 365 fireplaces and the pièce de résistance — a unique double spiral staircase. More castles await your discovery in *Frommer's France*, available wherever books are sold or at www.frommers.com.

WILEY

Sales

Contact Wiley
at (800) 762-2974
or (317) 572-4002.

PRAISE FOR VISUAL BOOKS...

"This is absolutely the best computer-related book I have ever bought. Thank you so much for this fantastic text. Simply the best computer book series I have ever seen. I will look for, recommend, and purchase more of the same."

—David E. Prince (NeoNome.com)

"I have several of your Visual books and they are the best I have ever used."

—Stanley Clark (Crawfordville, FL)

"I just want to let you know that I really enjoy all your books. I'm a strong visual learner. You really know how to get people addicted to learning! I'm a very satisfied Visual customer. Keep up the excellent work!"

—Helen Lee (Calgary, Alberta, Canada)

"I have several books from the Visual series and have always found them to be valuable resources."

—Stephen P. Miller (Ballston Spa, NY)

"This book is PERFECT for me — it's highly visual and gets right to the point. What I like most about it is that each page presents a new task that you can try verbatim or, alternatively, take the ideas and build your own examples. Also, this book isn't bogged down with trying to 'tell all' – it gets right to the point. This is an EXCELLENT, EXCELLENT, EXCELLENT book and I look forward to purchasing other books in the series."

—Tom Dierickx (Malta, IL)

"I have quite a few of your Visual books and have been very pleased with all of them. I love the way the lessons are presented!"

—Mary Jane Newman (Yorba Linda, CA)

"I am an avid fan of your Visual books. If I need to learn anything, I just buy one of your books and learn the topic in no time. Wonders! I have even trained my friends to give me Visual books as gifts."

—Illona Bergstrom (Aventura, FL)

"I just had to let you and your company know how great I think your books are. I just purchased my third Visual book (my first two are dog-eared now!) and, once again, your product has surpassed my expectations. The expertise, thought, and effort that go into each book are obvious, and I sincerely appreciate your efforts."

—Tracey Moore (Memphis, TN)

"Compliments to the chef!! Your books are extraordinary! Or, simply put, extra-ordinary, meaning way above the rest! THANK YOU THANK YOU THANK YOU! I buy them for friends, family, and colleagues."

—Christine J. Manfrin (Castle Rock, CO)

"I write to extend my thanks and appreciation for your books. They are clear, easy to follow, and straight to the point. Keep up the good work! I bought several of your books and they are just right! No regrets! I will always buy your books because they are the best."

—Seward Kollie (Dakar, Senegal)

"I am an avid purchaser and reader of the Visual series, and they are the greatest computer books I've seen. Thank you very much for the hard work, effort, and dedication that you put into this series."

—Alex Diaz (Las Vegas, NV)

Credits

Project Editor
Jade L. Williams

Acquisitions Editor
Tom Heine

Product Development Supervisor
Courtney Allen

Copy Editor
Kim Heusel

Technical Editor
Vanessa L. Williams

Editorial Manager
Robyn Siesky

Business Manager
Amy Knies

Permissions Editor
Laura Moss

Manufacturing
Allan Conley
Linda Cook
Paul Gilchrist
Jennifer Guynn

Book Design
Kathryn Rickard

Production Coordinator
Adrienne Martinez

Layout
Jennifer Click
Melanee Prendergast
Heather Ryan
Amanda Spagnuolo

Screen Artist
Jill Proll

Quality Control
Leeann Harney
Brian H. Walls

Indexer
Anne Leach

**Vice President and Executive
Group Publisher**
Richard Swadley

Vice President and Publisher
Barry Pruett

Composition Director
Debbie Stailey

About the Author

Steven Holzner Ph.D. (Ithaca, New York) is the author of 100 technology books, including bestsellers such as *Ajax for Dummies* and *Inside JavaScript*. His books have been translated into 18 languages and have sold more than 2 million copies. He specializes in writing about online applications, and has authored popular books on the components of Ajax including JavaScript, XML, browser objects, and Web services. He teaches classes to programmers around the country on the central skill in Ajax, using XML online and in-depth. He has been a contributing editor to *PC Magazine*, and was on the faculty at Cornell University and MIT.

Author's Acknowledgments

The book you hold in your hands is the work of many people. I'd especially like to thank my project editor, Jade Williams, for keeping this book on track; my copy editor, Kim Heusel, for his precise editing; my technical editor, Vanessa Williams, for her keen eye and helpful comments; my acquisitions editor, Tom Heine, for his support throughout the writing of the book; and all the people in Wiley's Composition Services Department who helped with the production of this book.

TABLE OF CONTENTS

4 GETTING MORE AJAX POWER 92

5 CREATING AJAX APPLICATIONS 122

TABLE OF CONTENTS

TABLE OF CONTENTS

HOW TO USE THIS BOOK

Ajax: Your visual blueprint for creating rich Internet applications uses clear, descriptive examples to show you how to work with Ajax. If you are already familiar with Ajax, you can use this book as a quick reference for many Ajax-specific tasks.

Who Needs This Book

This book is for the computer user who wants to find out more about Ajax. It is also for more experienced computer programmers who want to expand their knowledge of the different features that Ajax has to offer. All the programming knowledge, from JavaScript on up, that you will need is already in this book.

Book Organization

Ajax: Your visual blueprint for creating rich Internet applications has 11 chapters.

Chapter 1, *"Getting into Ajax,"* gets you started with Ajax. Ajax can do many things, and this chapter provides an overview, from fetching data from the server behind the scenes to auto-completing text the user enters, this chapter gives you the Ajax story.

Chapter 2, *"Creating Ajax Using JavaScript,"* gives you the JavaScript foundation you are going to need throughout the book. If you are already familiar with JavaScript, you can feel free to skip this chapter and go on to the good stuff.

Chapter 3, *"Writing Ajax Code,"* Gives you your start writing Ajax in JavaScript. This chapter shows you the fundamentals of Ajax, and how to write Ajax applications. You are going to see how to fetch data from the server without causing a page refresh in the browser here.

Chapter 4, *"Getting More Ajax Power,"* Digs deeper into the Ajax story, showing how to use Ajax to create browser mouseovers, download and execute JavaScript from the server, connect to Google Suggest's Ajax interface, and more.

Chapter 5, *"Creating Ajax Applications,"* puts the separate Ajax skills together to build full, larger-scale Ajax applications — an Ajax-driven shopping cart application, and an Ajax-driven menu system. Both of these applications show how to work with Ajax in a substantial program.

Chapter 6, *"Exploring the Basic Ajax Frameworks,"* examines the basic Ajax frameworks available. These frameworks exist to let you avoid writing Ajax code yourself, and the basic Ajax frameworks are all written in JavaScript, to be used in the browser.

Chapter 7, *"Using More Powerful Ajax Frameworks,"* looks at the more powerful Ajax frameworks available. These Ajax frameworks are all more heavy-duty than the ones you will find in Chapter 6.

Chapter 8, *"Handling Server-Side Ajax Frameworks,"* is a guided tour of the Ajax frameworks you install on the server, rather than in the browser. Most of these Ajax frameworks use PHP on the server, and they will write the JavaScript you need to execute in the browser for you.

Chapter 9, *"Handling XML in Ajax,"* is all about working with XML in JavaScript. Ajax relies on using XML, and it is used in Ajax applications throughout the book. This chapter gives you the full story on using XML with JavaScript.

Chapter 10, *"Using CSS with Ajax,"* is all about using Cascading Style Sheets, CSS, with Ajax. Ajax applications frequently use CSS — enabling the user to drag items in the Web page, displaying items in various colors, creating drop-down menus, and more.

Chapter 11, *"Supporting Ajax on the Server with PHP,"* is a PHP primer. You use Ajax with a Web server, and most frequently, that means using server-side programming. PHP is probably the most common choice for server-side scripting in Ajax programs, and this chapter gives you the skills you will need to use PHP and Ajax.

What You Need to Use This Book

You are going to need a Web browser that can run JavaScript, and access to a Web server to use this book profitably. For the best results, you are going to have to be able to run server-side scripts to get the most out of this book. This book uses PHP on the server, and gives you a working knowledge of PHP as well.

The Conventions in This Book

A number of styles have been used throughout *Ajax: Your visual blueprint for creating rich Internet applications* to designate different types of information.

Courier Font

Indicates the use of Ajax code such as tags or attributes, scripting language code such as statements, operators, or functions, and code such as objects, methods, or properties.

Bold

Indicates information that you must type.

Italics

Indicates a new term.

Apply It

An Apply It section takes the code from the preceding task one-step further. Apply It sections allow you to take full advantage of Ajax code.

Extra

An Extra section provides additional information about the preceding task. Extra sections contain the inside information to make working with Ajax easier and more efficient.

What's on the Web Site

The Web site accompanying this book contains the sample files for the book that you can use to work with *Ajax: Your visual blueprint for creating rich Internet applications*. You can access the Web site at www.wiley.com/go/ajaxvisualblueprint.

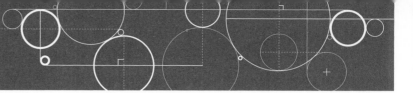

Get into Ajax

Everyone agrees that the World Wide Web is taking off. Everywhere you look, the talk is all about going online. Even cell phones are online these days. The online revolution is here, and it is permanent. No matter what ultimate shape it takes, the Web is going to be around a long, long time. People are addicted to it — online browsing, shopping, gaming — you name it, it is on the Web.

The online revolution has been a long time in the making, and many people were not convinced that it was going to last, but there is no doubt today. Many millions of users are online at any given time, and the online community is international in scope and size. With that many potential users just waiting to work with your Web site, you naturally want to give them the best experience possible. It turns out that in some areas, Web browsing leaves a lot to be desired.

Whenever you want to perform some action in a browser, such as update a table or select a new color, you must send the entire page back to the server online to which your browser is connected, and then the server sends the page back. That means that the page in front of you blinks, the figures and text in it move around as the page is rebuilt while you watch, and then the new results are presented.

Downloads Take Time

Not only does it take time to download an entire page from the Web server each time you click a button or perform some action in the page, it is also annoying. The whole display flickers and your location in the page resets back to the top. You must scroll back to where you were working with the page and find what you were doing again. As the page reloads from the server, you must watch as the page redisplays in front of you, meaning that text and images can squirm around the screen until ending up in their final positions.

Enter Ajax

Ajax allows you to fetch data from the server behind the scenes without a full-page refresh. You can communicate with the server and fetch text or call online code, all while the browser keeps displaying the current page. When you fetch the data you want from the server, you can use dynamic HTML techniques (such as writing to a `<div>` element) to update the part of the text or a table in a Web page that you want to change.

The Desktop Feel

That feels very little like an application that is loaded onto your computer, such as Microsoft Excel or Word. When you perform an action with that kind of application, you can see the results immediately in the application, and the whole screen does not flicker as the page reloads. If you type a word into Microsoft Word, for example, the word appears at the location of the cursor. The entire page does not reload each time you type a word, and the cursor does not reset to the top of the page.

These days, browsers can display many of the controls (those interactive elements you use: buttons, list boxes, scroll bars, and so on) that you see in desktop applications. However, there has been a continual problem with the feel of Web applications that display in browsers. They feel like Web applications, not desktop applications. It would be great if you could create online applications that do not need to refresh the entire display each time they need to grab some new data from the server.

Improve User Experience

Imagine how that improves the user's experience —
instead of clicking a button to update the display and
then watching as the entire display is reset from
scratch, they see just the text or data they were working
with change. That is just what happens with Ajax — you
can communicate with the server behind the scenes,
and the user never need know about it. Ajax represents
another step along the way of making online programs
look and feel like programs that run directly on the
user's computer.

Origin of Ajax

Adaptive Path's Jesse James Garrett coined the term
Ajax. The idea was that Web designers became
envious of desktop programmers, who did not have to
put up with page refreshes and extra round trips to the
server to collect data. Desktop applications have a
solid feel that Web applications have problems
duplicating, because you have to rely on the Send
button so often along with the delay that entails.
However, Ajax is working to close the gap between
desktop and Web applications.

What Is Ajax?

Ajax stands for Asynchronous JavaScript + XML. It is
about a basic shift in the way Web applications work.
Ajax itself is not a single technology, it is a group
of technologies working together to bring a rich
experience to the user. Ajax is made of HTML and
XHTML, Cascading Style Sheets (CSS) and dynamic
HTML, as well as auxiliary technologies like XML and
XSLT. JavaScript holds everything together. Ajax is
bringing the kind of dynamic application you see on
the desktop to the Web, and not only are users the
better off for it, Web programmers are as well.

Ajax Beginnings

The ability to use Ajax has been available since 1998.
However, Ajax did not really catch on until early
2005 when some very popular Web applications
started using it, such as Google Suggest and
Google Maps. Jesse James Garrett wrote an article on
Ajax, bringing the term and the technology into the
spotlight. Since this new release, Ajax has burst onto
the popular computing stage and is being used in
more and more places.

How Ajax Works

Ajax works by using JavaScript and the
`XMLHttpRequest` object that most modern
browsers support to communicate with the server
without having to refresh the Web page currently
displayed. You write code in a Web page that includes
JavaScript, which will fetch data from the server. That
data can be in XML or text format, and it is
downloaded into an object supported by the browser,
an `XMLHttpRequest` object. This object not only
handles the download behind the scenes, but also
stores the data fetched from the server. After the data
is downloaded, you can use JavaScript to retrieve that
data from the `XMLHttpRequest` object and display
or otherwise use that data.

Because the download happens behind the scenes, the
application the user is working with does not have to
come to a screeching halt while data is fetched from
the server. What makes Ajax *asynchronous* is the data
fetching that goes on behind the scenes without
making everything stop and wait. A synchronous
interact is waiting for data to be fetched before
proceeding, as in a standard, non-Ajax Web application.

Using an
Ajax-Based Application

You can see the difference in Ajax applications very clearly. As you know, Ajax's specialty is fetching data from Web servers behind the scenes. Ajax applications are based on JavaScript, and they run in Web browsers.

With standard Web applications, you click a button — usually a Submit button — and your data is sent to a Web server. Typically, that data is sent to a program on the Web server, and that program then creates a new Web page, which the server sends back to you. Because all the data handling is performed on the server, the page you see in the browser must be fully refreshed to display any changes. In other words, the browser just displays data; it takes no real part in handling or working with that data.

When you use Ajax, the browser becomes an active participant. That happens because you add JavaScript to your Web pages so those pages can work with the browser's XMLHttpRequest object to communicate with the server, download data, and display or work with that data as needed. JavaScript is a substantial language, and you can create powerful applications using it.

Ajax represents a revolution in Web design. There is nothing else like it, and it is going to become standard in Web applications. Using Ajax, you can download data behind the scenes from the Web server, before the user needs it. Then, when you want to, you can display that data as needed. This is a very useful way of operating, and it is much more in line with the desktop way of doing things — you can display data in most cases without waiting for a page refresh in the browser, which users find annoying.

① Open a non-Ajax Web application in your browser.

② Click Submit to fetch data from the server.

Wait as the new page is entirely downloaded from the server.

③ Read the fetched data in the newly displayed Web page.

   In this example, it is the text Here is the data.

Note: The entire Web page has to be refreshed in this case.

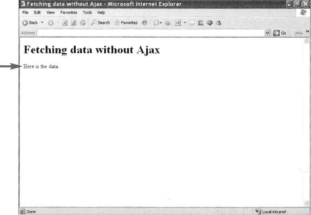

4 Open an Ajax-enabled application in your browser.

5 Click Display Message.

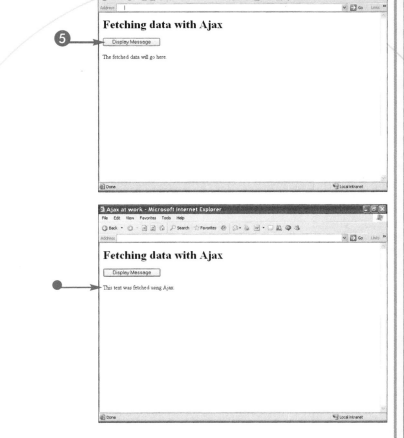

● The results appear in the current Web page — with no page refresh needed.

Extra

It is important to bear in mind that Ajax relies on JavaScript to do what it does. All browsers today, such as Internet Explorer, Firefox, Mozilla, Safari, and Opera, support JavaScript. Internet Explorer is the most common browser today, but browsers based on Mozilla, including Firefox and Firebird, are gaining ground. All of these browsers already support JavaScript.

Some browsers may have JavaScript turned off. Users sometimes turn off JavaScript support in their browsers for security reasons. One of the most annoying capabilities of JavaScript is that it can be used to display pop-up ads, and many people turn off JavaScript for that reason. Sometimes, JavaScript is used to perform legal, but very annoying things, such as opening dozens of new windows in a way that effectively jams the computer and freezes it. JavaScript can even be used in illegal ways when browser bugs are exploited and hackers can grab control of the computer. In Chapter 2, you learn how to handle situations where the user has turned off JavaScript.

Run a
Live Search

You can find many live-search Ajax-enabled applications online. These applications take advantage of the capabilities of Ajax to fetch data as you search for matches to specific keywords.

For example, when you perform a search on Google, you type your search term, and then click Google Search to perform your search. Your search term is sent to Google's server. The programs on that server search for matches to your search term among the billions of archived Web pages on the server. If a match is found, it is sent back to your browser. Without Ajax, however, an entirely new page appears in front of you in the browser when your search is complete.

Because Ajax specializes in fetching data from the server behind the scenes, Google can use Ajax to help speed up searches. That is the purpose of a new Google page, Google Suggest. As you type your search term, the Web page can send what you have already typed to the Google server, which can then suggest matches to your term. That can save you a great deal of time — if Google has already found what you are searching for, all you have to do is click the suggested word instead of typing the full word, and Google performs the search for you. That is very handy.

That is a good indication of the power of Ajax — you can use Ajax to fetch data behind the scenes without having to wait for a page refresh. In this case, the Web page fetches data from Google without making the user wait. Users like that kind of utility because it helps speed the Web interaction.

Run a Live Search

❶ Navigate to the non-Ajax-enabled Google Web site, www.google.com.

❷ Type a term for which to search.

This example uses the term Ajax.

❸ Click Google Search.

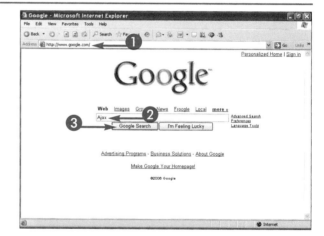

The pages that Google finds that match your search appear.

④ Navigate to the Ajax-enabled Google site at www.google.com/webhp? complete=1&hl=en.

⑤ Type **ajax** into the search term field.

⑥ Click ajax from the drop-down list that appears.

This page uses Ajax to get those suggested search terms from the Google server.

● The number of matches to the various selected terms appears, making it easier to select the term you want.

Google finds pages that match your search.

Extra

Google Suggest can save you time when you type search terms simply because when you type the first few letters of your term, the whole term may appear and you can click it, saving you the trouble of typing the rest of the term. The terms that Google suggests to you are not based on your previous searches; they are based on whichever matching terms provide the most hits, which are the most frequently searched for, and so on.

You can make Google Suggest your home page if you really like it (thousands of people use the main Google page as their home page). In Internet Explorer, you can do this by selecting Tools, then Internet Options. On the Internet Options menu, look for the Home Page section, find the Address: text field, and enter www.google.com/webhp?complete=1&hl=en. Click OK. In Firefox, you can find this menu by choosing Tools➔Options. In Mozilla, you can find it by choosing Edit➔Preferences. In Opera, you can find it by choosing Edit➔Options.

Autocomplete What You Type

You can also use Ajax to *autocomplete* your data entry, which means that when you start typing a word, the autocomplete capability in an Ajax-enabled Web page can offer suggestions to complete the word. For example, if you type Aj, a Web page that supports autocomplete may suggest Ajax as the full term. Clicking Ajax in the drop-down list in which it appears replaces Aj with the full term, Ajax.

In other words, autocomplete is much like the live search you just saw in the previous task at Google Suggest. However, autocomplete is different, and the two terms are different in Ajax usage. While live searches offer suggestions specifically for search terms, autocomplete offers suggestions for any words you enter. Selecting an autocomplete term from the offered list completes the

word you have been typing; it does not perform a search. That is useful for applications of all kinds, besides search applications. If you keep a store of words online, you can offer the user a list of possible completions for the word or term the user is currently typing.

You can find an Ajax autocomplete example at www.papermountain.org/demos/live/. There are three Ajax demonstrations worth looking at: an autocomplete example, a live search example, and a Live Action example. The live search example searches http://dictionary.reference.com instead of Google. The Live Action is the term www.papermountain.org uses when data is fetched using Ajax and displayed in a Web page without a page refresh. (See the section "Using an Ajax-Based Application.") You are going to see how to create all three of these Ajax applications in this book.

Autocomplete What You Type

① Navigate to www.papermountain.org/demos/live/.

② Type **Aj** in the text field in the Autocomplete section.

The demo displays a number of autocomplete suggestions that are retrieved from the server.

③ Click the Ajax autocomplete suggestion.

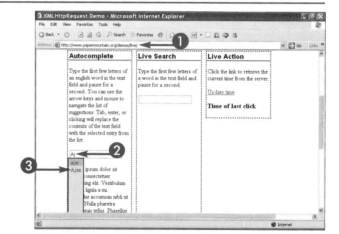

● The letters you typed are replaced by the word Ajax.

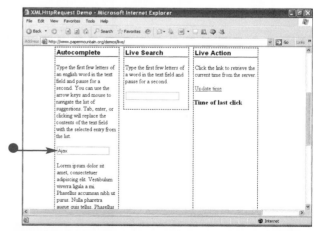

④ Type **Aj** in the Live Search section's text field.

● The application displays possible search terms.

If you select a suggested search term, that term's definition from http://dictionary.reference.com opens in your browser.

⑤ Click the Update Time link in the Live Action section of the page.

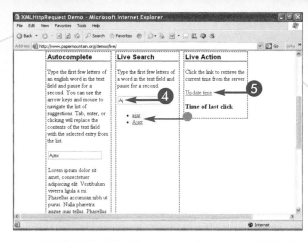

● Using Ajax techniques, the application displays the time without refreshing the page.

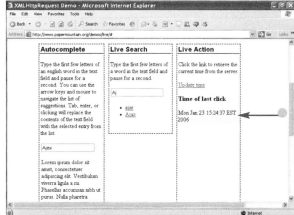

Extra

The www.papermountain.org site was created by Leslie and Cassondra Hensley. Their Ajax demonstration page at www.papermountain.org/demos/live/ is all about what you can do with Ajax and the XMLHttpRequest object using JavaScript, showing how you can update Web pages without resorting to page refreshes in the browser. If you want to look at the actual JavaScript that supports this demonstration, you can find it at http://cvs.sourceforge.net/viewcvs.py/lakeshore/lakeshore/resources/liveUpdater.js?view=markup. The Hensleys say you can adapt it and use it as you like (and if you have suggestions or make improvements, you can e-mail them at hensleyl@papermountain.org). The server-side code responsible for finding search terms and offering suggestions can be found online at www.papermountain.org/demos/live/live-demos-source.html. That code is written in the Ruby language, however, which you may not be familiar with (server-side programming in this book uses a small amount of PHP). The Hensleys discuss these examples and more about Ajax at www.papermountain.org/blog/index.cgi/Tech/Javascript/PoorMansAjax.txl and www.papermountain.org/blog/index.cgi/Tech/Ruby/AutoCompleteXMLHttpRequest.txl.

Modify Web Pages without Page Refreshes

You can use Ajax to modify Web pages on the fly as the user watches. When you fetch data from the server behind the scenes and store that data, you want to display the fetched data in the Web page itself. There are many different ways of doing that, most of which involve some form of dynamic HTML or Cascading Style Sheets (CSS). These methods of displaying data are very powerful, because they let you display new data without needing a page refresh in the browser.

Dynamic HTML lets you update the elements in a Web page dynamically. In the early days of Web browsers, all the elements (such as the HTML elements <h1>, <p>, and so on) in the displayed pages could not be altered after they were displayed. Years ago, however, dynamic HTML became the standard, and using dynamic HTML enables you to alter the contents of any HTML element in the page.

That is great when you are using Ajax, because when you grab some data from the server, you can display that data by assigning it to the contents of an element. You see this technique at work frequently in this book.

The other technique you use to display data in a Web page without a page refresh is CSS. CSS allows you to create and display pop-up windows like those used in the previous task and in the Google Suggest task to display suggestions for words from the server. That is also a very powerful technique, and it gives Web applications the feel of desktop applications.

You see both dynamic HTML and CSS used with Ajax, which lets you update a page in the browser with data you get from the server. A site that uses both dynamic HTML and CSS together with Ajax in a series of demonstrations is http://openrico.org/rico/demos.page.

Modify Web Pages without Page Refreshes

① Navigate to http://openrico.org/rico/demos.page.

② Click the Inner Html demo link.

- The Ajax Rolodex example opens.

③ Click Holloman, Debbie.

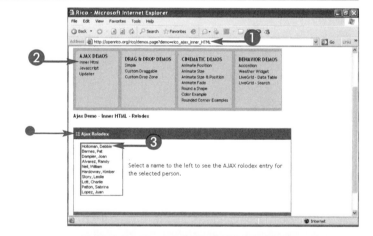

- Using CSS, the application displays what looks like a business card in the Web page.

④ Click the JavaScript Updater link.

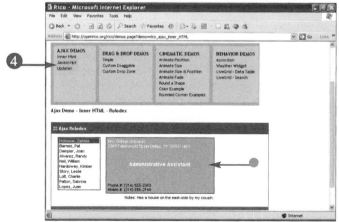

An Ajax Form Letter appears with default entries for the person's name, address, and so on.

⑤ Click Holloman, Debbie.

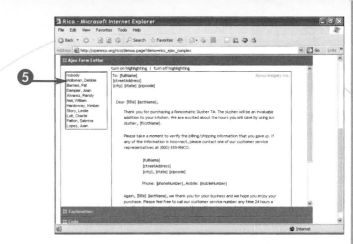

● Using dynamic HTML, the blank items in the letter are updated with data fetched from the server for the person you selected.

Extra

You can do the same kinds of things that you see in this Rico demonstration. It is easier than you might expect, because these examples are part of the ajaxEngine Ajax framework that Rico offers.

There is a considerable amount of programming involved in writing Ajax applications — and even more if you want to produce the kind of effects you see in the Rico demonstrations. Ajax frameworks are full libraries of code that handle much of the programming for you. When you use an Ajax framework, all you have to do is install it and customize the code as you want it.

Some Ajax frameworks are written in pure JavaScript, and you use them in the browser only. Those are the easiest of the frameworks to use. There are also a number of Ajax frameworks that you can use on the server that are written in a server-side language, most often PHP. The server-side frameworks actually write JavaScript code to do what you want and send that code to the browser. You see both kinds of Ajax frameworks in this book.

Drag and Drop with Ajax

You can use Ajax to simplify hundreds of standard tasks that users perform every day online. For example, consider the process of buying something online and then checking out. The shopping process involves moving from page to page. You look at an item on one Web page, and then move to another item's page, all of which involves a great deal of navigation using the browser, which means many page refreshes. The screen is continually being refreshed.

Finally, when you select an item, the shopping cart page appears, showing the item you added to the cart. The check-out process also involves three or more page refreshes. First, you open the checkout page, then you move to a page that gets your personal data, then another page pops up that asks about shipping, and then you get a confirmation page. This process can become very tiresome to the user, who is tired of watching the browser window clear and then having to wait for the elements in the page to reappear.

The whole process involves many page refreshes, and that is one of the unpleasant aspects of shopping online — you continually see pages flash and flicker. Ajax specializes in avoiding page refreshes, so it is a natural technology to use here. Every aspect of the online shopping experience can be improved with Ajax — for example, instead of moving from page to page to see new items, the new items can just appear in the current page. When you want to check out, everything can be handled on the same page. Even adding items to the shopping cart benefits from using Ajax. Instead of clicking Add to Cart and then viewing the shopping cart page, you can simply drag an item onto the shopping cart icon.

Drag and Drop with Ajax

① Navigate to a shopping page where you see an item that you want to buy.

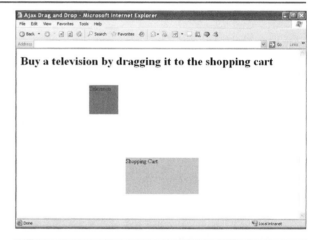

② Click and drag the television to the shopping cart.

You no longer have to use a separate shopping cart page to add the item to the shopping cart.

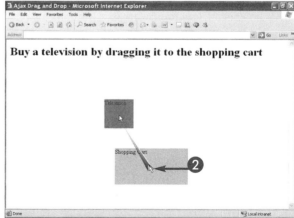

③ Drop the television into the shopping cart and release the mouse.

The Ajax application contacts the server behind the scenes to inform the server that you added an item to the cart.

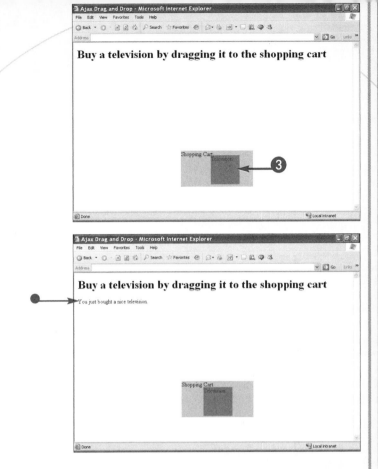

● The server sends confirmation, which appears in the upper-left corner of the Web page.

You added an item to the shopping cart without leaving the current shopping page.

Extra

This way of using Ajax can revolutionize processes like online shopping. Using Ajax can make the entire online shopping experience just like a desktop application, because it appears that you never left the current page. Not only can the process of adding items to a shopping cart work as in this example, but it is particularly important to realize that the check-out process can be simplified as well. Surveys have shown that users find the check-out process, which involves moving between at least three different Web pages, particularly annoying. After you type your credit card number, for example, and you wait for the next page, there is always that thought that the server will lose your information and the transaction may fail, which is the kind of thing that makes the online shopping experience feel so fragile and error-prone. When everything takes place on the same page, however, it makes the experience feel much more solid and trustworthy.

Get Instant Login Feedback

You can also use Ajax to make the online login process much easier. Logging in to a site is another one of those online tasks that can benefit from using Ajax to avoid page refreshes.

For example, say that you are dealing with a Web site to which you must supply a username and password before you can gain entry. Suppose that you misspell your username. You are directed to a new page that explains the problem with a message something like, "No such user." You probably must click the Back button in your browser, go back to the login page, and retype both your username and password. Once again, you face several screen refreshes to get through the process, and that can be very annoying as well as time-consuming — which is something you would like to avoid if possible.

With Ajax, it is a different story. You type your username and password into an Ajax-enabled login page. Using Ajax techniques, the login page sends the username and password to the server without making you go to a new page. If your username and password are correct, you are logged in without having to leave the current page.

On the other hand, if you make a mistake in the login process, you get immediate notification and can retype your username or password — all without having to leave the login page. Using Ajax, the login page sends your username and password to the server. If they are incorrect, you are immediately notified. You can correct what you typed at once, without having to get a page refresh that takes you to a login error page. You can see an example at www.jamesdam.com/ajax_login/login.html.

Getting Instant Login Feedback

① Navigate to www.jamesdam.com/ ajax_login/login.html.

The login page appears.

A correct username is user1, and the matching password is pass1.

② Type an incorrect name in the Username text field.

This example uses steve.

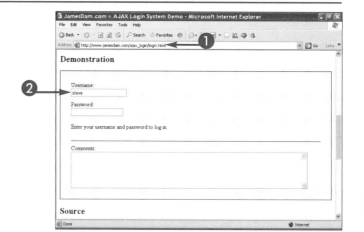

③ Type an incorrect password in the Password field.

④ Click anywhere outside the Username or Password text fields.

● The login page displays the text Invalid username and password combination.

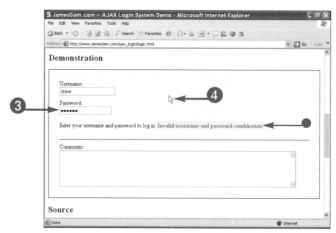

⑤ Type **user1**, the correct username, in the Username text field.

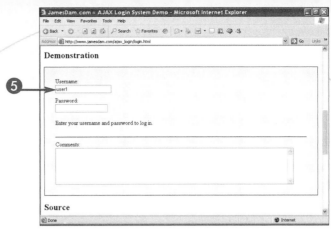

⑥ Type **pass1**, the correct password, in the Password text field.

● The login page indicates that you are logged in.

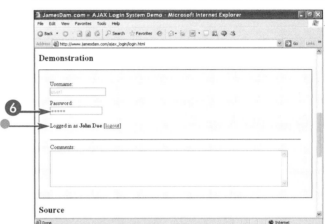

Extra

One of the problems with an Ajax-enabled login page is that you must make sure that you send username and password information to the server in a secure way. Do not send that information freely over the Internet without any security, because it can be easily read. To create an Ajax-enabled login page, provide some password security.

The login page in this example, www.jamesdam.com/ajax_login/login.html, uses the MD5 encryption algorithm to send its username and password data to the server. There are links in the page at www.jamesdam.com/ajax_login/login.html that show you the code on how to do this. On the other hand, as the text in this page itself notes, the MD5 encryption algorithm is not secure, which means it is not the best way to send username and password information. If you want to make sure your data is sent securely, use a strong encryption algorithm such as SHA-1.

Create Rich Displays with Ajax

You can create rich displays with Ajax. When the server returns information, you can use it to add elements to the current data you display to the user. For example, your site may display a generic map of an area so that users can orient themselves. Users may be interested in a particular location on your map. You can simply leave the map as it is and assume users can figure out where the location is.

On the other hand, you can use Ajax to make it easier to find a specific location. When users ask about a particular location, for example, your page can send the request to the server using Ajax techniques. Your page can use those techniques to retrieve information from the server to help the user find the exact location on the map.

In other words, you display a map of an area, and you know the location in the map that the user is interested in (the server may send you the map x and y coordinates, in pixels, of the location that the user is inquiring about). Using Cascading Style Sheet (CSS) techniques, you can move a marker, such as an image of an arrow or a pushpin, to mark the exact location in the map in which the user is interested.

Such an application already exists at Google Maps, which you can find at http://maps.google.com/. This application uses Ajax to position markers and text to point out the location on a map the user is interested in. As you would expect, you do not need a page refresh in order to make it work; all you have to do is use it, and Ajax will handle all the details for you.

Create Rich Displays with Ajax

① Navigate to Google Maps at http://maps.google.com/.

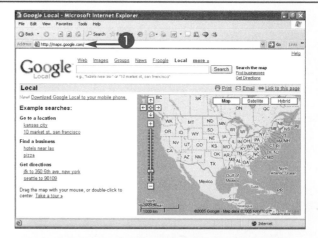

② Click Hybrid.

Google Maps displays not just maps, but also actual satellite images of the area as the background.

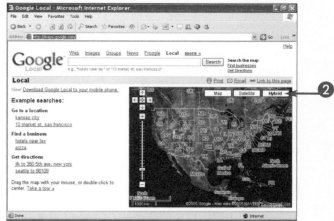

③ Type a location you are interested in into the search box.

In this example, 10 Market St, San Francisco is used.

④ Click Search.

Google Maps displays the location.

The position of the marker and the text information superimposed on the map are fetched using Ajax, and the page is not refreshed.

⑤ Click the To here link in the text bubble if you want more directions, and type the location you are starting from.

⑥ Click Get Directions.

Google Maps displays directions from your current location to the location pinpointed on the map.

Extra

Getting directions from Google Maps also involves using Ajax. Typing the location you want to start from in the text field in the text bubble and clicking Get Directions sends the information to the Google servers using Ajax — the page is not refreshed.

Google calculates how you can travel from the location you type to the location pinpointed on the map by using its large database of streets and distances. The server then sends that information back to the Web page in your browser, which displays the driving directions using a panel of text inside the Web page. In that way, Google Maps uses Ajax again to avoid making the user deal with page refreshes where the map would jump around in the browser view.

Look at this application at http://maps.google.com/. It is a very good introduction to using Ajax programming techniques.

Create Games
with Ajax

You can create online games with Ajax. Online games that interact with the server are easy to create with Ajax. If you wanted to create an online game, your choices were limited to creating your own software that communicates over the Internet, because browsers were not up to the task.

In the old days, if you relied on using a browser to create a game, you ran up against the same problem discussed throughout this chapter — page refreshes. When you made a move, the entire page refreshed as your new move was sent to the server, and the server sent back a whole new page. That was bad because the entire page jumped and reset its position back to the top left, which meant that you had to scroll down to your earlier position to continue the game. Rapidly interactive games, as when you had to avoid rocket ships or torpedoes, were

impossible because of those page refreshes. Slower games, like chess, were barely possible. Creating interactive graphical games required that you create your own software, which the user had to download and install in order to run the entire game using that software (no Internet connection necessary), or use the software to communicate with the server itself.

Ajax has improved the situation dramatically. You can use dynamic HTML and CSS to move elements around in the browser window, and you can use Ajax to communicate with the server to find out what should be happening in the game. One such example is at http://pandorabots.com/pandora/talk?botid=c96f911b3e3 5f9e1, where Tom Riddle's diary reads what you write and answers you — all without a page refresh.

Create Games with Ajax

1 Navigate to Tom Riddle's diary at http://pandorabots.com/pandora/talk ?botid=c96f911b3e35f9e1.

A cursor appears, waiting for you to type something.

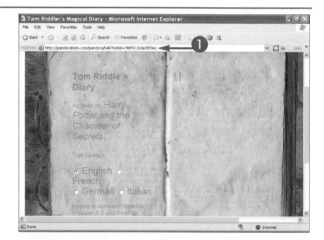

2 Type **Hello** at the cursor.

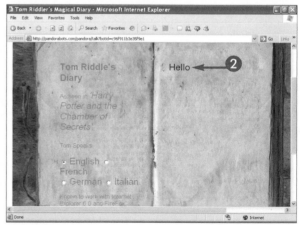

Tom Riddle's diary reads what you write and deletes it.

The cursor also disappears because the diary is not asking for input at this time.

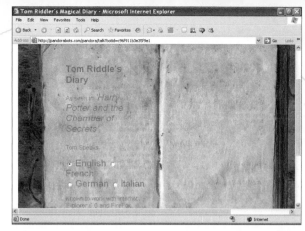

● The diary answers with a response that it types as you watch.

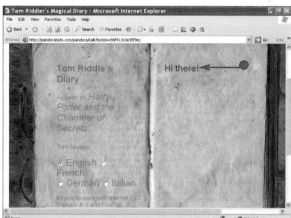

Extra

Tom Riddle's diary is an impressive game, and its answers are usually surprisingly accurate. It is a good example of a game that would be difficult to write purely in JavaScript because the database for the answers is so large that to download it into the browser would be difficult. Moreover, you can communicate with the diary in English, German, French, or Italian. Imagine downloading all that into a browser. That points out one of the useful aspects of Ajax games online: You can store a huge database of game moves on the server and access that database using Ajax. That is useful when your game needs such a database, as when you have a chess game that relies on a library of standard opening moves from the great games of the past.

There are also other Ajax games available today. For example, The Fonz and Ajax at http://mrspeaker.webeisteddfod.com/2005/04/17/the-fonz-and-ajax/ is a word game that lets you move around using typed commands. In addition, there is a Monopoly-like game available at http://llor.nu/ as well.

Chat Online
Using Ajax

You can use Ajax's ability to let browsers display and update Web pages without page refreshes in many different kinds of applications. Any online application where you need to communicate with the server behind the scenes is a good candidate for Ajax. Here is another example: online chat applications. Such applications let you type text that is seen by everyone who is logged on at the time. Whatever you type can be seen by others; whatever others type can be seen by you.

The reason this is a good candidate for Ajax techniques is that you need to communicate with the server in order to download what other people are typing and to upload what you have typed. This is how it works: You type your message and click a button to upload that text to the server. The server displays your text in the chat application's Web page. When others view that page

in their browsers, it automatically updates itself every few seconds using Ajax so that they can see what other people have been typing. Ajax is perfect here, because you need to communicate with the server while avoiding screen refreshes.

There is an example showing how an Ajax chat works at www.plasticshore.com/projects/chat/. To use this chat application, type your name and your comments, and click Submit. Your comments are displayed in the main part of the page. Anyone else viewing the page can also see your comments and can reply to you with their own answers to your comments. This is a perfect example of Ajax at work. You do not need any screen refreshes to execute this example, just pure Ajax code that automatically updates the screen.

Chat Online Using Ajax

① Navigate to www.plasticshore.com/projects/chat/.

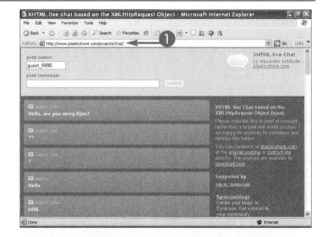

② Type your name in the your name text field.

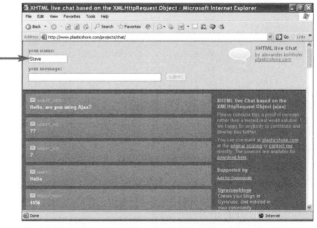

③ Type your comments in your message text field.

④ Click Submit.

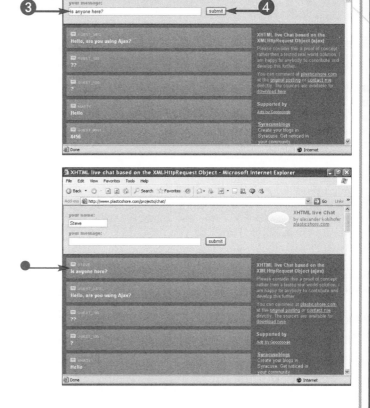

● Your comments appear in the chat application.

You and everyone else viewing that page can see the comments.

This kind of instant communication using Ajax is a very exciting technology that allows you to write tools such as instant messenger-type programs using nothing more than Web browsers. There are all kinds of possibilities here. Using this kind of technology can enable a person to communicate instantly with someone who has posted something in a Web page. For example, if someone publishes a blog (a Web log of commentary), he or she might include a comment button that allows you to communicate with him or her directly. Alternatively, if someone lists an item in an online auction and you have questions about the item (such as the whether a DVD player supports both 4:3 and 16:9 screen ratios), you could contact that person immediately, and get a response in the same Web page. You can also use this technique to broadcast live events, where everyone looking at your Web page can see it instantly updated, without page refreshes, with the latest news of a sporting event, for example.

Download Images
with Ajax

You can also use Ajax to download images from the server and display them. You can also use Ajax to download text or XML from the server.

You cannot download images directly using Ajax, but if you are clever, you can see how to use Ajax together with dynamic HTML to download images without refreshing the Web page. Normally, when you display an image in a Web page, you use an `<img>` element this way: `<img src="image1.jpg">`.

If the server wants you to display a different image to match some new data, you can download the name (or URL if that new image is not in the same directory as the Web page itself on the server) of the new image file using Ajax — say it is image2.jpg. Now that you have the name

of the new image file you can display it using dynamic HTML by rewriting the contents of the `<img>` element so that the `src` HTML attribute, which gives the name of the image you want to display, is assigned the name of the new image like this: `<img src="image2.jpg">`.

When the browser sees that the image it is supposed to display has been changed, it downloads the new image and displays it. You just used Ajax to download the name of the new image, or its URL, to display and relied on dynamic HTML to make the browser display that new image. The effect is the same. You have been able to fetch those images behind the scenes without a page refresh, and it looks as if you have used Ajax to download images.

Download Images with Ajax

① Open a Web page that lets you swap images.

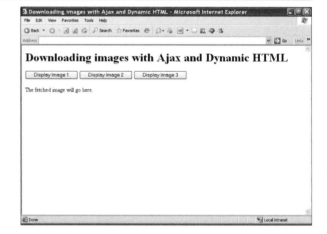

② Click Display Image 1.

Image 1 is downloaded and displayed using a combination of Ajax and dynamic HTML.

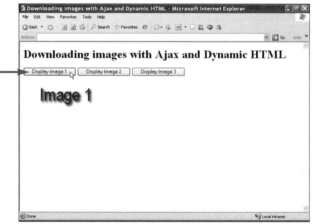

③ Click Display Image 2.

Image 2 is downloaded and
displayed.

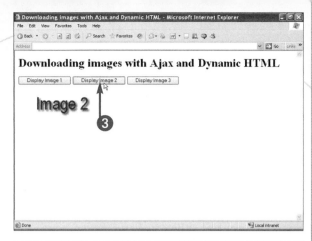

④ Click Display Image 3.

Image 3 is downloaded and
displayed.

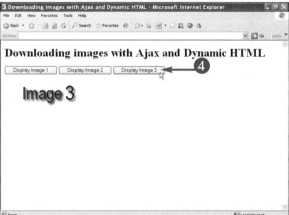

Extra

This technique of using the browser to do the downloading is an interesting one. While Ajax itself is
restricted to downloading text or XML data, as you see in this example, you can use Ajax to force
the browser to download image data that is in binary format, not text format. You can extend this
technique to any kind of binary file, not just images, as long as the browser knows what to do with
such files. For example, you can download podcast MP3 files and have the browser play them (or
automatically launch software that can play them). You can do the same with video files like AVI or
MPEG, and the browser can play them (or launch software that can play them). The same goes for
other binary formats, such as Adobe PDF files. Overall, this is a very handy technique to remember
when working with Ajax if you want to work with other data formats besides text or XML.

Create a Script

You can place JavaScript code directly into your HTML Web pages if you enclose the code inside an HTML `<script>` element. The `<script>` element itself usually is placed in the `<head>` element of a Web page. You use the language attribute of the `<script>` element to indicate what scripting language you are using. When you use JavaScript, you can assign the language attribute the value "javascript". Capitalization does not matter here — you can also assign a value of "JAVASCRIPT". When you place your JavaScript code inside the `<script>` element, it appears as `<head> <script language="javascript"> </script> </head>`.

To write the message "Welcome to JavaScript" to a Web page, you can use the JavaScript `document.write` method. The term document here corresponds to the built-in document *object* in JavaScript. An object can

contain both *methods* and *properties*. A method is a *function* that is part of an object. A function is a segment of code that you can refer to by name. A property holds a single data item. The document object stands for the Web page itself, and you can use the `write` method to write to the page.

Data is passed to JavaScript functions and methods by enclosing that data in parentheses. All lines of JavaScript end with a semicolon (;). For example, using the JavaScript `document.write("Hello");` writes "Hello" to the Web page. In this case, the text "Hello" is passed to the document object's write method, which displays that text in the Web page. You can also set properties of the document object; for example, a property such as `document.bgcolor` holds the background color of the Web page, and you can assign it colors such as `document.bgcolor="red"`.

Create a Script

① Create a new Web page using your text editor, and add a `<script>` element.

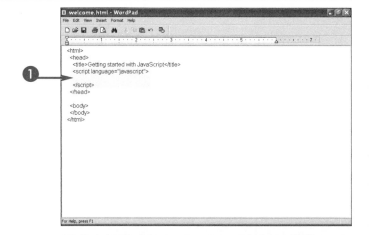

② Inside the `<script>` element, add the JavaScript code `document.write("<h1>Welcome to JavaScript</h1>");`.

This JavaScript will write the text `"<h1>Welcome to JavaScript</h1>"` to the Web page. Note that this text is enclosed in an `<h1>` header element, so the text appears in a large, bold font.

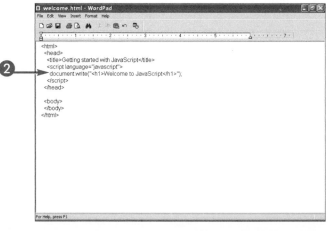

3 Add a JavaScript comment to make your script easier to read.

Comments are annotations to your code that make that code easier for people to read. JavaScript ignores the text of comments.

The most common type of JavaScript comment begins with //, which makes JavaScript ignore anything that follows, all the way to the end of the current line.

4 Open the Web page in your browser.

JavaScript displays the text "Welcome to JavaScript" in <h1> header style.

Extra

Not all browsers support JavaScript. Although it is quite rare now, some early browsers have no way of running JavaScript. More importantly, some users turn JavaScript off to avoid security issues. If this is a concern, you can use the <noscript> element to display a message in case there is no JavaScript support in the browser. To avoid having your JavaScript code simply appear as text in such browsers, you can enclose your JavaScript inside an HTML comment, which starts with <!-- and ends with --> (and you prefix the --> part with a JavaScript comment marker, //, because -- is legal JavaScript, which may confuse your browser). In browsers that do not support JavaScript, this example displays the message "Sorry, your browser does not support JavaScript."

Example:
```
<script language="javascript">
<!--
  document.write("<h1>Welcome to JavaScript</h1>")
//-->
</script>
<noscript>Sorry, your browser does not support JavaScript.</noscript>
```

View JavaScript Errors

When you are creating JavaScript files, there is always the possibility of errors. If you make an error while writing your JavaScript, you can use your browser to determine what the problem is. In other words, your browser not only runs your JavaScript, it can function as a debugging aid.

For example, you make a mistake typing `document.write`, and instead type
`documet.write: <html> <head> <title>Getting started with JavaScript</title> <script language="javascript"> documet.write("<h1>Welcome to JavaScript</h1>"); </script> </head> <body> </body> </html>`.

You will introduce a bug in your JavaScript code, which means your JavaScript will not run properly in a browser. In fact, your Welcome to JavaScript message will not display.

When you do not get the results you expect, you can use your browser to determine what the trouble is. Most browsers that can run JavaScript have some debugging capability, such as Internet Explorer and Firefox. However, how you access that debugging information varies by browser.

When there is a JavaScript error, Internet Explorer sometimes displays a small yellow triangle at lower left. Sometimes, it displays the text "Done, but with errors on the page." To open a dialog box with more information about the error, double-click the icon at lower left in Internet Explorer. To view a JavaScript error in Firefox, click Tools and then click the JavaScript Console menu item. When you view the JavaScript error, you can see what went wrong, and then correct the problem by editing your JavaScript code. Note that Firefox offers more useful debugging and helpful information than Internet Explorer.

View JavaScript Errors

① Create a new Web page with the misspelled `documet.write` instead of `document.write`.

② Save the document.

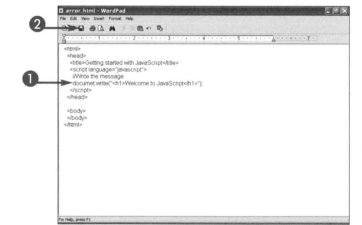

③ Open the document in a Web browser.

This example uses Internet Explorer.

Because there is a JavaScript bug, no text appears in the browser.

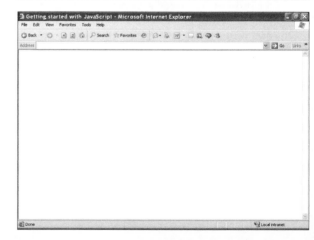

④ Double-click the small icon that appears in the lower-left corner in Internet Explorer.

A dialog box appears, explaining the reason for the JavaScript problem.

You can use that information to correct the problem.

⑤ Open the same Web page in Firefox, if you have that browser.

There is no display in the browser, indicating there is a problem.

⑥ Click Tools→JavaScript Console.

● The JavaScript Console appears, displaying debugging information.

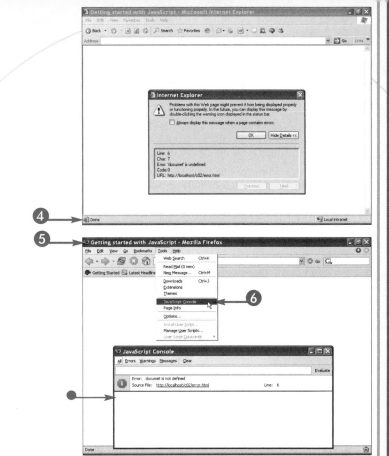

Extra

One way to make debugging easier is to divide long JavaScript programs into smaller sections and store them externally in JavaScript files, which have the extension .js, for example, myscript.js. Say that you place this JavaScript in a file named script.js:

```
document.write("<h1>Welcome to JavaScript</h1>");
```

You can refer to script.js in an HTML file by using the `<script>` element's `src` attribute:

```
<html>
  <head>
    <title>Getting started with JavaScript</title>
    <script language="javascript" src="script.js">
  </head>

  <body>
  </body>
</html>
```

The `src` attribute points to the external file holding JavaScript code. You can assign a URL to the `src` attribute, or, if the file holding the JavaScript is in the same directory as the Web page that uses it, you only need to assign the name of the external JavaScript code file to the `src` element.

Handle Browser Events

You can write JavaScript to respond to various *events* in the browser. A browser event can be a mouse click, a keystroke, a button click, a page load event when a page is opened in the browser, and so on.

Ajax applications often use events to respond to the user. For example, when the user clicks a button to update the display, an Ajax application may fetch data from the server and display it. Or clicking part of the page with the mouse may also trigger a script to use Ajax to communicate with the server.

You can determine when such an event occurs so that your JavaScript can handle that event. For example, you can determine when the user has clicked the Web page. To do that, you use the *HTML event attributes*, and connect them to your JavaScript. For each type of event, there is an event attribute. For example, when the user

clicks the mouse, the JavaScript connected to the onmousedown event attribute is executed.

All visual HTML elements support event attributes like onmousedown, and you can assign JavaScript code to those event attributes. For example, if you want to execute JavaScript when the user clicks the body of a page, you can use this code in the <body> tag: <body onmousedown="[*JavaScript Goes Here*]">.

For example, you can make a JavaScript dialog box — an alert box that displays a message — appear when the user clicks the page. To display alert boxes, you use the built-in JavaScript function named alert. To use the alert function, you simply pass the text you want to display in the dialog box to the alert function, and the browser makes the dialog box appear.

Handle Browser Events

① In a text editor, create a new Web page with the title Using Browser Events.

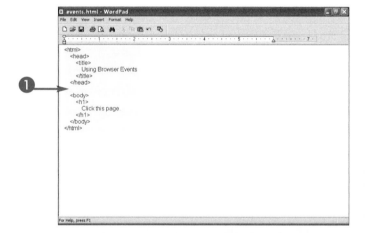

② Assign the JavaScript to display an alert box with the text "Hello from JavaScript" to the onmousedown attribute of the <body> tag.

You must assign quoted text to event attributes. Here, that is "alert('Hello from JavaScript')". Note that if you have quoted text inside your JavaScript (that is "Hello from JavaScript" here), use single quotes around that text ('Hello from JavaScript') so the Web browser is not confused by too many quotation marks.

③ Save the new Web page.

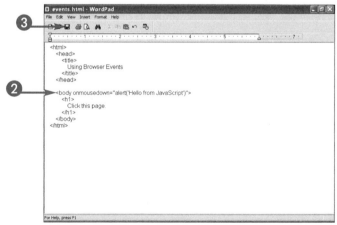

④ Open the new Web page in your browser.

⑤ Click the new Web page.

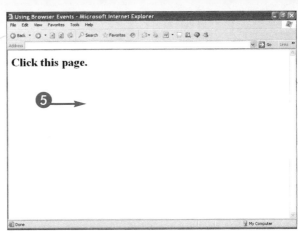

● The alert box appears, displaying the message you assigned to it.

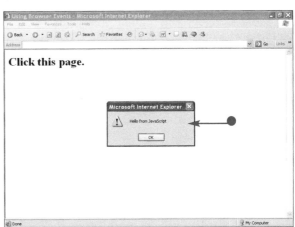

Extra

Here are some common event attributes that you might see in Ajax applications:

ATTRIBUTE	OCCURS WHEN	ATTRIBUTE	OCCURS WHEN
onchange	Data in a control, like a text field, changes	onmousedown	A mouse button goes down
onclick	An element is clicked	onmousemove	The mouse moves
ondblclick	An element is double-clicked	onmouseout	The mouse leaves an element
ondragdrop	A drag–and-drop operation is undertaken	onmouseover	The mouse moves over an element
onkeydown	A key goes down	onmouseup	A mouse button goes up
onkeypress	A key is pressed and the key code is available	onresize	An element or page is resized
onkeyup	A key goes up	onsubmit	The user clicks a Submit button
onload	The page loads	onunload	A page is unloaded

Create JavaScript Functions

You can specify when your JavaScript code is run by the browser. So far, the JavaScript code you put inside a `<script>` element has been run as soon as the browser loads the page, like this:

```
<html> <head> <title>Getting started with
JavaScript</title> <script
language="javascript">
document.write("<h1>Welcome to
JavaScript</h1>"); </script>
```

That is fine as far as it goes. But running your JavaScript as soon as the page containing that JavaScript is loaded is not a good idea in some cases — you may want to execute your JavaScript, downloading data from the server, only when the user clicks a button or types some data into a text field.

In other words, you need a way to make sure that your JavaScript does not run until you want it to run. The way that works in JavaScript is that you place your JavaScript inside a JavaScript function. A function is a section of code given a name that you can use to *call* that function. When you call the function, the code in the function runs.

To create a function, you use the keyword function, give the name of the function followed by a pair of parentheses, and surround the code that makes up the body with curly braces, { and }: function *functionName*() { [*JavaScript Goes Here*] }. The JavaScript you enclose inside the curly braces is executed only when the function is called. By placing your JavaScript inside a function, you can execute that JavaScript at the time you choose instead of automatically when the page loads. That way, you can respond to user-driven events, such as mouse-down events in the Web page as those events occur.

Create JavaScript Functions

① Create a new Web page with the title Using JavaScript Functions.

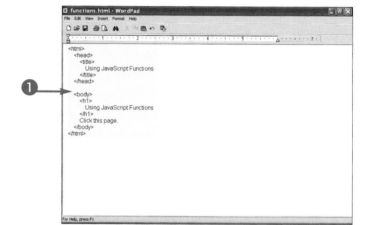

② Add code to call a function named `displayText` when the `onmousedown` event happens in the page.

You call a function by name in JavaScript. When the mouse goes down in this page, the `displayText` function is called.

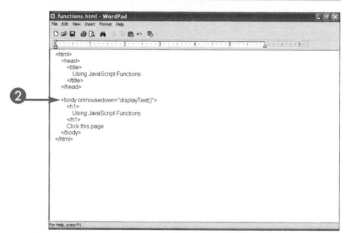

3 Add the code for the `displayText` function, and make it display an alert box.

3

4 Open the Web page in a browser and click the page.

● The `displayText` function is called, which displays the alert box.

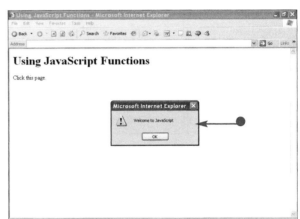

Extra

Functions are not limited to a single line of code. There was only one line of code in this function:

```
function displayText()
{
  alert("Welcome to JavaScript");
}
```

However, functions can have an unlimited number of lines of code in them. For example, if you want to first display an alert box with the text "Welcome to JavaScript" followed by a second alert box, which is displayed after the user dismisses the first alert box and displays the text "And welcome to Ajax", you can use this code in the `displayText` function:

```
function displayText()
{
  alert("Welcome to JavaScript");
  alert("And welcome to Ajax");
}
```

Display Results Where You Choose in a Page

You can use JavaScript and a little dynamic HTML to display text and even images where you want them to appear in a Web page. For example, you may have a table of data that you want to display and need to update a particular item in that table, which means you need to target a specific location in a page to display your data.

You can use an alert box to display text in a dialog box, but that hardly lets you target individual locations in a Web page. You may think that the document.write method is a good candidate here, but that method does not work well when you try to display or update data. First of all, you cannot target a specific location in the page to display your data using that method. But more importantly, document.write only writes to the current

location in a Web page. As you open a Web page, the browser lets you use document.write to write to the page; if you execute document.write using JavaScript in the <head> section of a document, it writes to the Web page first, and then any HTML elements in the body of the page appear. But if you try to use document.write after the page appears (and is now considered "closed"), the whole Web page opens again, and whatever you write with document.write replaces what is already there.

The best way to write to a specific location in a Web page is to use dynamic HTML, where you overwrite the contents of a <div> or <span> element. You can use a <div> element to enclose any section of a Web page, and <span> elements are usually used inline to enclose a section in part of a line of text.

Display Results Where You Choose in a Page

1 Create a new Web page with a `<div>` element.

2 Add code to connect the `onload` event to a JavaScript function named `displayText`.

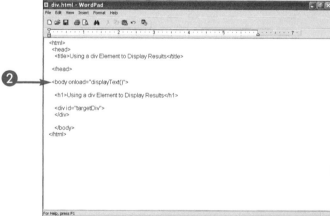

③ Add JavaScript to display the text "This message brought to you by JavaScript" in the target `<div>` element.

To access that `<div>` element, use the JavaScript expression `document.getElementById('targetDiv').innerHTML`-- the `getElementById` method gives you an object corresponding to the `<div>` element, and the `innerHTML` property of that object lets you access the HTML inside the `<div>` element directly.

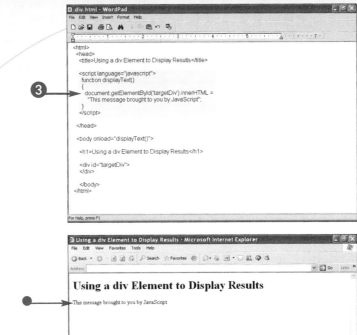

④ Open the Web page in your browser.

● The text "This message brought to you by JavaScript" in the target `<div>` element appears when the `onload` event occurs.

Extra

The JavaScript expression `document.getElementById('targetDiv').innerHTML` bears a little more examination and elaboration. This expression starts by using the document object's `getElementById` method. The method lets you search a Web page for a particular HTML element, and it gives you — that is, it returns — a JavaScript object corresponding to that HTML element. That is how you can deal with the HTML elements in a Web page in JavaScript — as JavaScript objects. In this case, you get a JavaScript object corresponding to the `targetDiv` `<div>` element. Such JavaScript objects have their own methods and properties, and to access the HTML inside the `<div>` element, you can use this object's `innerHTML` property.

Besides `innerHTML`, you can also use the `outerHTML` property. The `outerHTML` property corresponds to the entire `<div>` element, including the `<div>...</div>` HTML markup that surrounds everything. If you assign new text to the `outerHTML` property, you replace the entire element (including the `<div>...</div>` part), which means you can change that element to anything you want.

Connect HTML Buttons to JavaScript

You can gain more control over your Web pages by specifically handling events caused by the user, as opposed to the `onload` event. For example, a common way to make things happen in Ajax applications is to click a button.

Up to this point, Web pages did something as soon as they were loaded into a browser. You had no control over the timing of events besides clicking a mouse, where you could click a page to display an alert box. On the other hand, you can use buttons in Ajax applications to avoid asking the user to click the Web page to make something happen.

You can connect button clicks to the execution of JavaScript code. You start by creating a `<form>` element, which is where all HTML controls, like buttons or text fields, must be enclosed in a Web page like this: `<form> </form>`.

It is important that all HTML controls, such as buttons or text fields, are enclosed inside an HTML `<form>` element.

You can create a button and give that button a caption, such as "Click Me," using an HTML `<input>` element like this:

```
<form> <input type="button" value="Click Me"> </form>
```

Then you can tie that button to a JavaScript function by using the button's `onclick` event attribute like this:

```
<form> <input type="button"
onclick="displayText()" value="Click Me">
</form>
```

When the button is clicked, the JavaScript function `displayText` is called in this case. Setting things up this way gives you the power of determining when your JavaScript functions are called, waiting for the user to click a button, rather than having your JavaScript code executed at the same time that the Web page loads.

Connect HTML Buttons to JavaScript

① Create a new Web page that supports the `displayText` function.

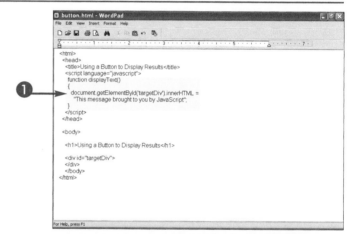

② Add an HTML `<form>` element to support the new button.

③ Add the `onclick` event attribute, tying that event to the `displayText` function.

④ Click the button in the Web page after opening the page in a browser.

● The `displayText` function is called and displays your text in the `targetDiv` `<div>` element.

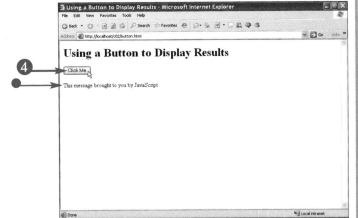

Extra

Besides button clicks, there are many other ways of handling events in HTML controls, such as when the user types text into a text field. In that case, you can use the onchange event to run JavaScript code when the text in a text field changes:

```
<form>
   <input type="text" onchange="displayText()">
</form>
```

In fact, you can catch such changes on a keystroke-by-keystroke basis if you use the onkeypress event attribute:

```
<form>
   <input type="text" onkeypress="displayText()">
</form>
```

You can even catch mouse movements, as when the mouse moves over a text field, using event attributes such as onmouseover:

Example:
```
<form>
   <input type="text" onmouseover="displayText()">
</form>
```

Display Text in Text Fields

You can interact with HTML controls besides buttons with JavaScript as well. One of the most popular HTML controls is text fields, those rectangular controls into which you type text. Besides buttons, text fields are the most common HTML control, and it is worth describing how you interact with text fields in JavaScript.

To access a text field, you can give it an ID using the HTML attribute `id`, and then access the text field using the JavaScript document object's `getElementById` method. That method returns an object corresponding to the text field, and you can use the properties of the object to work with the text field. For example, say you have an HTML button in a form: `<form> <input type="button" onclick="displayText()" value="Click Me"> </form>`, which calls the `displayText` function when the button is clicked.

Then you can add a text field to the form, giving that text field an ID such as text1, like this:

```
<form> <input type="button"
onclick="displayText()" value="Click Me">
<input type="text" id="text1"> </form>
```

In JavaScript code, you can access the text field with the expression `document.getElementById('text1')`, which returns an object corresponding to the text field. Now that you have an object corresponding to the `text1` text field, you need to know how to access the text in that text field. That turns out to be simple — the names of JavaScript properties of objects corresponding to HTML elements match their HTML attributes. For example, to set the text in a text field using HTML, you use the value attribute, and in JavaScript you can do the same. Here is how you can set the text in a text field using JavaScript: `document.getElementById('text1').value = "Hello from JavaScript";`. All you need to do is to place that JavaScript inside the `displayText` function to execute it when the user clicks the button.

Display Text in Text Fields

① Create a new Web page with an empty `displayText` function.

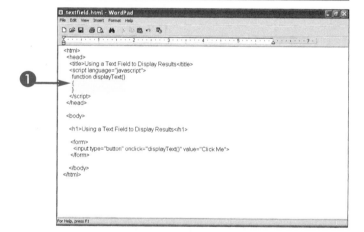

② Add a text field with the ID `"text1"` to the Web page.

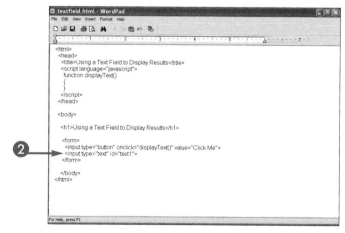

③ Add the JavaScript code that displays text in the text field to the `displayText` function.

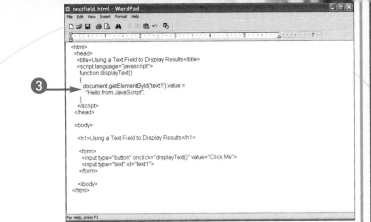

④ Open the Web page in a browser and click the button.

● The message "Hello from JavaScript" appears in the text field.

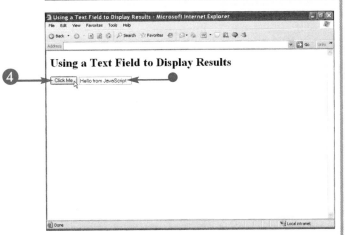

Extra

Besides displaying text in a text field, you can also read the text in a text field using JavaScript. The JavaScript expression `document.getElementById("text1").value` stands for the text in the text field with the ID `"text1"`. Instead of using that expression to set the text in the text field, you can use it to read the text in the text field. For example, to display the text currently in the text field in an alert box, you can type this in JavaScript:

```
function readText()
{
    alert(document.getElementById("text1").value);
}
```

You can even take the contents of the text field with the ID `text1` and copy those contents over to another text field, which has the ID `text2`, this way:

```
function readText()
{
    document.getElementById("text2").value =
        document.getElementById("text1").value;
}
```

Pass Arguments to Functions

You can send data to JavaScript functions for those functions to work with. JavaScript functions are segments of code that run only when the function is called. And so far, the code in those functions is self-contained — the message that each function is supposed to display is already built into those functions.

But you do not always want a function to do the same thing each time you call it. If you want to use the function to add two numbers, for example, you may want to tell the function which two numbers to add. To do that, you can *pass* those numbers to the functions.

The parentheses that you see after the names of functions, such as in `onclick="displayText()"`, are there to allow you to pass data to the function. The data items you pass to the function are called *arguments*.

For example, if you want to pass the text "Hello from JavaScript" to the `displayText` function, you can do it this way:

```
<form> <input type="button"
onclick="displayText('Hello from
JavaScript')" value="Click Me"> </form>
```

Note that inside the quoted text, you use single quotes to avoid confusing the browser. That passes the text "Hello from JavaScript" to the function `displayText`, and in the code inside that function, you can read that passed text. For example, if you create the `displayText` function this way: `function displayText(text){ }`, then you can refer to the text passed to the function using the variable name text inside the body of the function, like this:

```
displayText(text){ alert(text); }
```

You do not have to use the name text for the argument here — you can use any variable name.

Pass Arguments to Functions

① Create a new Web page, and add the `displayText` function.

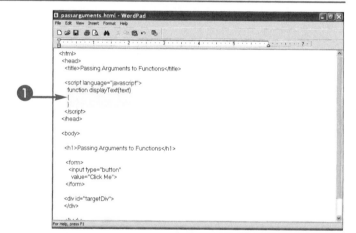

② Add the code to pass the message "Hello from JavaScript" to the `displayText` function when the button is clicked.

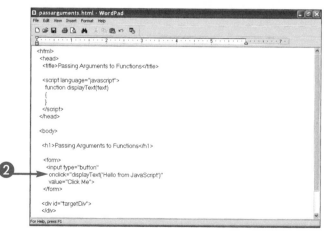

3 Add the code to handle the text passed to the `displayText` function.

The name inside the parentheses, `text`, is the name you can use in the body of the function to refer to the data passed to you. To display that data in the `target` `<div>` element, you use the JavaScript `document.getElementById ("targetDiv").innerHTML = text`.

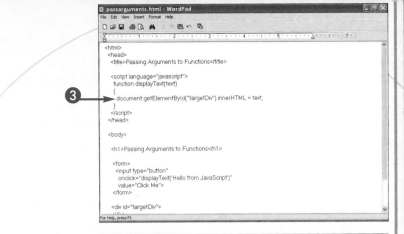

4 Open the Web page in your browser and click the button.

● The text message is passed to the `displayText` function, and the message appears.

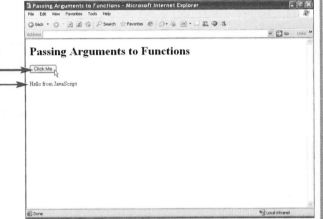

Extra

You can pass multiple arguments to functions. This example passes only one argument to the function:

```
displayText("Hello from JavaScript");
```

You can pass as many arguments as you want to a function if you separate them with commas. Here's how to pass three numbers — 55, 99, and 22 — to a function named add:

```
add(55, 99, 22);
```

The add function looks something like this:

```
function add(argument1, argument2, argument3)
{
    [Javascript goes here]
}
```

In the add function's code, argument1 would stand for 55, argument2 for 99, and argument3 for 22. In this way, you can support multiple arguments passed to the same function. You simply need to give each one a name when you create the function.

Return Data from Functions

You can pass arguments to JavaScript functions for functions to work on, and those functions notify you of the results of their work. For example, say that you have a function named add that takes two arguments and is supposed to add them together, like this:

```
function add(argument1, argument2) { }
```

To add together two numbers, such as 2 and 3, you can pass those values to the add function like this: `add(2, 3)`. And inside the body of the function, you can refer to the value of the arguments passed to you as `argument1` and `argument2`. To add those values together, you can use the JavaScript addition operator, + like this:

```
function add(argument1, argument2) {
argument1 + argument2; }
```

You can make the add function return the result of the addition using the JavaScript return keyword this way:

```
function add(argument1, argument2) { return
argument1 + argument2; }
```

Using the return keyword makes the function code send back the result you specify as the *return value* of the function.

When you use an expression like `add(2, 3)`, 2 and 3 are passed to the add function and their sum is returned — which means that the expression `add(2, 3)` is replaced with the result of the addition, 5. For example, the JavaScript statement `alert(add(2, 3));` displays an alert box displaying 5.

That is the way the return statement works — it allows you to specify the result returned from a function. You pass data to a function, work on that data, and use the return keyword to return the result of that work. In this way, functions cannot only accept data, but can return results as well, making them more useful.

Return Data From Functions

① Create a new Web page with an empty `displayText` function.

② Add the text 2 + 3 = and a `<span>` element that displays the result.

You use a `<span>` element here so that the results will appear on the same line as the text 2 + 3 =. If you used a `<div>` element, the results would appear on the next line in the Web page.

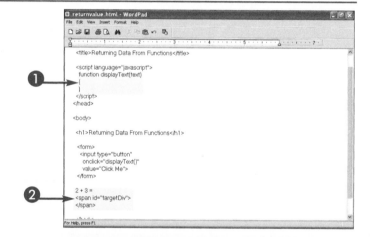

③ Add the `displayText` function to call the add function to add 2 + 3.

You can have multiple JavaScript functions in the same `<script>` element.

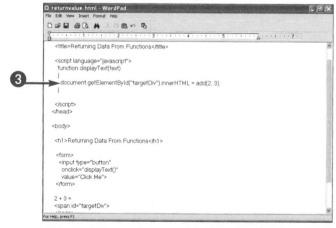

④ Type the code for the add function to add the two arguments passed to it and return their sum.

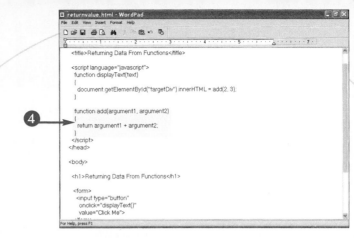

⑤ Open the new page in a browser and click the button.

● The `displayText` function passes the values 2 and 3 to the add function, which returns the sum 5.

Extra

In this example, the add function returns the sum of two numbers that are passed to it:

```
function add(argument1,
argument2)
{
   return argument1 +
argument2;
}
```

You can pass multiple arguments to a function; however, you cannot return multiple values where the values you want to return are separated by a comma, as you use when you pass multiple arguments to a function:

```
{
   return argument1,
argument2;
}
```

In JavaScript, you cannot return multiple values from the same function, at least not directly. There is one way to return multiple values indirectly. You can return a JavaScript *array*, which holds multiple values.

Store Data in Variables

You can store the data you work with in your JavaScript code in *variables*. If you do any programming, variables are familiar to you — they hold your data for you. Using variables in JavaScript is very easy, because you can store anything you want in them — text, numbers, even JavaScript objects.

For example, say you want to store the temperature in a variable. You name variables when you create them, so to create a variable named temperature in JavaScript, you can do this: `var temperature;`.

The JavaScript `var` keyword lets you create variables, and this JavaScript statement creates a variable named temperature. Now you can store values in that variable, like this, which stores the number 25 in the variable: `var temperature; temperature = 25;`.

The variable named temperature now holds the number 25. When you use the temperature variable in your code from now on, JavaScript replaces it with the value it

contains. For example, this new statement displays the value in temperature, 25, in the target `<div>` element: `var temperature; temperature = 25; document.getElementById("targetDiv").innerHTML = temperature;`.

You can also modify the data in the temperature variable at any time. This new code stores a new value, 16, in the temperature variable (overwriting the 25 there now), and that is the value that appears in the target `<div>` element when the last line here is executed: `var temperature; temperature = 25; temperature = 16; document.getElementById("targetDiv").innerHTML = temperature;`.

In other words, variables are the placeholders in your JavaScript. They store data for you, and you can access that data by name. Variables are handy whenever you want to work with data that changes or that is set at runtime.

Store Data in Variables

① Create a new Web page with an empty `displayText` function.

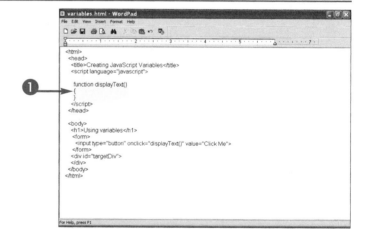

② Add code to create a new variable named text.

This variable will hold the text "Welcome to JavaScript".

You can create a variable and assign it a value in the same JavaScript statement.

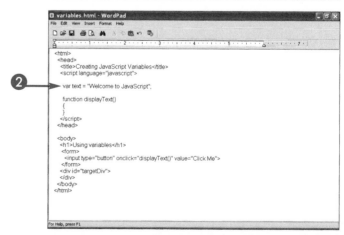

③ Add the code to display the value in the new variable in the target `<div>` element.

④ Open the Web page in a browser and click the button.

● The `displayText` function is called, which displays the value in the text variable.

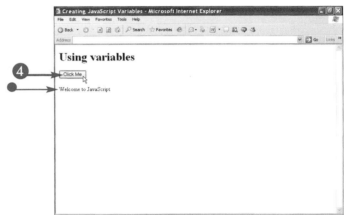

Extra

There are some rules about the names you can use for variables in JavaScript. You can use names like `text`, `temperature`, or `numberOfPizzas`. But you cannot use any of the JavaScript reserved words that appear at `http://javascript.about.com/library/blreserved.htm`, such as `var`, `do`, `delete`, and so on. JavaScript variable names may not start with a number (so you cannot say `1944battles`, for example).

The convention is to start variable names with a lowercase letter, as in the variable name text or temperature. If your variable name is made up of a number of words, there are two ways of handling that: you can use underscores, _, to separate the words, as in number_of_snowflakes, or you can use the "Java" naming convention, which capitalizes each word after the first, as in numberOfSnowflakes. The Java naming convention is becoming standard, and that is the convention used in this book.

It is also interesting to know that you do not have to declare variables at all; that is, you can omit the `var` statement altogether — just using a variable declares it. But it is considered good practice to use the `var` statement.

Work with Operators

An operator is a tool used to manipulate data. It can perform mathematical calculations, data comparisons, and assign data values to variables. Generally, operators are represented by mathematical symbols and sometimes words.

You can use JavaScript operators to manipulate the data stored in your variables. For example, you have already used the = *assignment* operator to assign values to variables, as in this case:

```
temperature = 25;
```

The assignment operator is an example of a JavaScript operator. It lets you store values in variables. In this example, you are assigning a value of 25 to the variable temperature, and the end result is that the value of 25 is stored in the variable temperature. Using JavaScript operators like this makes it easy to work with and manipulate the data stored in variables.

There are many other operators available, such as the addition operator, +. If you want to use the addition operator to add 5 to the current temperature, for example, you can do this:

```
temperature = 25;
temperature = temperature + 5;
```

The second statement adds 5 to the current value in the temperature variable and stores the result back in the temperature variable. Note that the second line of code used two operators, the = assignment operator, and the + addition operator. First, a value of 5 was added to the value in the temperature variable, and then the resulting sum is assigned to the temperature variable, leaving a value of 30 in that variable in this case.

Using Shortcut Operators

You can use the shortcut assignment operator, +=, and combine both the addition operation and the assignment operation. Here is what that looks like:

```
temperature = 25;

temperature += 5;
```

The result of these two statements is the same as the result of the previous two statements — a value of 30 is stored in the temperature variable.

You can also use the multiplication operator, *, to multiply two numbers. Here is an example, where 3 is multiplied by 5:

```
var result;

var operand1 = 3;

var operand2 = 5;

result = operand1 * operand2;
```

After these lines of JavaScript code are executed, the variable result is left with the value 15 in it.

Using the Increment and Decrement Operators

The ++ operator adds one to the value in the variable you use it on. In this case, the value in fish starts at 219, and the value in fish will be 220 after this code executes:

```
var fish = 219;

fish++;
```

The -- operator subtracts one from the variable you use it with, so this code leaves 218 in the fish variable:

```
var fish = 219;

fish--;
```

You can use the ++ and -- operators in front of a variable's name (--fish) or after (fish--), and there's a difference. When you use it before a variable's name, it is executed before the rest of the statement is executed, and when you use it after the variable's name, it is executed after the rest of the statement. In this example, the -- operator is applied to the variable a after the rest of the statement containing that expression executes, so at the end of this code, a is left with a value of 9, and b with a value of 10:

```
var a = 10;

var b;

b = a--;
```

Here is a table of the most common JavaScript operators and what they do:

OPERATOR CATEGORY	OPERATOR	DESCRIPTION
Arithmetic Operators	+	(Addition) Adds two numbers.
	++	(Increment) Increments by one the value in a variable.
	–	(Subtraction, negation) Subtracts one number from another. Can also change the sign of its operand like this: `-variableName`.
	– –	(Decrement) Decrements by one the value in a variable.
	*	(Multiplication) Multiplies two numbers.
	/	(Division) Divides two numbers.
	%	(Modulus) Returns the remainder left after dividing two numbers using integer division.
String Operators	+	(String addition) Joins two strings.
	+=	Joins two strings and assigns the joined string to the first operand.
Logical Operators	&&	(Logical AND) Returns a value of true if both operands are true; otherwise, returns false.
	||	(Logical OR) Returns a value of true if either operand is true. However, if both operands are false, returns false.
	!	(Logical NOT) Returns a value of false if its operand is true, true if its operand if false.
Assignment Operators	=	Assigns the value of the second operand to the first operand, if the first operand is a variable.
	+=	Adds two operands and assigns the result to the first operand, if it is a variable.
	–=	Subtracts two operands and assigns the result to the first operand, if it is a variable.
	*=	Multiplies two operands and assigns the result to the first operand, if it is a variable.
	/=	Divides two operands and assigns the result to the first operand, if it is a variable.
	%=	Calculates the modulus of two operands and assigns the result to the first operand, if it is a variable.
	&=	Executes a bitwise AND operation on two operands and assigns the result to the first operand, if it is a variable.
Comparison Operators	==	(Equality operator) Returns true if the two operands are equal to each other.
	!=	(Not-equal-to) Returns true if the two operands are not equal to each other.
	= = =	(Strict equality) Returns true if the two operands are both equal and of the same type. Used with objects.
	!= =	(Strict not-equal-to) Returns true if the two operands are either not equal and/or not of the same type. Used with objects.
	>	(Greater-than) Returns true if the first operand's value is greater than the second operand's value.
	>=	(Greater-than-or-equal-to) Returns true if the first operand's value is greater than or equal to the second operand's value.
	<	(Less-than) Returns true if the first operand's value is less than the second operand's value.
	<=	Less-than-or-equal-to operator. Returns true if the first operand's value is less than or equal to the second operand's value.

Use JavaScript Operators

You can use JavaScript operators to perform all kinds of operations on your data. You can create a calculator that uses the multiplication operator (*) to multiply two numbers that the user types, using JavaScript operators. To enable the user to type the two numbers to multiply, you can use two text fields: `<input type="text" id="operand1"> <input type="text" id="operand2">`.

The field text field has the ID `operand1`, and the second operand has the ID `operand2`. You can read the data the user has entered directly from those text fields in your JavaScript code.

After the user types the two numbers to multiply, the user can click a button you supply to multiply those two numbers: `<input type="button" onclick="displayText()" value="=">`.

You will need a third text field to display the results of the multiplication operation: `<input type="text" id="result">`. You can read the two numbers the user

types into the text fields, how to multiply those numbers, and display the result.

You can get the values entered into the `operand1` text field this way: `document.getElementById ("operand1").value` and the value typed into the `operand2` text field like this: `document.getElement ById("operand2").value`

To multiply the two operands together and display the results in the result text field, you can use this code which uses the * multiplication operator:

```
document.getElementById("result").value =
document.getElementById("operand1").value *
document.getElementById("operand2").value;
```

This code fetches the value of the two operands from the `operand1` and `operand2` text fields, multiplies those values, and stores the result in the result text field. You can arrange things so the calculation is performed when the user clicks a button in a Web page.

Use JavaScript Operators

1 Create a new Web page with an empty `displayText` function.

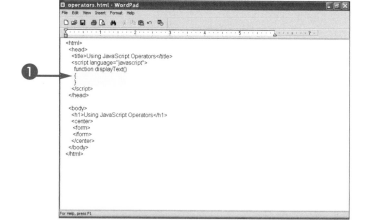

2 Add the code for two text fields with an * sign between them to show this example performs multiplication, a button with an equals sign caption, and a result text field.

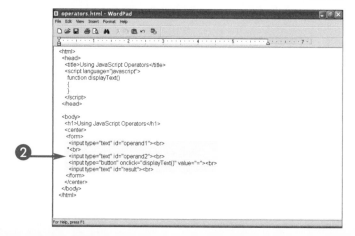

③ Add the JavaScript code that reads the numbers the user types, multiply them with the * operator, and display the result in the result text field.

④ Open the Web page in a browser, and type two numbers to multiply.

This example uses the numbers 2 and 3.

⑤ Click the button.

● The result of the multiplication appears in the results text field.

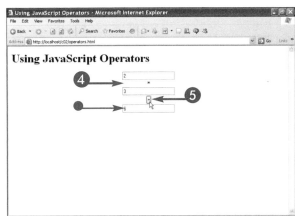

Extra

You can modify this example to perform more than just multiplication. All you need to do is to add additional buttons. Here is how you change the HTML controls displayed to display both a + and a - button:

```
<input type="text" id="operand1"><br>
<input type="button" onclick="add()" value="+"><br>
<input type="button" onclick="subtract()" value="-"><br>
<input type="text" id="operand2"><br> = <br>
<input type="text" id="result"><br>
```

You need two JavaScript functions, add and subtract, as well:

```
function add() {
   document.getElementById("result").value =
   document.getElementById("operand1").value +
   document.getElementById("operand2").value; }
function subtract() {
   document.getElementById("result").value =
   document.getElementById("operand1").value -
   document.getElementById("operand2").value; }
```

Create Local Variables

You can create both local and global variables in JavaScript. A local variable is one inside a function or an object's method, and a global variable is a variable outside any function or method. A local variable may only be used inside the function or method where it has been declared, while a global variable may be used anywhere in the script.

For example, look at this JavaScript code: `var count1 = 0; function displayText() { var count2 = 0; }`. The variable named `count1` is a global variable, and the variable named `count2` is a local variable. You can use `count1` anywhere in the script, inside the `displayText` function or outside it. On the other hand, you can only use the `count2` variable inside the `displayText` function.

There is another consequence of declaring local variables inside functions and methods. Each time a function is called, all the local variables inside it are reset to their original values. For example, if you had this code and called it repeatedly: `var count1 = 0; function displayText() { var count2 = 0; count1++; count2++; }`, then `count1`, the global variable, holds 0, 1, 2, 3, and so on as `displayText` is called over and over. But because `count2` is a local variable, it is reset to 0 each time `displayText` is called, which means that it holds 0, then 1 as the ++ operator adds 1 to it, then 0, then 1, then 0, then 1, as `displayText` is called over and over. In other words, `count2` is initialized to 0 each time the function is called, so the value in that variable is not retained, it is reinitialized each time.

Create Local Variables

① Create a new Web page with a button in it.

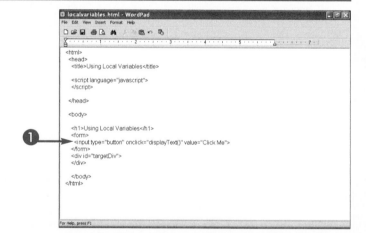

② Add the global variable `count1` and the `displayText` function.

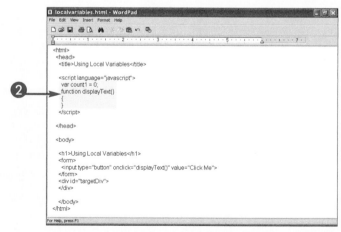

③ Add the `count2` local variable, the code to increment both the `count1` global variable and the `count2` local variable, and display their values in a `<div>` element.

④ Open the Web page in your browser and click the button repeatedly.

● The global `count1` variable continues incrementing in value from 1 to 2 to 3 and so on, and the local variable `count2` resets each time you call the `displayText` function, so it always displays a value of 1.

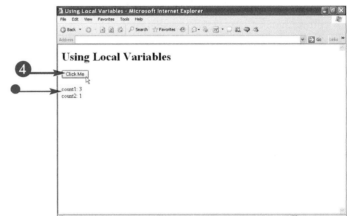

Extra

JavaScript allows you to create variables even if you do not explicitly declare them with the `var` keyword. That can be a problem sometimes, because you may end up declaring a new variable when you think you are working with one that already exists. In this code, `count2` is a local variable inside the `displayText` function, but the code right after that function also uses `count2`:

Example:
```
function displayText()
{
   var count2 = 0;
   count2++;
}
count2 = 10;
```

What happens is that JavaScript creates a new variable when you refer to `count2` outside the function, and names that new variable `count2`. Therefore, although you may think you are still working with the same `count2` that was inside the `displayText` function, this new `count2` function is an entirely new variable not related to the one inside the function.

Make Choices with the if Statement

You can make choices with the JavaScript if statement. The code in your JavaScript scripts can be executed sequentially, one statement after the next, without the possibility of different paths of execution. However, the if statement changes this by enabling your code to branch in different directions depending on the results of tests you make in your code. Here is what the if statement looks like in general: if(*condition*) { *[JavaScript goes here]* }.

The *condition* part is a true/false test that is evaluated when your code runs. If it is true, the JavaScript contained inside the curly braces ({ }) is executed. If the condition is false, the code inside the curly braces is not run. This means your code can branch — either executing the code inside the braces or skipping it — depending on the condition.

You use JavaScript's logical and comparison operators here. For example, if you need more than 100 votes to win an election and the variable votes contains more than a value of 100, you are elected.

Here is how you can check with an if statement: if(votes > 100) { }. For example, if you have more than 100 votes, you could display a message like this:

```
if(votes > 100) { document.getElementBy
Id("targetDiv").innerHTML = "You were
elected!"; }
```

Using an if statement in this way lets you make choices and execute code depending on the results of those choices. That means that your code can be interactive in a way that it could not be otherwise, responding to conditions current at runtime.

Make Choices with the if Statement

① Create a new Web page with an empty displayText function.

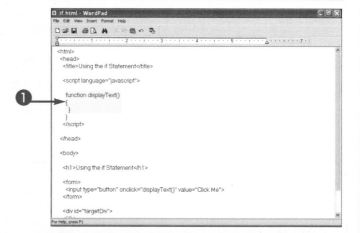

② Create a variable named votes and give it the value 101.

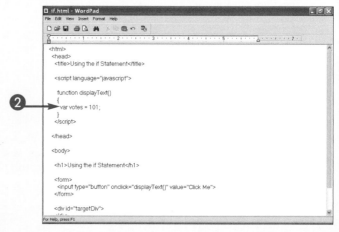

③ Add code to check if you have more than 100 votes using the `if` statement.

④ Open the Web page in your browser and click the button.

● The `if` statement determines that you have enough votes to win and displays the corresponding message.

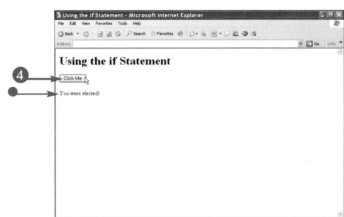

Extra

There is an additional part of the `if` statement you should know about — the optional `else` clause. This clause contains code to execute if the `if` statement's condition is false. In that case, the code in the `if` statement is not executed, but the code in the `else` clause, which must immediately follow, is

```
if(condition) {
   [JavaScript goes here]
}
else {
   [Alternate JavaScript goes here]
}
```

If you have more than 100 votes, this code tells you that you are elected; otherwise, you see the message "Sorry, you were not elected!":

```
var votes = 101;
if(votes > 100) {
   document.getElementById("targetDiv").innerHTML =
      "You were elected!";
}
else {
   document.getElementById("targetDiv").innerHTML =
      "Sorry, you were not elected!";
}
```

Using Comparison Operators

You can use JavaScript to make choices in the condition part of an `if` statement, for example: `if(votes > 100) { document.get ElementById("targetDiv").innerHTML = "You were elected!"; } else { document .getElementById("targetDiv").innerHTML = "Sorry, you were not elected!"; }`.

This code uses the greater than operator (`>`). The expression `a > b` is true if the value stored in the variable `a` is larger than the value stored in variable `b`, and false otherwise. There are other comparison operators that you should know about as well in order to write functioning Ajax code.

For example, the expression `a == b` is true if the value in `a` equals the value in `b`, and false otherwise. Using the `==` comparison operator in this way lets you compare two values, and get a true or false result, depending on

whether they were equal or not. You can use the true or false result in `if` statements to execute certain code if the two values were equal, or other code if the two values were not.

The expression `a != b` is true if the value in `a` is not equal to the value in `b`, and false otherwise. Unlike `==`, using the `!=` operator allows you to check whether two values are *not* the same. Like all comparison operators, the `!=` operator returns a value of true or false that you can use in `if` statements.

The `>=` operator lets you compare whether one value is larger than or equal to another. In particular, the expression `a >= b` is true if the value in `a` is greater than or equal to the value in `b`, and false otherwise. Other comparison operators are the less than operator (`<`) and the less than or equal to operator (`<=`).

Using Comparison Operators

① Create a new Web page that checks whether you have more than the 100 votes needed to be elected.

In this example, 99 votes is listed as the variable.

```
comparison.html - WordPad
File Edit View Insert Format Help

<html>
  <head>
    <title>Using Comparison Operators</title>

    <script language="javascript">

      function displayText()
      {
        var votes = 99;
        if(votes > 100) {
          document.getElementById("targetDiv").innerHTML =
            "You were elected!";
        }
      }
    </script>

  </head>
  <body>
    <h1>Using Comparison Operators</h1>

    <form>
      <input type="button" onclick="displayText()" value="Click Me">
    </form>

    <div id="targetDiv">
    </div>

  </body>
</html>
```

② Add an `else if` statement to check if you have exactly 100 votes, using the `==` operator.

```
comparison.html - WordPad
File Edit View Insert Format Help

<html>
  <head>
    <title>Using Comparison Operators</title>

    <script language="javascript">

      function displayText()
      {
        var votes = 99;
        if(votes > 100) {
          document.getElementById("targetDiv").innerHTML =
            "You were elected!";
        }
        else if (votes == 100){
          document.getElementById("targetDiv").innerHTML =
            "You almost got elected!";
        }
      }
    </script>

  </head>
  <body>
    <h1>Using Comparison Operators</h1>

    <form>
      <input type="button" onclick="displayText()" value="Click Me">
    </form>

    <div id="targetDiv">
```

3 Add another `else if` statement to check if you have less than 100 votes, using the < operator.

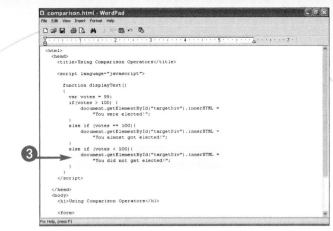

4 Open the Web page in your browser and click the button.

● The code determines that in this case you do not have enough votes to get elected.

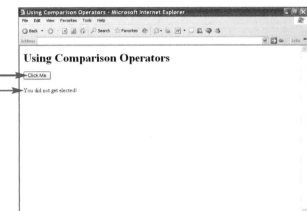

Extra

You can also use the JavaScript comparison operators together with the JavaScript logical operators. The `&&` logical AND operator connects two expressions and gives you a value of true if both expressions are true, and false otherwise. For example, say that you want to make sure the temperature is above 50 and below 80. You can connect the two expressions `temperature > 50` and `temperature < 80` this way:

```
if(temperature > 50 && temperature < 80) {
  document.getElementById("targetDiv").innerHTML =
    "The temperature is OK.";
}
```

Now the message "The temperature is OK." is displayed if the value in the temperature variable is greater than 50 and less than 80.

On the other hand, the `||` logical OR operator connects two expressions and gives you a value of true if either is true, and false otherwise. For example, `temperature < 50 || temperature > 80` is true if the temperature is either less than 50 or greater than 80.

The final logical operator is `!`, the logical NOT operator, which changes true to false and false to true. For example, `!(temperature > 50)` is true if the temperature is not greater than 50.

Determine Browser Type and Version

You can use JavaScript to determine the type and version of the browser that your Ajax application is executing in. This can be useful at times because different browsers support different capabilities. For example, Internet Explorer supports a scrolling banner <marquee> element that other browsers do not.

To determine the type of the browser, you can use the JavaScript navigator object's `appName` property. This property holds "Microsoft Internet Explorer" for that browser or "Netscape" for Firefox. To determine the browser version, you can examine the navigator object's `userAgent` property, which is a text string that holds version and other information. To extract the version number, you must search the text in the `navigator.userAgent` property.

To search that text, you should know that text strings in JavaScript are considered objects, and so have methods

and properties built in. For example, you can use the length property of the string in the `navigator.userAgent` property to determine the length of that string like this: `navigator.userAgent.length`. You can use the `indexOf` method of that string to search for matches to a substring — this method returns -1 if there is no match. And the substring method lets you extract a substring from a larger string.

Using the `navigator.appName` property, the `navigator.userAgent` property, the length property of text string objects, and the `indexOf` and substring methods of string objects, you can extract the browser name and version. Doing so lets you know what browser you are in and what browser your code is executing inside. After you have the browser name and version number, you can use `if` statements to execute different code for different browsers and different versions of those browsers.

Determine Browser Type and Version

① Create a new Web page and add the code needed to determine if the user is using Firefox, and if so, what version.

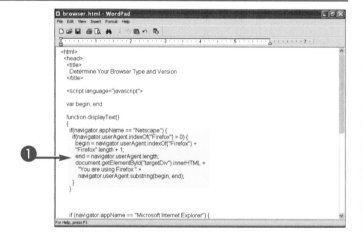

② Add the code shown to determine if the user is using Internet Explorer, and if so, what version.

③ Open the Web page in Internet Explorer and click the button.

● The browser type and version appear.

④ Open the Web page in Firefox and click the button.

● The browser type and version appear.

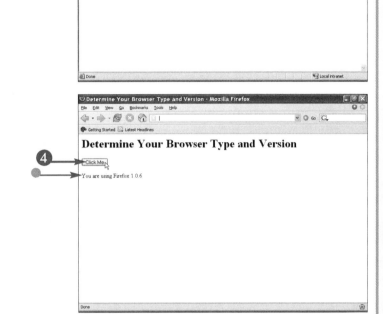

Extra

You can adapt the code in this example to execute certain code for Internet Explorer and other code for Firefox. For example, if you want to run certain code in Firefox only, you can check if the JavaScript navigator object's `appName` property equals "Netscape", and if so, you can find the text "Firefox" in the navigator object's `userAgent` property:

Example:
```
{
    if(navigator.appName == "Netscape") {
        if(navigator.userAgent.indexOf("Firefox") > 0) {
            [JavaScript for Firefox goes here.]
        }
    }

    if (navigator.appName == "Microsoft Internet Explorer") {
        [JavaScript for Internet Explorer goes here.]
    }
```

Repeat Code Execution with the for Loop

One of the best parts of programming is the ability to execute code over and over. For example, you may have a list of thousands of students, all of whom have a test grade, and you may want to find the average score. Instead of writing code to handle each student individually, which would take thousands of lines of code, you can write code to *loop* over all the scores.

Looping means iterating over code and executing it more than once. Here is an example showing how to use the for loop. Say that you want to display the text "Hello from JavaScript." ten times in a Web page. You can do that easily with a for loop. To use a for loop, you must use a loop index variable, which keeps track of how many times you execute the loop.

To create a for loop, you use the keyword for, followed by a pair of parentheses and the code to execute each

time through the loop enclosed in curly braces ({ }). Inside the parentheses, you list three items separated by semicolons: the initialization code to execute when the loop starts (usually, you set the loop index variable to a starting value here, such as loopIndex = 1); the condition that must become true to make the loop end, such as loopIndex <= 10 for ten loops; and the code you want executed after each time through the loop (usually code to increment the loop index by one, such as loopIndex++). Here is what the for loop would look like to display the message ten times: The first time through the loop, the loopIndex variable will hold 1, the next time 2, and so on. The loop ends when loopIndex exceeds a value of 10: var loopIndex; for(loopIndex = 1; loopIndex <= 10; loopIndex++) { document.write("Hello from JavaScript.
"); }.

Repeat Code Execution with the for Loop

1 Create a new Web page that lets you sum the integers from 1 to 50, using a for loop, creating a loop index variable.

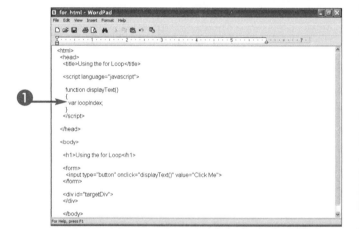

2 Set up a for loop to loop 50 times.

③ Add a new variable named sum that holds a running sum, and set it to 0.

④ Each time through the loop, add the current loopIndex value to it, which holds the values 1, 2, 3, and so on, and then display the final sum.

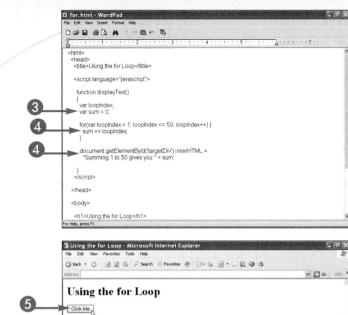

```
<html>
  <head>
    <title>Using the for Loop</title>

    <script language=")javascript">

    function displayText()
    {
      var loopIndex;
      var sum = 0;

      for(var loopIndex = 1; loopIndex <= 50; loopIndex++) {
        sum += loopIndex;
      }

      document.getElementById('targetDiv').innerHTML =
        "Summing 1 to 50 gives you " + sum;

    }
    </script>

  </head>

  <body>

    <h1>Using the for Loop</h1>
```

⑤ Open the Web page in your browser and click the button.

● The for loop loops 50 times. The total sum displays the sum of the integers from 1 to 50.

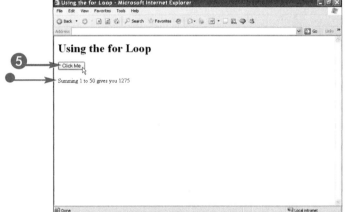

Using the for Loop

⑤ Click Me

Summing 1 to 50 gives you 1275

Extra

The for loop has a shortcut, making it easier to declare the loop index variable. Although the loopIndex variable is explicitly declared in this task's example:

```
var loopIndex;
for(loopIndex = 1; loopIndex <= 10; loopIndex++) {
  document.write("Hello from JavaScript.<br>");
}
```

You do not need to declare the loopIndex variable outside the loop. You can use the var keyword in the part of the for loop that initializes the loopIndex variable to declare that variable:

```
for(var loopIndex = 1; loopIndex <= 10; loopIndex++) {
  document.write("Hello from JavaScript.<br>");
}
```

Note also that the loop index variable does not have to be named loopIndex — you can use any valid JavaScript name for the name of this variable, such as count:

```
for(var count = 1; count <= 10; count++) {
  document.write("Hello from JavaScript.<br>");
}
```

Handle Multiple Data Items at Once Using Arrays

ou can handle multiple data items at the same time using arrays in JavaScript. So far, the variables you have seen only contain a single data item, but an array can handle multiple data items at once. You give an array a single name, but can store multiple items (numbers, strings, or objects) in that array, which you access using a numeric index. For example, you can create an array called names that holds five elements like this: `var names = new Array(5);`.

Then you can place elements — strings that hold names in this case — in the array, indexed by number. That number is given in square brackets ([ ]) like this:

```
names[0] = "Steve"; names[1] = "Edward";
names[2] = "Sam"; names[3] = "Nancy";
names[4] = "Susan";
```

Now you can access any of the names stored in the array by number inside the square brackets. For example, to display `names[2]`, `"Sam"`, you can use code the code `document.getElementById('targetDiv').innerHTML = names[2];`.

If you want to find the length of an array, you can use the array's length property. For example, `names.length` holds the value 5 because the names array is declared to hold five elements.

Arrays are particularly good to use in loops like `for` loops because you can use the loop index as the index in the array, allowing you to loop over all the elements in an array easily. That means you can add the elements in an array easily by accessing each element in the array, display each element in the array, or find the average value of the elements in the array, and so on.

Handle Multiple Data Items at Once Using Arrays

① Create a new Web page and declare an array named scores that holds the test scores of five students.

② Fill the array with student scores, and create the `for` loop that loops over the array and sums the scores.

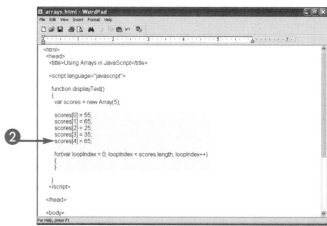

③ Create a new variable named `sum` to hold the sum of the scores.

④ Add the code to the `for` loop to update the running sum each time through the loop.

⑤ Add the average score by dividing the summed test scores by the number of students.

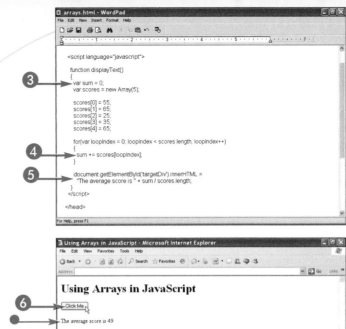

⑥ Open the Web page in your browser and click the button.

● The average test score appears.

Extra

In JavaScript, arrays are zero-based. Filling the five elements in the scores array in this task started with item number 0 in this array:

```
scores[0] = 55;
scores[1] = 65;
scores[2] = 25;
scores[3] = 35;
scores[4] = 65;
```

This does not work if you omit the zero and do it this way:

```
scores[1] = 55;
scores[2] = 65;
scores[3] = 25;
scores[4] = 35;
scores[5] = 65;
```

Because arrays are zero-based in JavaScript, you access the first element with the index value 0, not 1. You can access an array with five elements with the index values 0 – 4, not 1 – 5. In fact, there is no element corresponding to index value 5, and trying to access it results in an error.

Using the while Loop

You can use the `while` loop to loop over data. The `while` loop keeps looping, which mean it continues to execute the code you have put into it as long as a certain condition remains true. That is different from the `for` loop because you do not need to use a loop index variable, as you do with the `for` loop.

The `while` loop is simple to use: You just use the keyword `while`, enclose the condition you want to be tested in parentheses, and the code you want to execute each time through the loop in curly braces ({ }). Here is an example: In this case, the `while` loop keeps executing while the value in a variable named `count` is less than 200: `while (count < 200) { [JavaScript goes here] }.`

When the value in `count` exceeds 200, the loop terminates, because the condition `count < 200` becomes

false, which ends the loop's execution. Here is another example: In this case, the code inside the curly braces executes over and over while the text field with the ID `"text1"` does not hold any text: `while (document. getElementById("text1").value == "") { [JavaScript goes here] }.`

You can use `while` loops anywhere you use any loop in JavaScript, where a loop index is not necessary. As long as you have a condition that remains true as long as you want the loop to keep looping, that is fine. When the tested condition becomes false, the loop stops.

For example, you can display the reciprocal (for example, one-fourth is the reciprocal of 4) of numbers in an array as long as the code does not encounter 0 in the array, because you cannot calculate 1/0.

Using the while Loop

① Create a new Web page with a JavaScript function named `displayText` and an array named `values` that includes one element with a value of zero.

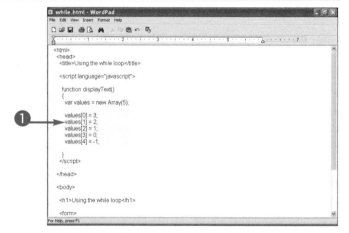

② Create a new variable named `index` that keeps track of where you are in the array.

③ Create a `while` loop that keeps looping while the current value in the array is not zero.

60

④ Type the code to display the reciprocal of the current value in the array.

⑤ Open the Web page in your browser.

The reciprocals appear until the JavaScript code is asked to find the reciprocal of 0.

The `while` loop quits and the display terminates.

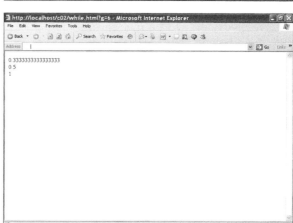

Extra

The `do...while` loop is a variant of the `while` loop. This loop is just like the `while` loop, but it checks its condition at the end of the loop like this:

```
do {
    display(count);
} while (count < 200)
```

That might seem just the same as a `while` loop, but it is not. In particular, you may only set the condition you want to test inside the body of the loop, and if you do, it is more appropriate to check that condition at the end of the loop instead of the beginning. Here is an example:

```
do {
    display(count);
    count = setCount();
} while (count < 200)
```

A `while` loop may not execute even once if the condition is false, but a `do...while` loop always executes at least once because the loop condition is tested at the end of the loop, not the beginning.

The whole point behind Ajax applications is that they can fetch data from the server behind the scenes without causing a page refresh. Normal Web applications communicate with the server simply by going to a new URL. For example, when you enter data into a Web page and click the Submit button in a form, what normally happens is that your data is sent to the URL specified in the form's action attribute. For example, in a form, say that you are asking the user to give their name and list their favorite fruits, and then to click a Submit button. The data in a text field and a `<select>` control are sent to the URL `www.ajaxisus.com/program.php`. `<form method="post" action="http://www.ajaxisus.com/program.php">` What is your name?

```
<input name="Name" type="text"> <br> <br>
Select your favorite fruit(s): <select name=
"Food[]" multiple>          <option>Apple</option>
<option>Orange</option> <option>Pear</option>
<option>Pomegranate</option> </select> <br>
<br> <input type="submit" value="Submit">
</form>
```
The form's action attribute will hold the URL `www.ajaxisus.com/program.php`, the URL to which the form's data is sent.

When the data is sent to the server, the program named program.php on the server reads the data from the form, processes it, and creates a new Web page, which is sent back to the browser. That new page causes a page refresh, and you see that familiar flicker as the new page appears.

Enter Ajax

Ajax applications are different. In Ajax applications, you use an `XMLHttpRequest` object — an object built into the browser that you have access to in JavaScript — to communicate with the server. In an Ajax application, you do not need an HTML form to communicate with the server. Everything is handled in JavaScript, and the user never needs to know about the details. If you wish, you can read the data in an HTML form and send it to the server, but that is not necessary — now, you are no longer restricted to working with HTML forms at all.

That means you are going to have to know how to work with the `XMLHttpRequest` object, which is the main topic of this chapter. The way you create and use `XMLHttpRequest` objects differs a little by browser, and you have to know how to handle various browser types so that your Web page functions in all of them. And you must know how to work with `XMLHttpRequest` objects in detail. For reference, you can see the methods and properties of this object in the following tables for various popular browsers. You can see how to use those methods and properties in this chapter.

The XMLHttpRequest object

When you use Ajax, the `XMLHttpRequest` object is responsible for everything you usually do with HTML forms: You can communicate with server-side code, such as program.php, on the server, and when you use Ajax, you write such server-side code to return data in text or XML format, not as complete Web pages. It is up to you to extract your data from the `XMLHttpRequest` object and to handle it as you see fit, such as displaying it in the current Web page.

This chapter is all about getting started creating Ajax applications and working with the `XMLHttpRequest` object.

METHODS FOR INTERNET EXPLORER	
METHOD	CONTAINS
abort	Aborts an HTTP request.
getAllResponse Headers	Returns all HTTP headers.
getResponseHeader	Returns an HTTP header.
open	Lets you configure an XMLHttpRequest object.
send	Sends an HTTP request to the server.
setRequestHeader	Sets an HTTP header name and value.

PROPERTIES FOR INTERNET EXPLORER

PROPERTY	CONTAINS
onreadystatechange	Contains the name of the function to be called when the value of the readyState property changes. Read/write.
readyState	Contains the state of a request. Read-only.
responseBody	Contains an HTTP response body. Read-only.
responseStream	Contains a response stream, which is a binary stream to the server. Read-only.
responseText	Contains the HTTP response body in string form. Read-only.
responseXML	Contains the HTTP response body in XML form. Read-only.
status	Contains the HTTP status code. Read-only.
statusText	Contains the HTTP response status text. Read-only.

PROPERTIES FOR MOZILLA, FIREFOX, AND NETSCAPE NAVIGATOR

PROPERTY	CONTAINS
channel	Contains the channel used to perform the request. Read-only.
readyState	Contains the current state of the request. Read-only.
responseText	Contains the HTTP response body in string form. Read-only.
responseXML	Contains the HTTP response body in XML form. Read-only.
status	Contains the HTTP status code returned by a request. Read-only.
statusText	Contains the HTTP response status text. Read-only.

PROPERTIES FOR APPLE SAFARI

PROPERTY	CONTAINS
onreadystatechange	Contains the name of the function to be called when the value of the readyState property changes. Read/write.
readyState	Contains the state of a request. Read-only.
responseText	Contains the HTTP response body in string form. Read-only.
responseXML	Contains the HTTP response body in XML form. Read-only.
status	Contains the HTTP status code. Read-only.
statusText	Contains the HTTP response status text. Read-only.

METHODS FOR MOZILLA, FIREFOX, AND NETSCAPE NAVIGATOR

METHOD	CONTAINS
abort	Aborts an HTTP request.
getAllResponseHeaders	Gets all HTTP headers.
getResponseHeader	Gets an HTTP header.
openRequestNative	A method to open a request not using scripts.
overrideMimeType	Sets the MIME type of the data the server returns.

METHODS FOR APPLE SAFARI

METHOD	CONTAINS
abort	Aborts an HTTP request.
getAllResponseHeaders	Returns all HTTP headers.
getResponseHeader	Returns an HTTP header.
open	Lets you configure an XMLHttpRequest object.
send	Sends an HTTP request to the server.
setRequestHeader	Sets an HTTP header name and value.

Create an XMLHttpRequest Object Using JavaScript

You can create XMLHttpRequest objects using JavaScript. The XMLHttpRequest object is the very heart of Ajax. There are two main browsers you have to handle, because creating an XMLHttpRequest object differs in two types of browsers.

The first type of browser is made up of all modern browsers except for Internet Explorer. You can check whether you are dealing with one of these browsers if the XMLHttpRequest property of the browser window object exists, which you can check with the if statement. To create an XMLHttpRequst object in this case, you simply use the JavaScript new operator, which is designed to create new objects. Here is how it looks in code:

```
var XMLHttpRequestObject; if (window.
XMLHttpRequest) { XMLHttpRequestObject =
new XMLHttpRequest(); } That creates an
XMLHttpRequest object and stores it in
the variable named XMLHttpRequestObject
```

If your application is running in Internet Explorer, on the other hand, the window.XMLHttpRequest property does not exist, but the window.ActiveXObject property does. If that property exists, you can create a new XMLHttpRequest object in Internet Explorer this way:

```
var XMLHttpRequestObject; if (window.
XMLHttpRequest) {      XMLHttpRequestObject =
new XMLHttpRequest(); } else if (window.
ActiveXObject) {      XMLHttpRequestObject =
new ActiveXObject("Microsoft.XMLHTTP");
```

When you create an XMLHttpRequest object and store it in a variable this way, you are ready to start working with Ajax. The XMLHttpRequest object is at the heart of Ajax, and you use this object to interact with the server to both upload and download data. You use the methods of this object in order to interact with the server behind the scenes, without needing a browser page refresh.

Create an XMLHttpRequest Object Using JavaScript

① Create a new Web page with a `<script>` section and create a new variable named XMLHttpRequestObject, setting it to false to indicate that the variable does not yet hold an object.

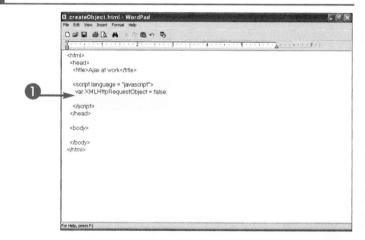

② Create the XMLHttpRequest object and store it in the XMLHttpRequestObject variable for non-Internet Explorer browsers.

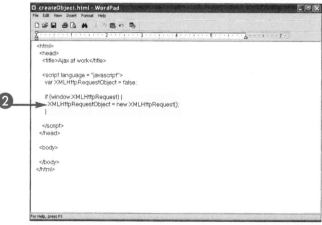

③ Type the code to create an `XMLHttpRequest` object in case the browser is Internet Explorer, and also type the code to display the message "Object created." if object is created.

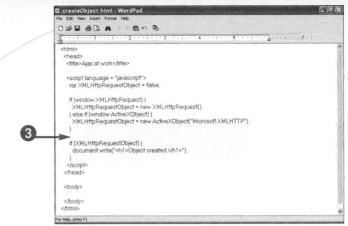

④ Open the Web page in a browser.

The message "Object created." appears in your browser; you have created a new `XMLHttpRequest` object.

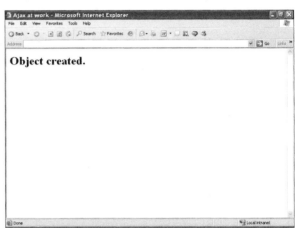

Extra

Take a look at the code that checks to see if the `XMLHttpRequest` object is created and stored in the `XMLHttpRequestObject` variable:

```
if (XMLHttpRequestObject) {
   document.write("<h1>Object created.</h1>");
}
```

Note that the condition of the `if` statement is simply the `XMLHttpRequestObject` variable. If that variable holds false — which it was initialized to do — the `XMLHttpRequest` object is not created. If it holds any other value, JavaScript treats its value as true, which means an `XMLHttpRequest` object was indeed created.

If you are not able to create an `XMLHttpRequest` object, you can display a message in the browser, or execute alternate code, indicating that the browser does not support Ajax:

```
if (XMLHttpRequestObject) {
   document.write("<h1>Object created.</h1>");
}
else {
   document.write("<h1>Your browser does not support Ajax.</h1>");
}
```

Open the XMLHttpRequest Object

You can work with an XMLHttpRequest object after you *open* it. Opening an XMLHttpRequest object prepares it for use to fetch data from the server — just opening the object does not fetch any data or connect to the server.

To open an XMLHttpRequest object, you use the open method, which takes these arguments — (the ones in square brackets are optional):

```
open("method", "URL"[, asyncFlag[,
"userName"[, "password"]]])
```

method is the HTTP method used to open the connection, such as GET, POST, PUT, or HEAD. URL is the URL you want to download from. asyncFlag is a Boolean value indicating whether the call is asynchronous. The default is true, which means the send method will not halt the rest of your code while waiting for data: userName — user name; password — password.

The method argument sets the way you want to access the data on the server. You can use various HTTP methods here — GET or POST, for example, are the most common. These methods match the ones you can use in an HTML form's method attribute. You learn more about GET and POST later in this chapter. If you are in doubt, you can always use the GET method to fetch data from the server.

The URL is the URL you want to use to fetch data from, which is the same URL you give in an HTML form's action attribute. The asyncFlag argument is set to true in Ajax, making the connection with the server asynchronous, which means the whole browser does not have to stop to wait for the data. The userName and password arguments let you log on to servers that require them.

After the XMLHttpRequest object is opened, you can see how to use its send method to communicate with the server in upcoming topics.

Open the XMLHttpRequest Object

① Add a form with a Display Message button connected to a function named getData.

In preparation for fetching data from the server, pass the name of the text file data.txt to the getData function, as well as the ID of the <div> element where results should be displayed, which is targetDiv.

② Add the <div> element with the ID targetDiv to the Web page to display results.

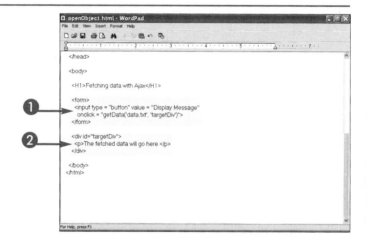

③ Create the getData function, and add an if statement to check if the XMLHttpRequest object has been created and is stored in the XMLHttpRequestObject variable.

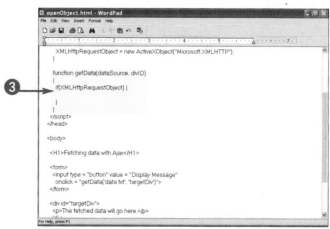

④ Open the `XMLHttpRequest` object, passing the open `Get` HTTP method and the name of the file on the server as stored in the `getData` function's dataSource argument. After the object is opened, display the message `"Object opened"` in the display `<div>` element.

⑤ Open the Web page in your browser.

The message "Object opened." appears.

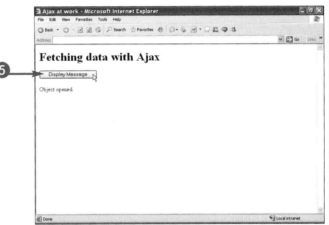

Extra

The HTTP method selected when the `XMLHttpRequest` object is opened in this task is the `GET` method. When you use the `GET` method, you can send data to code on the server by encoding that data in the URL passed to the `XMLHttpRequest` object's open method. For example, if you have an HTML text field named text1 and you want to let your program on the server know that that text field contains the text "Now is the time", you can send your data to this URL:

```
http://www.servername.com/user/scriptname?text1=Now+is+the+time
```

That works fine, and you can see more on how to send data to the server using the `GET` and `POST` methods at the end of this chapter. Note that storing your data in the URL like this — which is called URL-encoding — makes that data visible as you send it over the Internet.

In contrast, when you send data to the server using the `POST` method, that data is hidden in the HTTP headers that are sent to the server, making the `POST` method somewhat more secure.

Get Ready to Download

You can download data from the server now that you have opened an XMLHttpRequest object. Ajax downloads take place behind the scenes, in an asynchronous way, which means they do not stop and wait for the data — they handle the data as it comes in from the server, when it comes in from the server.

When data comes in from the server that an XMLHttpRequest object has fetched, that object's readyState property changes. Here are the possible values of the readyState property — (note that a value of 4 means your data is all downloaded): 0, uninitialized; 1, loading; 2, loaded; 3, interactive; 4, complete.

Also, you can check the XMLHttpRequest object's status property, which holds the status of the download. This is the standard HTTP status of a download, and you need to make sure that it is set to a value of 200. That value means that the download was successful, and the XMLHttpRequest object got the data.

You know when the readyState and status values of an XMLHttpRequest object change when you can connect a JavaScript function to the XMLHttpRequest object's onreadystatechange property. There is an easy way to do that: You can create an anonymous — that is, unnamed — JavaScript function to this property like this:

```
XMLHttpRequestObject.onreadystatechange =
function() { }
```

This creates a function without a name — that is, an anonymous function. This function is connected to the XMLHttpRequest object's onreadystatechange property, which means that when there is a change in that property, this function is called automatically.

The code you want to execute in this function is placed inside the curly braces. This is where you place the code to handle the downloaded data in the next topic.

Get Ready to Download

① Connect an anonymous function to an XMLHttpRequest object.

The anonymous function handles downloads from the server.

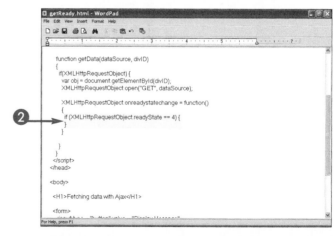

② Check to see if the readyState property is set to 4, indicating the download is complete.

3 Check to make sure that the status property holds 200, indicating that there were no problems; also, add code to display the message "Ready to download".

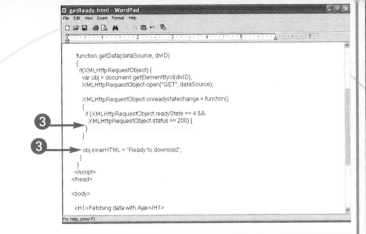

4 Open the Web page in a browser.

● The message "Ready to download" appears.

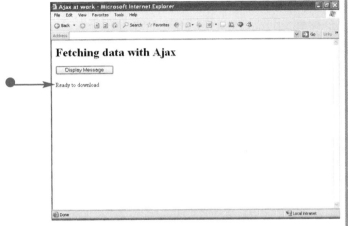

Extra

The `XMLHttpRequest` object's status property holds the HTTP result of your download. A value of 200 means that your download is successful. But there are other possible values you might see listed here so that you can tell the user what is wrong. Here is a list of some common HTTP errors:

204 No Content

206 Partial Content

401 Unauthorized

403 Forbidden

404 Not Found

407 Proxy Authentication Required

408 Request Timeout

413 Requested Entity Too Large

414 Requested URL Too Long

415 Unsupported Media Type

500 Internal Server Error

503 Service Unavailable

504 Gateway Timeout

505 HTTP Version Not Supported

Download Data with the XMLHttpRequest Object

Y ou can download data from the server using the XMLHttpRequest object. Say that you have created a new XMLHttpRequest object, opened it to configure it for the download, and connected it to an anonymous function to handle the actual download when that download is done.

Using the open method, you can configure the XMLHttpRequest object to fetch a file named, for example, data.txt from the server. When a button is clicked, a function named getData is called, and that function is passed the name of the file to fetch, data.txt:

```
<input type = "button" value = "Display
Message" onclick = "getData('data.txt',
'targetDiv')">.
```

The getData function is declared as getData(dataSource, divID), so the filename data.txt is placed in the dataSource argument when the getData function is called. That name is then passed to

the XMLHttpRequest object's open method as

```
function getData(dataSource, divID)
{ XMLHttpRequestObject.open("GET",
dataSource); }
```

On the server, you must place the file data.txt in the same directory as the Web page that fetches that file. The reason for that is that this example only uses the name "data.txt" as the file on the server, without giving a full URL — "data.txt" is a relative, not absolute, URL. If you gave the full URL pointing to data.txt, you would not have to place data.txt in the same directory as the Web page that fetches it. The file data.txt in this example simply has the text "This text was fetched using Ajax." in it. To download data.txt, you use the XMLHttpRequest object's send method. Because you are using the GET method to fetch data, you pass the send method a value of null, which means you have no additional data to send.

Download Data with the XMLHttpRequest Object

① Use the XMLHttpRequest object's send method, passing it a value of null, to fetch data.txt from the server.

The XMLHttpRequest object downloads the data in data.txt from the server.

Note: Make sure data.txt is in the same directory as this Web page on the server or the code will not be able to find it.

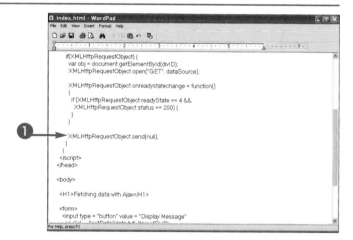

② Use the XMLHttpRequest object's responseText property to read the downloaded text, and display the downloaded text in the display <div> element in the Web page.

In this example, text in the file data.txt is downloaded from the server, which means you recover that text using the XMLHttpRequest object's responseText property.

70

3 Open the new Web page in your browser, and click the Display Message button.

● Using Ajax techniques, the Web page fetches the contents of the file data.txt behind the scenes and displays the contents "This text was fetched using Ajax."

This example must be run on a Web server.

4 Open the Web page in another browser and click the Display Message button.

This example uses Firefox.

● When you click the Display Message button, the same message appears.

Apply It

As written, this example handles the downloaded data in the anonymous function connected to the `XMLHttpRequest` object's `onreadystate` property by displaying that data in the Web page:

```
XMLHttpRequestObject.onreadystatechange = function()
{
  if (XMLHttpRequestObject.readyState == 4 &&
    XMLHttpRequestObject.status == 200) {
      obj.innerHTML = XMLHttpRequestObject.responseText;
  }
}
```

If your code to handle the downloaded data is long, you do not have to place all that code inside the anonymous function. You can simply call another function, and place your data-handling code there. Here is an example that passes the downloaded text to a function named `handleData` that you can write:

```
XMLHttpRequestObject.onreadystatechange = function()
{
  if (XMLHttpRequestObject.readyState == 4 &&
    XMLHttpRequestObject.status == 200) {
      handleData(responseText);
  }
}
```

Select Relative or Absolute URLs

Y ou can use relative or absolute URLs when pointing to the data you want to read from the server. Ajax techniques can download the contents of a file, data.txt, from the server by passing the name of the file to download to the `getData` function this way: `<form> <input type = "button" value = "Display Message" onclick = "getData ('data.txt', 'targetDiv')"> </form>`.

In the `getData` function, the name of the file is stored in the `dataSource` argument, which is passed to the `XMLHttpRequest` object's open method this way:
```
function getData(dataSource, divID)
{           if(XMLHttpRequestObject)
{ var obj = document.getElementById(divID);
XMLHttpRequestObject.open("GET",
dataSource);.
```

The reason you can access data.text using only its filename is that data.txt is in the same directory on the server as the Web page that fetches that file. You only need to use the filename, because the browser assumes that you are looking for that file in the same directory on the server as the Web page that references that file. On the other hand, if the data you are fetching is not in the same directory in the Web server, you have to provide a path to the data you want, which can mean using a URL like this:

```
<form> <input type = "button" value =
"Display Message" onclick = "getData
('http://www.fxaz.com/data.txt',
'targetDiv')"> </form>
```

The filename alone is a relative URL (relative to the location of the Web page), and using the full URL is using an absolute URL. If you try to reach an absolute URL that is in an entirely different Web domain than the Web page is in, the browser issues a security warning by displaying a warning dialog box to the user.

Select Relative or Absolute URLs

1 Use a relative URL to point to the data.txt file.

In this example, data.txt is in the same directory as the Web page itself on the server, so you can use just the name of the file, data.txt.

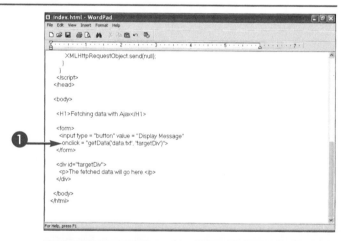

2 Open the Web page in your browser to make sure that it works as it should.

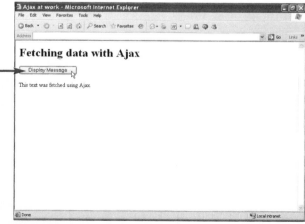

③ Type the full URL of the data.txt file.

Now you are using an absolute URL.

④ Open the Web page in your browser again to make sure that the code can find the data.txt file using the absolute URL.

Extra

A relative URL can also contain a pathname. For example, if the file data.txt is in the data subdirectory of the directory that contains the Web page, you can access it using the relative URL /data/data.txt:

```
<input type = "button" value = "Display Message"
  onclick = "getData('/data/data.txt', 'targetDiv')">
```

On the other hand, some Web servers require backslashes instead like this:

```
<input type = "button" value = "Display Message"
  onclick = "getData('\data\data.txt', 'targetDiv')">
```

You can also use the syntax .. (two periods) to navigate to the directory above the current directory on many servers. For example, if the file you want to reach is in the data subdirectory of the current directory's parent directory, you can use this code:

```
<input type = "button" value = "Display Message"
  onclick = "getData('..\data\data.txt', 'targetDiv')">
```

Create Newer XMLHttpRequest Objects in Internet Explorer

You can get newer versions of the XMLHttpRequest objects in Internet Explorer, and in future releases of Internet Explorer, such objects may offer more advanced capabilities. A newer XMLHttpRequest object may be created with the expression new ActiveXObject("MSXML2.XMLHTTP"), for example.

To try to create a newer object with that expression, you can use the JavaScript try/catch statement. If the code in a try section fails, the code in the following catch section will be executed. Here is an example. If this code cannot create a newer XMLHttpRequest object, it creates a standard one:

```
var XMLHttpRequestObject = false; try {
XMLHttpRequestObject = new ActiveXObject
("MSXML2.XMLHTTP"); } catch (exception1)
{ try { XMLHttpRequestObject = new
ActiveXObject("Microsoft.XMLHTTP"); } catch
(exception2) { XMLHttpRequestObject =
false; } }
```

The way this code works is by attempting to create an MSXML2.XMLHTTP XMLHttpRequest object first, inside a try block, by using this code: XMLHttpRequestObject = new ActiveXObject("MSXML2.XMLHTTP"). If that does not work, the code in the catch block is executed, which tries to create a Microsoft.XMLHTTP XMLHttpRequest object using this code: XMLHttpRequestObject = new ActiveXObject("Microsoft.XMLHTTP")

If that does not work, the code was unable to create an XMLHttpRequest object, and sets the XMLHttpRequestObject variable to false. In this way, you provide for failure to create the most recent XMLHttpRequest object in a smooth way, falling back on the most common way of creating that object. If this does not work, you set the XMLHttpRequestObject variable to false, because there is no other option.

Create Newer XMLHttpRequest Objects in Internet Explorer

① Add the code to create a newer
XMLHttpRequest object.

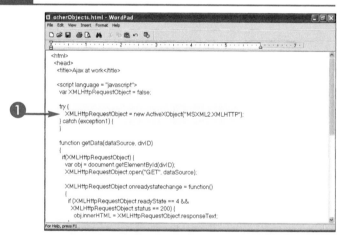

② Add the code to create a standard
XMLHttpRequest object if a newer
one cannot be created.

74

③ Add the code to handle browsers other than Internet Explorer.

④ Open the Web page in your browser and click the button.

The page works as before, but this time uses a more recent XMLHttppRequest object.

Newer XMLHttpRequest objects available in Internet Explorer offer no new functionality, but that may change in the future.

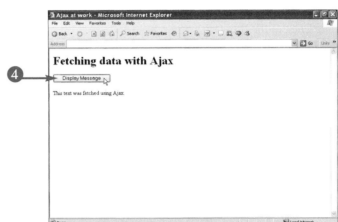

Extra

Note the exception objects exception1 and exception2 in the JavaScript code in this task. These exception objects contain more information about the error that occurred, and you can determine the name of the error with the exception object's name property and get the error's message with the exception object's message property. Here is some code that insists on creating an MSXML2.XMLHTTP XMLHttpRequest object, and if it cannot, it displays an error message in an alert box:

```
var XMLHttpRequestObject = false;

try {
   XMLHttpRequestObject = new ActiveXObject("MSXML2.XMLHTTP");
} catch (exception1) {
   alert("There was a " + exception1.name + " error. Error message: " +
      exception1.message); }
}
```

You can use server-side programming to create the data read by your Ajax scripts. The examples you have seen to this point have read a simple text file, data.txt, from the server. However, Ajax can also be used to interact with programs on the server.

Most commonly, Ajax is used with PHP programs on the server when server-side scripting is used; this book uses PHP as well. You do not have to understand PHP to read this book, and the PHP examples are simple. For example, you can use an easy PHP script — data.php — to send data back to the browser: `<?php echo "This text was fetched using PHP and Ajax."; ?>`.

This script starts enclosed in the PHP markup `<?php` and `?>` (you can also use `<?` and `?>`) so that the server knows you are using PHP and that the enclosed text is PHP code. In this case, the code simply uses the PHP

echo statement to send the text "This text was fetched using PHP and Ajax." to the browser. That text is sent back to the browser, which reads it using Ajax techniques, not with a page refresh.

To use Ajax to read the text, simply open the file data.php, not data.txt: `<form> <input type = "button" value = "Display Message" onclick = "getData('data.php', 'targetDiv')"> </form>`. When you open the file data.php, the data.php script is run on the browser, and the text "This text was fetched using PHP and Ajax." is sent back to the browser.

Note that data.php must be in the same directory as the Web page in this case, and you must use a server that is PHP-enabled. In other words, your server must be able to run PHP scripts. If you are unsure if your server can run PHP, check with your server's technical staff.

Start Using Server-Side Scripts

① Create a new file named data.php, and type the PHP markup `<?php` and end the file with the PHP markup `?>`.

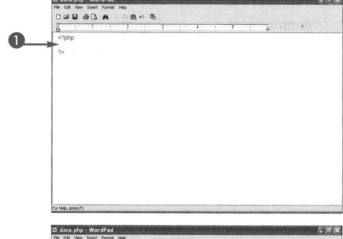

② Add the PHP code to send the text "This text was fetched using PHP and Ajax." back to the server.

③ Access data.php on the server.

Make sure the data.php file is in the same directory as the new Web page on your PHP-enabled server.

④ Click the button in the Web page after opening that page in a browser.

- The data.php script on the server returns the message to the browser.

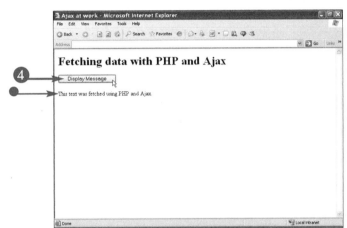

Extra

You can also use HTML in your PHP scripts. The PHP script in this task, data.php, simply looks like this:

```
<?php
    echo "This text was fetched using PHP and Ajax.";
?>
```

However, the <?php and ?> markup is only there to tell the server where the PHP code is. If you wanted to, you could rewrite this code something like this:

```
Hello.
<?php
    echo " This is a test. ";
?>
<i>This is only a test.</i>
```

In addition, the text "Hello. This is a test. <i>This is only a test.</i>" is sent to the browser. In this way, you can mix text, including HTML, together with your PHP code. The text and HTML outside the <?php and ?> markup is sent to the browser verbatim.

Create XML Documents for Download

Y ou can download data in XML format and use that data in your Ajax application. The X in Ajax stands for XML, and much of the data downloaded by Ajax applications uses XML data. All XML documents must begin with an XML declaration that starts with `<?xml` and ends with `?>`. You must also list the XML version in the XML declaration; by far the most common version of XML in use today is 1.0, so this is what the XML declaration looks like: `<?xml version= "1.0"?>`.

XML documents look much like the elements you use in HTML, except you make up the element names yourself. See Chapter 9 for the full details. Each XML document must contain a document element, which contains all the other elements in the document. In this case, say you are creating an XML document containing various sandwich types. For example, if the document element is named `<sandwiches>`, you would code the document like this:

```
<?xml version="1.0"?> <sandwiches>
</sandwiches>
```

Finally, you add the XML elements named `<sandwich>` that contain the sandwich types. Each `<sandwich>`

element starts with an opening tag, `<sandwich>`, contains a sandwich type, and ends with a closing tag, `</sandwich>`, so here is what the final document might look like:

```
<?xml version="1.0"?> <sandwiches>
<sandwich>ham</sandwich>
<sandwich>turkey</sandwich>
<sandwich>cheese</sandwich> </sandwiches>
```

This document contains three `<sandwich>` elements corresponding to three different types of sandwiches: ham, turkey, and cheese.

Note that all three `<sandwich>` elements are inside the `<sandwiches>` document element (all XML elements must be contained inside the document element). In addition, each `<sandwich>` element itself might contain child elements, like this:

```
<sandwich> <type> ham </type> <dressing>
mayonnaise </dressing> </sandwich>
```

where the `<sandwich>` element contains `<type>` and `<dressing>` child elements.

Create XML Documents for Download

① Create a new XML document, and place an XML declaration in it.

② Add the document element `<sandwiches>` to the new XML document.

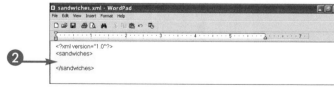

③ Add the `<sandwich>` elements that contain the types of sandwiches to the XML document.

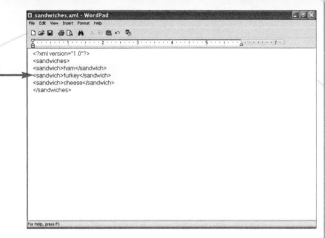

④ Open the XML document in Internet Explorer to examine the XML document.

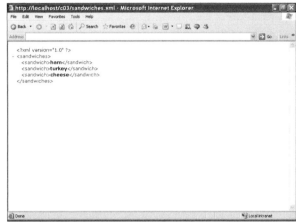

Extra

You can also create XML documents using server-side scripts like PHP scripts. Here is an example that creates the same XML document that you created in this task. Note that the default data PHP scripts sent is assumed to be HTML, so if you want to send XML, you use the PHP `header("Content-type: text/xml")` first:

```
<?
header("Content-type: text/xml");
echo '<?xml version="1.0"?>';
echo "<options>";
echo "<sandwiches>";
echo "<sandwich>ham</sandwich>";
echo "<sandwich>turkey</sandwich>";
echo "<sandwich>cheese</sandwich>";
echo "</sandwiches>";
echo "</options>";
?>
```

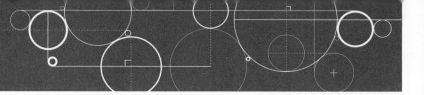

Download XML from the Server

You can use Ajax to download XML from the server. In particular, you might download an XML document named sandwiches.xml, which contains a number of different sandwich types. To download the XML, you can use a new JavaScript function named `getSandwiches`. The `getSandwiches` function is called when a button labeled "Get sandwiches" is clicked. Here is the HTML for the "Get sandwiches" button: `<form>` `<input type = "button" value = "Get sandwiches" onclick = getSandwiches()"> </form>`.

The code in the `getSandwiches` function downloads sandwiches.xml and displays them in a drop-down HTML select control. Here is what that `<select>` control looks like:

```
<form>   <input type = "button" value =
"Get sandwiches" onclick =
"getSandwiches()"> <select size="1"
id="sandwichList"> <option>Select a
sandwich</option>   </select> </form>
```

When you download XML, you do not read that XML from the `XMLHttpRequest` object's `responseText` property, but from its `responseXML` property. When downloading XML, use the `XMLHttpRequest` object's `responseXML` property, not the `responseText` property. Here is what the JavaScript to download XML into a variable named `xmlDocument` looks like:

```
XMLHttpRequestObject.onreadystatechange =
function() { if (XMLHttpRequestObject.
readyState == 4 && XMLHttpRequestObject.
status == 200) { var xmlDocument =
XMLHttpRequestObject.responseXML; }. The
XML data in the xmlDocument variable is
stored as a JavaScript XML document object
```

After you download XML into the `responseXML` property, you can extract data from the XML, working with the methods and properties of JavaScript XML document objects.

Download XML from the Server

① Create a button with the caption "Get sandwiches" and connect it to a function named `getSandwiches` and a drop-down list control to display sandwich types.

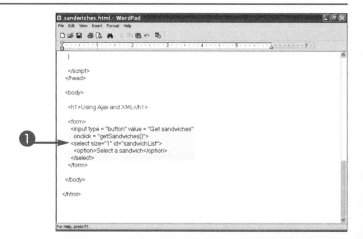

② Configure the `XMLHttpRequest` object to fetch the sandwiches.xml document in the `XMLHttpRequest` object's open method.

The sandwiches.xml document developed must be in the same server directory as the Web page you are developing in this task.

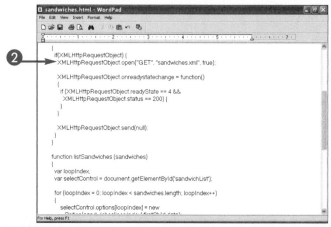

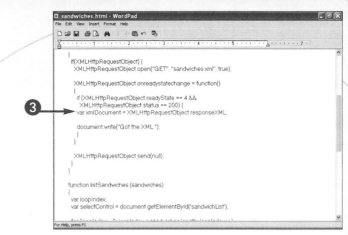

③ Add code to extract the downloaded data from the `XMLHttpRequest` object's responseXML property into a variable named `xmlDocument`, and add code to display the message "Got the XML." when the XML is successfully downloaded.

④ Open the Web page in your browser and click the Get sandwiches button.

The text message "Got the XML." appears in the browser, indicating that you successfully downloaded the XML from sandwiches.xml.

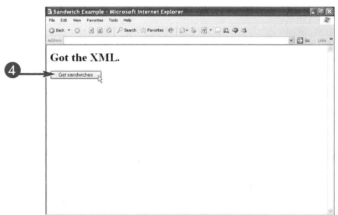

Extra

The way you downloaded your XML looks like this:

```
function getSandwiches()
{
  if(XMLHttpRequestObject) {
    XMLHttpRequestObject.open("GET", "sandwiches.xml", true);

    XMLHttpRequestObject.onreadystatechange = function()
    {
      if (XMLHttpRequestObject.readyState == 4 &&
        XMLHttpRequestObject.status == 200) {
        var xmlDocument = XMLHttpRequestObject.responseXML;
      }
    }
```

However, the XML you downloaded, which is the content of the sandwiches.xml document, is not as easily understandable as the text you downloaded earlier. The downloaded XML is in a JavaScript XML document object, and you must learn how to extract XML from that document to get the data you want. See the following topics to learn how to do that.

Create a Function That Adds Numbers

You can extract the XML elements you are looking for from the XML document object that you download from the server. When you download XML data from the server, it is stored in a JavaScript XML document object. To work with that object, you must use the methods of that object. In this example

```
<?xml version="1.0"?> <sandwiches>
<sandwich>ham</sandwich> <sandwich>
turkey</sandwich> <sandwich>cheese
</sandwich> </sandwiches>
```

you have downloaded XML data containing various sandwich types that is stored using `<sandwich>` elements inside a `<sandwiches>` document element. The data here is the type of sandwiches in the `<sandwich>` elements, and your goal is to extract that data. You can get all the `<sandwich>` elements and store them in a new object named, say, sandwiches, if you use the JavaScript `getElementsByTagName` method. You can use this

method on the document object to extract elements from an HTML page or from an XML document. All you have to do is to pass this method the name of the elements you want, which in this example is "sandwich". For example, this JavaScript extracts all `<sandwich>` elements from an XML document and stores them in an array named sandwiches:

```
XMLHttpRequestObject.onreadystatechange =
function() { if XMLHttpRequestObject.
readyState == 4 && XMLHttpRequestObject.
status == 200) { var xmlDocument =
XMLHttpRequestObject.responseXML;
var sandwiches = xmlDocument.
getElementsByTagName("sandwich"); } }
```

This loads an array of `<sandwich>` elements into the sandwiches variable. You can assess the various `<sandwich>` elements using a numeric index, like this: `sandwiches[10]`.

Create a Function That Adds Numbers

① Extract an array of XML elements, such as `<sandwich>` elements using the `getElementsByTagName` method, and store that array in a variable named sandwiches.

② Add the code to pass the sandwiches array to a new function, `listSandwiches`.

Most Ajax applications do not handle the downloaded XML in the anonymous function that monitors the download from the server, but pass the downloaded data to a new function.

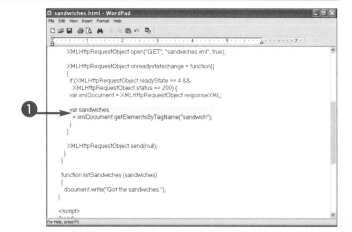

③ Type the code for the new listSandwiches function.

At this point, only make that function display the messages "Got the sandwiches."

Note: See the section "Extract Data from XML Elements" to learn how to use the listSandwiches function to extract the types of sandwiches.

④ Open the new page in a browser and click the Get sandwiches button.

The XML document sandwiches.xml is downloaded and the message "Got the sandwiches." appears.

Extra

Fetching data from Web servers is a delicate operation: If there is no working Internet connection, or the server is down, you might not get any data. That's why you check the readyState and status properties. But even if the download works, the data you get may still have problems. If you want to check for possible errors, check the sandwiches object, which is supposed to hold an array of <sandwich> elements: If that object exists, you can pass it on to the listSandwiches function. If it is set to JavaScript null value, on the other hand, no <sandwich> elements were found, and you can alert the user to the problem:

```
if (sandwiches) {
  listSandwiches(sandwiches);
}
else {
  alert("Did not find any sandwiches!");
}
```

Extract Data from XML Elements

You can extract data from XML elements using JavaScript. For example, if you have an array of `<sandwich>` elements named sandwiches, you might pass that array to a function named `listSandwiches`, where you can extract the type of each sandwich and display it in the list control in the Web page. Doing so involves deciphering the data in the `<sandwich>` elements.

Each element in the sandwiches array is an XML element object. You will read more about how to handle such objects in Chapter 9, but you also see here how to extract the data from such elements. Each `<sandwich>` element contains a sandwich type: Here are the three downloaded `<sandwich>` elements in the sandwiches array:

```
<sandwich>ham</sandwich>
<sandwich>turkey</sandwich>
<sandwich>cheese</sandwich>
```

The goal here is to extract each sandwich type from the various `<sandwich>` elements. The text inside each element is considered a *text node*. A text node is a data item whose only content is text. For example, the text node containing the text "ham" in the first `<sandwich>` XML element is considered a text node that is a child node of the `<sandwich>` element it is inside. To extract that node, you can use the expression `sandwiches[0].firstChild`. That gives you the XML text node that holds the text "ham". The next step is to actually read the word "ham" from that text node. To do that, you can use the text node's data property. In other words, to extract the word "ham" from the first element in the sandwiches array, you can use this JavaScript expression: `sandwiches[0].firstChild.data`. After you extract the names of the sandwiches, you can display them in the list control in this example's Web page.

Extract Data from XML Elements

① Write the a JavaScript function, such as `listSandwiches` so that it stores the drop-down list control in a variable named `selectControl`, and add a loop over all `<sandwiches>` elements in the sandwiches array.

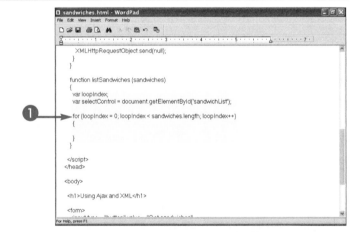

② Add code to add `<option>` elements to the select control.

The select control's options property holds an array of the `<option>` elements inside the control, which display the items in the control.

To create a new `<option>` object, use the JavaScript new operator.

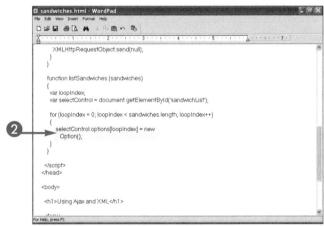

3 Insert the expression to get the name of the current sandwich type.

You pass the text you want to appear in an `<option>` element to the Option *constructor* method.

To create an object, you can use a constructor as seen here.

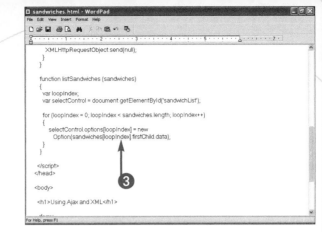

4 Open the Web page in a browser and click the Get sandwiches button.

The data in sandwiches.xml is downloaded from the server fully unpacked and loaded into the list control.

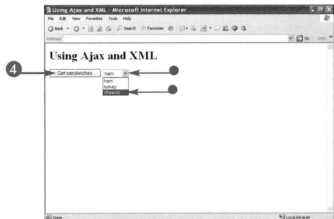

Extra

It is worth looking at error handling here. Say there are `<sandwich>` elements that have been downloaded, but there is a problem with them. For example, a `<sandwich>` element does not contain any text. In this example, you should not add it to the items displayed in the drop-down list control, which you can avoid with code like this:

```
var loopIndex;
var selectControl = document.getElementById('sandwichList');
for (loopIndex = 0; loopIndex < sandwiches.length; loopIndex++)
{
  if(sandwiches[loopIndex].firstChild.data != ""){
    selectControl.options[loopIndex] = new
      Option(sandwiches[loopIndex].firstChild.data);
  }
}
```

Read Data Sent to the Server

You can also write your scripts on the server to read data passed from the browser to the server. It can be very important to Ajax applications to communicate with the server: You might have to tell the server what data you want to fetch or pass to the server the data that the user has entered in your Web page.

For example, say that you want to let the user select either sandwiches or vegetarian sandwiches in the Web page you developed. How can you tell the server which type of sandwiches you want? You may pass an argument named `type` to the server and make the server-side script pass you back the correct type of sandwiches — standard sandwiches if the `type` argument holds a value of 1, for example, or vegetarian sandwiches if the `type` argument holds a value of 2.

If you use the `GET` method to fetch your data, you can encode the type parameter in the URL you access on the server. If you use a PHP script on the server named sandwiches.php, for example, you could pass a `type` argument with the value of 1 by using this URL `sandwiches.php?type=1` (or, if you want to make that URL absolute, include the full HTTP address, such as `http://www.fzax.com/steve/sandwiches.php?type=1`).

In the sandwiches.php script, you can read the value of the `type` argument by using the PHP array `$_GET`. For example, if the `type` argument equals 1, you can create a PHP array named `$sandwiches` (variables in PHP begin with `$`) to hold the names of the standard sandwiches, and then send that data back to the browser: `<? if ($_GET["type"] == "1") $sandwiches = array('ham', 'turkey', 'cheese');` *[PHP to send these sandwich names to the browser goes here]* `?>`.

Read Data Sent to the Server

① Create a new PHP script, and type the code to indicate that the data the script sends back to the server is in XML format.

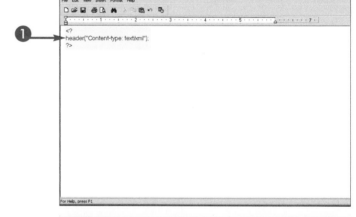

② Add the PHP code to check the `type` argument sent to the script and create an array named `$sandwiches` to contain the appropriate sandwiches.

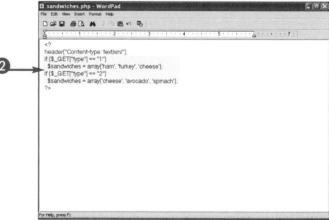

③ Add the PHP code to loop over the
`$sandwiches` array.

This PHP code takes the elements in the
`$sandwiches` array and places the
sandwich types in the XML it sends back
to the browser.

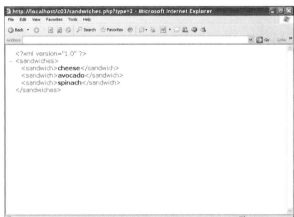

④ Place sandwiches.php on a PHP-enabled
server, and open the script in your browser
to test it.

The XML for the vegetarian sandwiches
appears in the browser.

Although this example is going to pass an argument named `type` that can contain a value of 1 or 2, you can
also read data from HTML controls in your Web page and pass that data to your server-side scripts. That is
very useful when you want to send any data the user entered to the server. For example, you may have a text
field with the ID named "text":

```
<form>
  <input type="text" id="text1">
</form>
```

In your JavaScript code, you can get the text from the text field and store it in a variable named, say, text:

```
function displayText()
{
    var text = document.getElementById("text1").value;
}
```

Now you have the text from the text field, and you are ready to send it to the server. To do that, you first
have to URL-encode that text. See the section "Pass Data to the Server with GET," for details.

Pass Data to the Server with GET

You can pass text data to server-side scripts from your Ajax application to tell that script what data you want to have sent back. Up to this point, when you open an XMLHttpRequest object to configure it with a URL, you just gave that URL, which is the relative URL sandwiches.php here:
XMLHttpRequestObject.open("GET", "sandwiches.php", true);.

Now, however, to send data to the server when you use the GET method, you have to *URL-encode* the data you send. Here is how it works: If you want to specify that the type argument for sandwiches.php holds the value 1, for example, you can use the URL
sandwiches.php?type=1: XMLHttpRequestObject.open("GET", "sandwiches.php?type=1", true);.

The text "?type=1" is the URL-encoded part. When data is URL-encoded, you add a question mark (?) to the end

of the URL. Then you add the data, in name=data format, after the question mark. Spaces in text are converted to a plus sign (+), and you separate pairs of name=data items with ampersands (&). To encode the data for the arguments "text1" and "text2" text fields and send it to http://www.servername.com/scriptname, you use this URL if text1 contains the text "Hi there" and text2 contains the text "Now is the time":

http://www.servername.com/scriptname?
text1 = Hi+there & text2=Now+is+the+time

Note that the data you send as URL-encoded is always text: Even if you are sending numbers, they are treated as text. Using URL-encoding lets you communicate with the server when using the GET method, uploading data as necessary so that that data may be read on the server. On the server, the URL-encoded data that you send is decoded and can be used by server-side scripts.

Pass Data to the Server with GET

① Create a Web page with a button, such as a Get sandwiches button connected to the function getSandwiches1, and a Get vegetarian sandwiches button connected to the function getSandwiches2.

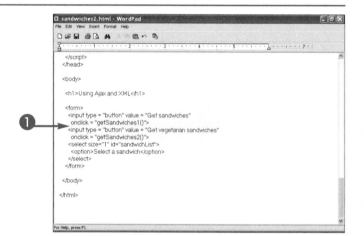

② Open the XMLHttpRequest object in the getSandwiches1 function by adding ?type=1 to the URL to open.

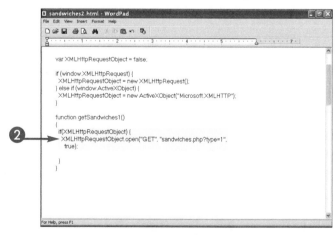

③ Add the rest of the getSandwiches1 function, calling the listSandwiches function after the XML data has been downloaded.

You can also create the getSandwiches2 function that is the same as getSandwiches1 except that it uses the URL sandwiches. php?type=2 to fetch the vegetarian sandwich names.

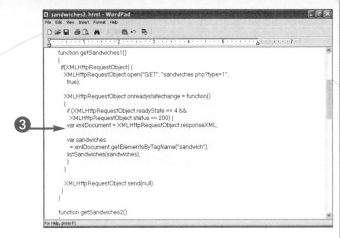

④ Open the Web page in your browser and click the Get vegetarian sandwiches button.

● The Web page sends the argument type, with the value 2, to the sandwiches.php script, which sends back the types of vegetarian sandwiches available, which are displayed in the list control.

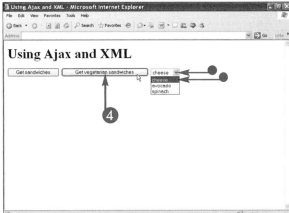

Extra

You can manually URL-encode data if you know what it looks like. All you have to do is replace spaces with + signs, or, as is becoming more common, with the code %20; separate name/value pairs with an &; and so on.

In fact, there is an easy way to URL-encode data that you should know about. JavaScript now contains a function named encodeURI that will URL-encode text for you ("URI" stands for Universal Resource Indicator, which is the XML-based name for URL). For example, say you have a text field with the ID "text1":

```
<form>
  <input type="text" id="text1">
</form>
```

You can URL-encode the data in that text field and send it to a URL this way:

```
var text1 = document.getElementById("text1").value;
var URL = "http://www.fzax.com/steve/sandwiches.php?data=" + encodeURI(text1);
XMLHttpRequestObject.open("GET", URL, true);
```

Pass Data to the Server with POST

You can send data to the server using the POST method instead of the GET method. You can specify the POST method instead of the GET method when you open the XMLHttpRequest object and do not include any URL-encoded data in the URL: `function getSandwiches1() { if(XMLHttpRequestObject) { XMLHttpRequestObject.open("POST", "sandwiches.php", true);`.

In addition, you should specify that you are sending your data using the POST method by using this additional code: `function getSandwiches1() { if(XMLHttpRequestObject) { XMLHttpRequestObject.open("POST", "sandwiches.php", true); XMLHttpRequestObject .setRequestHeader('Content-Type', 'application/x-www-form-urlencoded');`.

You call the XMLHttpRequest object's open method with a value of "POST" to indicate that you want to send your data using POST rather than GET. You also use the XMLHttpRequest object's setRequestHeader method to set the Content-Type request header to application/x-www-form-urlencoded when you use the POST method. Doing so informs the server that your data is encoded using the POST method and that the server should look for that data.

After preparing the XMLHttpRequest object, you use the send method to send your data. If you are using the GET method, you send a value of null, but with the POST method, you send the data you want to send to the server. In this case, you want to send an argument named type with a value of 1: `XMLHttpRequestObject. send("type=1");`. If you have a second argument to send, such as color, you can post data for both the type and color arguments this way: `XMLHttpRequestObject .send("type=1&color=red");`. In other words, you use the same URL-encoding syntax when sending data using POST as when you send data using GET, except that you do not append that data to the end of the URL.

Pass Data to the Server with POST

① Modify the Web page to use the POST method when you open the XMLHttpRequest object, and use the setRequestHeader method as outline ready to support the use of the POST method.

```
sandwiches3.html - WordPad
File Edit View Insert Format Help

    function getSandwiches1()
    {
    if(XMLHttpRequestObject) {
     XMLHttpRequestObject.open("POST", "sandwiches3.php",
     true);
     XMLHttpRequestObject.setRequestHeader('Content-Type',
     'application/x-www-form-urlencoded');

     XMLHttpRequestObject.onreadystatechange = function()
     {
      if (XMLHttpRequestObject.readyState == 4 &&
       XMLHttpRequestObject.status == 200) {
      var xmlDocument = XMLHttpRequestObject.responseXML;

      var sandwiches
       = xmlDocument.getElementsByTagName("sandwich");
      listSandwiches(sandwiches);
      }
     }

    }
    }
For Help, press F1
```

② Modify the send method to send an argument of "type=1" instead of null.

```
sandwiches3.html - WordPad
File Edit View Insert Format Help

    function getSandwiches1()
    {
    if(XMLHttpRequestObject) {
     XMLHttpRequestObject.open("POST", "sandwiches3.php",
     true);
     XMLHttpRequestObject.setRequestHeader('Content-Type',
     'application/x-www-form-urlencoded');

     XMLHttpRequestObject.onreadystatechange = function()
     {
      if (XMLHttpRequestObject.readyState == 4 &&
       XMLHttpRequestObject.status == 200) {
      var xmlDocument = XMLHttpRequestObject.responseXML;

      var sandwiches
       = xmlDocument.getElementsByTagName("sandwich");
      listSandwiches(sandwiches);
      }
     }

     XMLHttpRequestObject.send("type=1");
    }
    }
For Help, press F1
```

③ Modify the PHP script called by this Web page to use the `$_POST` array instead of the `$_GET` array.

In PHP, arguments sent using the POST method are read from the `$_POST` array instead of the `$_GET` array.

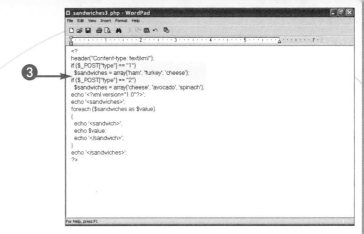

④ Open the Web page in your browser, and click the Get vegetarian sandwiches button.

- The vegetarian sandwiches are requested via the POST method and appear in the list box.

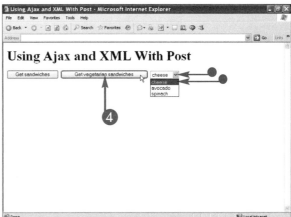

Extra

You have seen how to send a single argument to the server using the POST method. But say that you want to know how to send more than one argument. For example, say that you have two text fields:

```
<input type="text" id="text1">
<input type="text" id="text2">
```

You can extract the text in these text fields this way in JavaScript:

```
var text1 = document.getElementById("text1").value;
var text2 = document.getElementById("text2").value;
```

Then you open the XMLHttpRequest object and prepare it to send your data:

```
XMLHttpRequestObject.open("GET", "sandwiches.php", true);
XMLHttpRequestObject.setRequestHeader("Content-Type",
    "application/x-www-form-urlencoded");
```

To send multiple arguments, you prepare the same string as you would send if you were appending that string to the end of a URL with the GET method, without the question mark, and send that string to the server with the send method:

```
XMLHttpRequestObject.send("text1=" + encodeURI(text1) + "&"
    + "text2=" + encodeURI(text2));
```

1'

Create Server-Side Mouseovers

You can use Ajax in endless situations that can enhance the user's experience. For example, you can use Ajax to fetch text as the user moves the mouse over a Web page. As the mouse moves over specific hot spots, such as images, you can use Ajax to fetch text data to be displayed in the page to match the mouse position.

The data downloaded from the server can be updated periodically; for example, it can reflect current weather conditions over a region, and when the user moves a mouse from location to location in a map of the region, the application can display the weather condition in each location. Alternatively, you could download current traffic conditions or monitor data flow in a network, and so on.

For example, you can display a set of movie reel icons, each one corresponding to a favorite movie. When the

user moves the mouse over a movie icon, the application uses Ajax to download the name of the movie, and the application displays that name.

To make this work, you can display the movie reel icons using HTML <img> elements, and handle the mouseovers with the <img> element's onmouseover attribute, connecting that attribute to JavaScript to download and display the name of each movie.

You can make this easy by modifying the index.html example from Chapter 3 because that application has a JavaScript getData function that downloads a text file from the server. For example, if the user moves the mouse over a movie reel icon corresponding to *Citizen Kane*, the application should use the getData function to display that movie's name in the Web page by downloading a file named, say, kane.txt.

Create Server-Side Mouseovers

① Create a Web page to display three movie reel images.

The image movie.jpg is available in the downloadable code for this book.

② Add the JavaScript code that will call the getData function with the text files that contain the names of three favorite movies of yours.

The text files that hold the names of the movies should be stored on the server in the same directory as the Web page you are developing here.

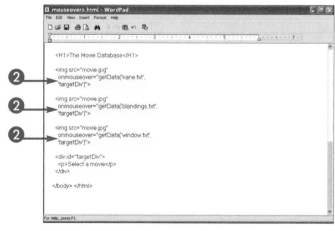

(3) Open the Web page in your browser.

You can see the movie reel images and the preliminary text, "Select a movie".

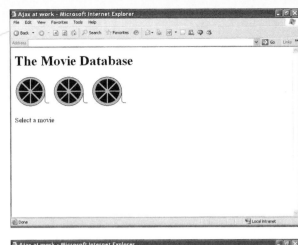

(4) Move the mouse over a movie reel image to see the name of the corresponding movie.

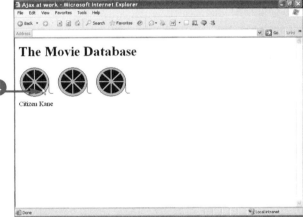

Extra

If you prefer, you can alter this example to download images instead of simple text. For example, you might display images of movie posters as the user moves the mouse over a specific movie's reel image. In this case, download from the server the name of an image file instead of the name of the movie. For example, you might download the name "kaneposter.jpg". Here is how you can use the name of the image file along with some dynamic HTML to display that image in the Web page:

```
var obj = document.getElementById(divID);

XMLHttpRequestObject.onreadystatechange = function()
{
  if (XMLHttpRequestObject.readyState == 4 &&
  XMLHttpRequestObject.status == 200) {
    var filename = XMLHttpRequestObject.responseText;
    obj.innerHTML = "<img src='" + filename + "'>";
  }
}
```

Download JavaScript Using Ajax

You can use Ajax to download JavaScript. That may seem odd, but it makes some sense. If your application is spread out over several Web servers, the JavaScript you decide to execute in the browser may depend on the current circumstances.

Say, for example, that your Ajax application has six different JavaScript functions, and it is up to the server to decide which of those functions should be called. It may make that decision based on current stock market prices, for example. In that case, the JavaScript you download from the server would simply be a statement calling that function. If such a function is named display, for example, the JavaScript you download might just be: display();. Executing that JavaScript calls the display function.

When you download this JavaScript as text, you can execute it with the built-in JavaScript eval function. You

just pass the JavaScript text you want to execute to this function, and it executes that text as JavaScript. If you are downloading JavaScript, you can simply pass the text downloaded to the responseText property to the eval function like this:

```
XMLHttpRequestObject.onreadystatechange =
function() { if (XMLHttpRequestObject.
readyState == 4 && XMLHttpRequestObject.
status == 200) {          eval(XMLHttpRequest
Object.responseText); }}.
```

That code will execute the text content of the XMLHttpRequestObject's responseText property as though that text was JavaScript.

Download and Execute Javascript

1 Download a document named javascript.txt, and on the server, place a plain text file named javascript.txt with the contents display(); in the same directory as the Web page you are developing.

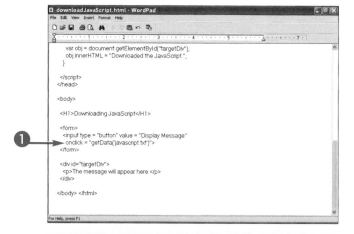

2 Add the code to execute the JavaScript when it is executed, using the eval function.

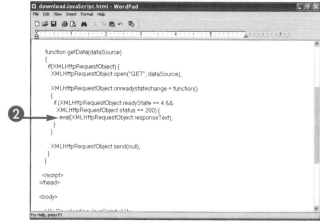

3 Enter a new JavaScript function in the Web page named `display` that displays the message "Downloaded the JavaScript." in a `<div>` element.

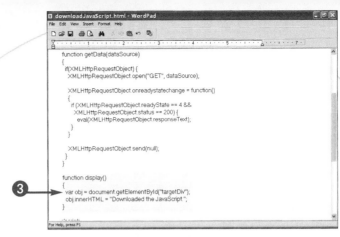

4 Open the Web page in your browser and click the button.

The message "Downloaded the JavaScript." appears as the JavaScript text is downloaded from the server and executed, which calls the `display` function.

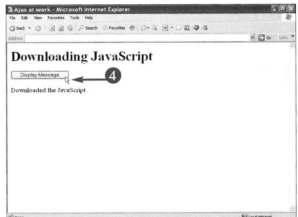

Extra

Although passing JavaScript to the browser is a common practice, it is not good programming practice. When you spread your code over several computers, you can make that code hard to understand, maintain, and debug. Ideally, your code should be self-contained and not execute code from possibly insecure networks. For example, it is often a better and safer idea to pass text data from the server to the browser, not JavaScript, and decide what JavaScript function to call based on the value of that data.

Example:
```
XMLHttpRequestObject.onreadystatechange = function()
{
  if (XMLHttpRequestObject.readyState == 4 &&
    XMLHttpRequestObject.status == 200) {
    if(XMLHttpRequestObject.responseText == "1"){
      displayOld();
    }
    else if (XMLHttpRequestObject.responseText == "2"){
      displayNew();
    }
  }
}
```

Create a Live Search Using Google Suggest

Y ou can connect to Google's Live Search yourself using Ajax, and you can see how to create an application that uses several new Ajax techniques in the next few tasks to enable you to do so. You saw Google's Live Search in Chapter 1. When you type the individual characters of a search term into Google Suggest at http://www.google.com/webhp? complete=1&hl=en, Google Suggest displays a drop-down list of search terms matching what you typed so far.

You can connect to Google Suggest in your own Ajax application. Google Suggest sends you the JavaScript you need to display the drop-down list of search terms that match what the user has typed so far.

Reading text as the user types it and sending it to the server as the user types is a common Ajax technique. In the following tasks, you learn how to send that text to

Google Suggest and display the search results that Google Suggest sends you in a drop-down menu.

For example, you can develop the JavaScript code to read the text that the user types into a text field as the user types that text. To do that, you can use the `onkeyup` attribute of the text field and assign the JavaScript function `getGoogleSuggest` to that attribute: Enter your search term: <input id = "text1" type = "text" name = "text1" onkeyup = "getGoogleSuggest(event)">.

After Google Suggest supplies you with matches to the current search term, you can display those results in a `<div>` element in your Web page like this:

`<div id = "targetDiv"><div></div></div>`

Such a `<div>` element can be used as a pop-up menu, for example.

Create a Live Search Using Google Suggest

① Type the HTML for a new text field, "text1", connected to a JavaScript function getGoogleSuggest, and add a <div> element named targetDiv to display the list of found matches to the current search term.

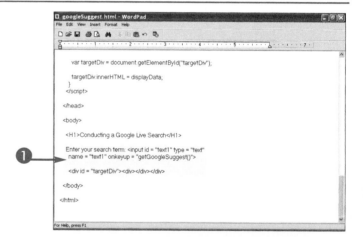

② Create the getGoogleSuggest function, and get an object corresponding to the text field control and use an alert box to display the text in the text field.

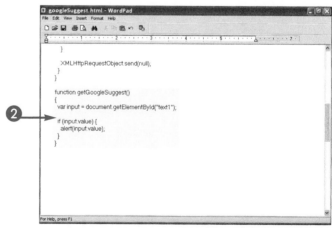

3 Delete the HTML in the display `<div>` element to start a new search if there is no text in the text field.

4 Open the Web page in a browser and type a character into the text field.

- The characters you type appear in an alert box.

You now are able to capture characters as the user types them.

Extra

In general, you should be careful about responding to every keystroke the user types, because it may slow your application's response significantly. If you send data to the server each time the user types a key, the server might not get all those keystrokes in a timely fashion or have enough time to respond. If your application appears sluggish, this may be the reason.

If you have more than one text field whose keystrokes you want to watch, there are various ways to do so in JavaScript. The easiest way to handle keystrokes from multiple text fields in JavaScript is to have multiple JavaScript functions — one per text field — to handle keystrokes:

```
<input id = "text1" type = "text" name = "text1"
   onkeyup = "function1()">
<input id = "text2" type = "text" name = "text2"
   onkeyup = "function2()">
<input id = "text3" type = "text" name = "text3"
   onkeyup = "function3()">
```

Connect to Google Suggest

You can send the keystrokes that users type when they are entering a search term, as they occur, to Google Suggest. For example, the user may type a, and you can send that character to Google Suggest to find matching search terms and then display those matches. If the user then types j, the search text field contains "aj", and you can send that to Google Suggest, and so on.

To connect to Google Suggest, this example uses a PHP script, googleSuggest.php. The actual URL you connect to is at www.google.com; for example, if you were looking for Google suggestions to match the partial search term "aj", you would go to this URL: http://www.google.com/complete/search?hl=en&js=true&qu=aj.

The problem as far as Ajax goes in this case is that www.google.com is not your domain — it is not the

same server as the server where your Web page resides. The browser displays a security warning if you try to navigate to the Google URL from JavaScript — that is, the browser is concerned that your script is trying to do malicious things behind the user's back, which is why this example uses a PHP script to connect to Google Select.

The PHP script operates on your server, not in your browser, so there is no security warning when it connects to Google. This is a common problem when you use Ajax to connect to a server that is not the same server where your Web page is located. For more information, see the section "Call a Different Domain Safely." By using a PHP script to interact with Google Suggest, you circumvent the problem — the PHP script connects to Google Suggest, not your JavaScript code, so there is no warning issued.

Connect to Google Suggest

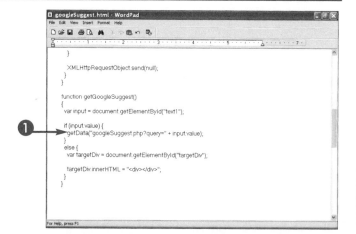

① Pass the getData function the URL googleSuggest.php?query=" + input.value.

This URL passes the partial search term the user has entered to the PHP script in this example, googleSuggest.php.

② In the getData function, add the code to display an alert box with the message "Connected to Google Suggest." after data is downloaded from the server.

③ Type the code shown in the PHP script googleSuggest.php.

This PHP script connects to Google Suggest, passing on the search term the user has entered, receiving an answer from Google Suggest, and passing that answer back to the browser.

Note: For more on PHP and how the code in a script like googleSuggest.php works, see Chapter 11.

④ Open the Web page in a browser, and type a search term.

● An alert box displaying the message "Connected to Google Suggest." appears.

You are connected to Google Suggest, and it sends back the search terms it found to match the partial search term the user typed.

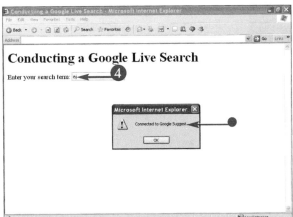

Apply It

So far, you have only sent your text data to Google Suggest using the assumption that there is only a single search term, such as "aj". Here is what that looks like (recall that input.value holds the current text in the text field where the users type their search terms):

```
if (input.value) {
   getData("googleSuggest.php?query=" + input.value);
}
```

On the other hand, the user may also enter spaces, and if you want to be able to handle spaces in the search term, you must URL-encode the data you send to Google Suggest.

The easiest way to do that is to use the JavaScript function encodeURI. For more information on encodeURI, see Chapter 3. To URL-encode the search term the user is looking for, you can use the encodeURI function like this:

```
if (input.value) {
   getData("googleSuggest.php?query=" + encodeURI(input.value));
}
```

Display the Google Suggest Results

You can display the results to the search term the user typed by using a little dynamic HTML. When Google Suggest sends back the matches it finds to the partial search term you have sent it, it actually sends back JavaScript that you can execute. The JavaScript relies on your Web page having a function named `sendRPCDone` in it.

This function extracts the data sent to it and displays the data by using an HTML table in the target `<div>` element. This HTML displays in the Web page. Besides the terms matching what the user has typed, the code adds a hyperlink back to Google for each term. If a user wants to look up a term, the user can click the hyperlink and the browser will navigate to Google to search the term. This table appears in a `<div>` element that is made to appear when the data in the table is ready. Making the `<div>` element appear is a clever way of giving the impression of a drop-down menu.

Each table cell displays the name of a search term, as well as a hyperlink to the Google site that pulls up that search term. After the table is created, its HTML text is assigned to the `innerHTML` property of the `targetDiv` `<div>` element, which corresponds to the drop-down menu under the search text field. When the drop-down menu opens, the user can select an item from it simply by clicking that item. Doing so makes the browser navigate to the Google Web site, where the clicked item is looked up automatically and all the Google search results are displayed.

It is very convenient to let Google create the JavaScript code to display the drop-down menu for you to display the Google Suggest results. By creating this JavaScript, Google Suggest helps you integrate their service into your Web pages easily and effectively, just as if you were looking at the Google Suggest Web site directly.

Display the Google Suggest Results

① Use a JavaScript `eval` statement to execute the JavaScript code you receive from Google Suggest.

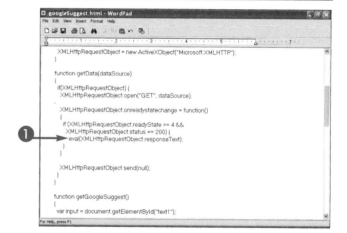

② Enter the `sendRPCDone` JavaScript function, which is executed by the JavaScript you download from Google Suggest.

③ Enter an HTML `<style>` element to give the target `<div>` element some background color.

The target `<div>` element is where the matching search terms are displayed.

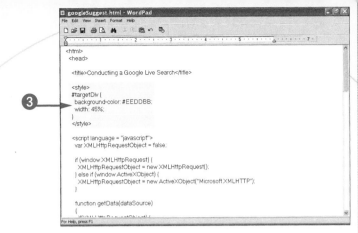

④ Open the Web page in your browser and type a partial search term.

In this example, the letters "aj" are typed.

● Matches to the search term you typed are supplied by Google Suggest, and your Ajax application lists them.

If you click one of the hyperlinks in the drop-down list, your browser navigates to Google and looks up the search term you clicked.

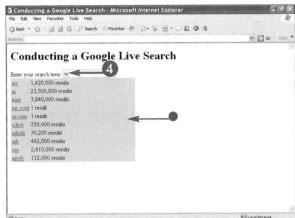

Extra

Because you may not be familiar with the use of the `<style>` element in this example, here is some more information. The `<div>` element that displays the results fetched from Google Suggest is displayed in a `<div>` element with the ID "targetDiv":

```
<div id = "targetDiv"><div></div></div>
```

To set up the styles this `<div>` element should use for display, you use a `<style>` element and refer to the target `<div>` with a #, which means you are referencing it by ID. Next, you list the style properties, such as width to set the width of the `<div>` as a fraction of the Web page, and the values you want to set those properties to:

```
<style>
#targetDiv {
  background-color: #EEDDBB;
  width: 45%;
}
</style>
```

For more on using styles with Ajax, see Chapter 10.

Read Input and Send It to the Server for Validation

You can use Ajax to send data to the server and get results back that indicate if there is some error in the user's input — and that can happen interactively. For example, say that you ask the user to select a new username to use to log on to your site. However, there is the chance that the user may select a username that someone else has already selected, resulting in a conflict.

You can use Ajax to check if the username the user enters, as the user types it, is already taken. This saves the user the time of clicking a Submit button and having to start all over again when the results come back from the server in a new page. To do that, you must first read what the user types, and send it to the server.

When the user types the intended username in an HTML text field, you can make the browser call a JavaScript function named, say, checker, to check what the user is typing as it is typed this way: Username: <input id = "textField" type = "text" name = "textField" onkeyup = "checker()">.

In the checker function, you can read what the user has entered so far and send it to the server to see if that username is already taken. In this example, the PHP script on the server that does the checking is named log.php (and the Web page to which the user is typing the username is named log.html), so you send the user's username to log.php. The log.php script will send back notification of whether the username is available or not.

Read Input and Send It to the Server for Validation

1 Create a new Web page, and add the HTML for a text field named `textfield` and a `<div>` element for display named `targetDiv`.

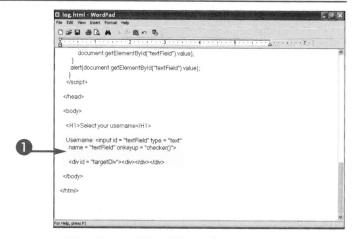

2 Add styling for the `<div>` element so that any text displayed in it stands out.

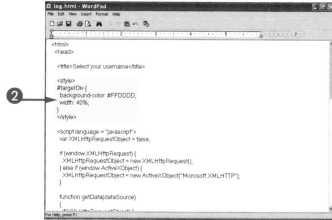

③ Add the `checker` function to your Web page, sending the user's username to the log.php script using the `getData` function and a parameter named "qu".

To verify that your page is handling each keystroke, you can also use an alert box to display what the user has typed so far.

④ Open the Web page in your browser and type some text.

● The text you type is echoed in the alert box.

Apply It

One issue for you to consider is that you may end up giving the user premature feedback. If, for example, the username "steve" is taken, and the user wants to use the name steve2007, there could be a problem here. When the user types "steve", the application provides feedback that that name is already taken, even though the user is not finished typing the intended username. The user will understand that your application is responding to what has been typed already, and not the full-intended username, steve2007. However, if you want to wait until the user is done typing, you can use the `onblur` event instead of `onkeyup`:

```
Username: <input id = "textField" type = "text"
    name = "textField" onblur = "checker()">
```

The `onblur` event happens when the text field loses the input focus, which means it is no longer the target of keystrokes, as when the user clicks some location outside the text field.

Return Validation from the Server

You can use server-side scripts to support server-side validation. For example, you can create an online PHP script that checks to see if a user's suggested username is taken. In this example, the script log.php checks if the user is trying to get the username steve. If so, it sends back the text "notOK". On the other hand, if the user is trying to get any other username, the script sends back the text "OK". Here is what the script looks like: `<?php if ($_GET["qu"] == "steve"){ echo "notOK"; } else { echo "OK"; } ?>`. As you can see, it simply checks to see if the name sent to it is "steve", and if so, sends back the message "notOK". Otherwise, it sends back the message "OK", meaning that the username is acceptable.

In the `getData` function, which handles downloads from the server, you can check to see if the downloaded text is "OK" or "notOK", and if it is "notOK" you can display a

message indicating to the user that the desired name is already taken. Here is what the code in the `getData` function looks like:

```
if (XMLHttpRequestObject.readyState == 4 &&
XMLHttpRequestObject.status == 200) {
if(XMLHttpRequestObject.responseText ==
"notOK"){ var targetDiv =
document.getElementById("targetDiv");
targetDiv.innerHTML = "<div>Sorry, that
name is taken.</div>"; } } }
```

As you can see, it is a simple matter to read the text returned from the server and check if that text is "notOK". If so, the code creates an object corresponding to the `targetDiv` `<div>` element and displays the message "Sorry, that name is taken." in that `<div>` element, indicating that the username the user is entering is not acceptable.

Return Validation from the Server

① Create a new file named log.php, and enter the PHP to make this script validate the data sent from the server.

② Remove the line of JavaScript that displays the alert box in the `checker` function.

③ Add the new JavaScript that checks the response from the server.

If the response is "notOK", display the message "Sorry, that name is taken." in the target display <div> element.

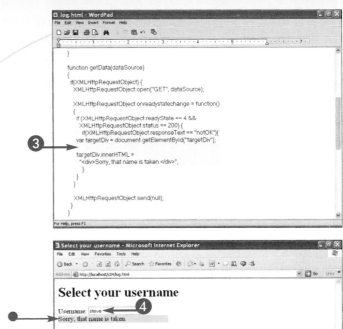

④ Open the Web page in a browser and type **steve**.

● A notification that the username is already taken appears.

Extra

Server-side validation is a useful technique, but you should not use it in all circumstances. In this case, the usernames that have already been taken are stored on the server. It is valid to check with the server each time a keystroke is entered to see if the username the user is selecting has been taken. In other words, when the data you want to use to validate the user's input is on the server, server-side validation can be appropriate. However, if you just want to make sure that the user enters a phone number or does not leave a field blank, you do not need server-side validation, because you can do that job in JavaScript.

When you can use JavaScript for validation of user input, you should, because it reduces the number of server accesses made by your application — and if Internet traffic is slow, server-side validation may have trouble responding to every keystroke. In addition, you may swamp your server if you ask it to check every username keystroke-by-keystroke. Imagine if a thousand users were trying to log in at the same time.

Get Header Information

You can use HTTP HEAD requests to get information about a document and about the server that you are interacting with from your Ajax script. Up to this point, you have used the GET and PUT methods to send data to and to fetch data from the server. However, that data has consisted of the contents of documents or the results returned from an online script. On the other hand, HEAD requests give you information supplied by the server about itself and about the documents on the server.

To make a HEAD request, you pass the text "HEAD" to the XMLHttpRequest object's open method. That might look something like this in the getData method, where this code requests HEAD data about the document whose URL you pass to the getData method:

```
function getData(dataSource, divID) {
if(XMLHttpRequestObject) {var obj =
document.getElementById(divID);
XMLHttpRequestObject.open("HEAD",
dataSource); }
```

When the data is returned from the server, you can access it using the XMLHttpRequest object's getAllResponseHeaders method, which displays the data in all the HTTP headers it has, like this: `targetDiv.innerHTML = XMLHttpRequest Object.getAllResponseHeaders();` which displays the header data in a `<div>` element named targetDiv.

Here is the type of data that is returned by this code: `Server: Microsoft-IIS/5.1 Date: Thu, 16 Feb 2006 18:10:23 GMT Content-Type: text/html Accept-Ranges: bytes Last-Modified: Thu, 16 Feb 2006 18:02:13 GMT ETag: "229d7d1d2333c61:977" Content-Length: 1263.`

Note that this text includes all the header information available, assembled together into a single string of text. You can search this string of text for the information you are seeking, which will help your Ajax application. As you can see, you can get information about the server and the documents it handles using HEAD requests.

Get Header Information

① Create a new Web page called head.html.

② Add a button giving it the caption, "Get header information".

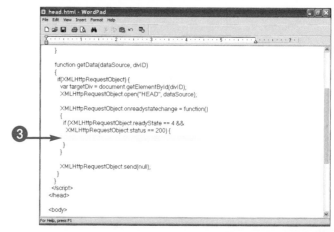

③ Remove the code in getData that displays the text downloaded from the server.

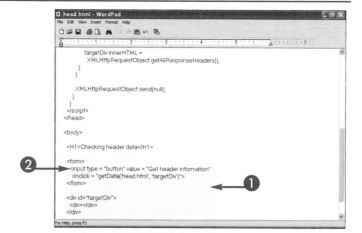

④ Add the call to the
`getAllResponseHeaders`
method to get all the HTTP headers,
and display them in the target
`<div>` element.

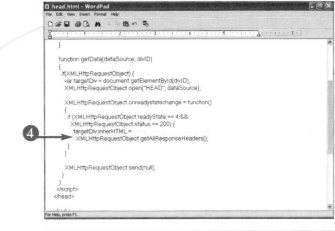

⑤ Open the Web page in your browser
and click the button.

- The HTTP header information
  from the server appears.

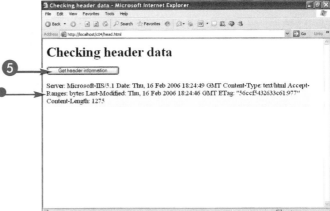

Apply It

The data you get back from the server when you call the `XMLHttpRequest` object's `getAllResponseHeaders`
method is a simple text string. You can extract specific data items using JavaScript's string functions. All you need
to do is store this text in a variable like this, which stores the header text in a variable named `headerData`:

```
headerData = XMLHttpRequestObject.getAllResponseHeaders();
```

Now you can use the JavaScript string functions and properties to extract the data you want from this string.
The length property gives you the length of the string, in characters. The `indexOf` method searches for the
occurrence of a substring and gives you the location of the first match or -1 if there is no match (the first
character of a string is considered character 0). The substring method lets you extract a substring from a
larger string. You can pass this method to the start and end locations of the substring you want to extract.

Extract Specific Header Data

Y ou can use header requests to determine a great deal about a specific document, such as the date the document was last modified. You can use the XMLHttpRequest object's getAllResponseHeaders method to get a text string with all the response headers for a particular document and server. If you want to extract just a specific response header's information — such as the date a particular document was last modified — you can use the getResponseHeader instead. This method returns only the text from a specific response header.

For example, the header that holds the last modified date is simply called "Last-Modified", and if you pass that text to the getResponseHeader method, you get the date on which the Web page was last modified. Here is what that might look like in code:

```
XMLHttpRequestObject.onreadystatechange =
function() { if (XMLHttpRequestObject.readyState
== 4 && XMLHttpRequestObject.status == 200) {
```

```
targetDiv.innerHTML =   "This document was last
modified on " + XMLHttpRequestObject
.getResponseHeader("Last-Modified"); } }
```

This code retrieves and displays the last-modified header. In this case, the last-modified date of the document you have requested HEAD information about is displayed in the targetDiv <div> element.

In order to make that request, you simply make a HEAD request for data about a particular document, which you can do using the getData function and passing "HEAD" to the XMLHttpRequest object's open method this way:

```
if(XMLHttpRequestObject) { var targetDiv =
document.getElementById(divID); XMLHttp
RequestObject.open("HEAD", dataSource);.
```
Doing so returns header data from the server, and you can then use the getResponseHeader method to retrieve the header information you are interested in. In this case, that information is the last-modified date, so you pass the getResponseHeader method the text "Last-Modified" here.

Extract Specific Header Data

① Create a date.html Web page.

② Add a button with the caption "Display the date of this document".

When the button is clicked, make the button pass the document date.html to the getData method.

③ Add code to the getData function to retrieve the HEAD data for the current document.

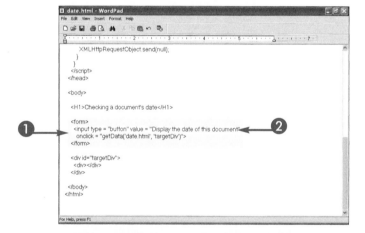

④ Use the `getResponseHeader` method to recover and display the value in the document's "Last-Modified" header.

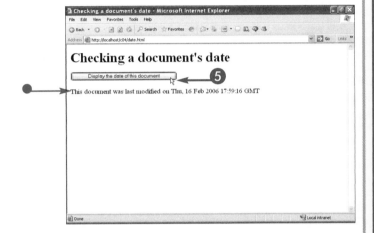

```
XMLHttpRequestObject = new ActiveXObject("Microsoft.XMLHTTP");
}

function getData(dataSource, divID)
{
  if(XMLHttpRequestObject) {
    var targetDiv = document.getElementById(divID);
    XMLHttpRequestObject.open("HEAD", dataSource);

    XMLHttpRequestObject.onreadystatechange = function()
    {
      if (XMLHttpRequestObject.readyState == 4 &&
        XMLHttpRequestObject.status == 200) {
        targetDiv.innerHTML =  "This document was last modified on " +
          XMLHttpRequestObject.getResponseHeader(
          "Last-Modified");
      }
    }

    XMLHttpRequestObject.send(null);
  }
}
</script>
```

⑤ Open the Web page in your browser and click the button.

● The date the current document was last modified appears.

Checking a document's date

Display the date of this document

This document was last modified on Thu, 16 Feb 2006 17:59:16 GMT

Apply It

This code lets you determine the length of a document, in bytes, using the Content-Length header:

```
if(XMLHttpRequestObject) {
  var targetDiv = document.getElementById(divID);
  XMLHttpRequestObject.open("HEAD", dataSource);

  XMLHttpRequestObject.onreadystatechange = function()
  {
    if (XMLHttpRequestObject.readyState == 4 &&
      XMLHttpRequestObject.status == 200) {
      targetDiv.innerHTML =  "Length of the document in bytes: " +
      XMLHttpRequestObject.getResponseHeader(
        "Content-Length");
    }
  }
}
```

Check If a Document Exists

You can use HEAD requests to check if a document exists and is accessible at a particular URL. It is a good idea to check if a Web resource exists before you rely on it in your Ajax application. If the document is not accessible, you will know about it before you need it. HEAD requests are often used to check if a document exists because you do not need to download the whole document in order to find out if the document exists.

All you have to do is to make a HEAD request for the document or Web resource you are interested in, and then check if the XMLHttpRequest object's status property holds 200, which means that the document exists, or 404, which means it cannot be found. You can do this by using the XMLHttpRequest object to request a particular document. In particular, you pass the argument "HEAD" to the open method of this object along with the

document's URL. That will enable you to check if a document exists on the Web server on which you want to work.

If the document exists, the XMLHttpRequest object's status property will hold 200, and the code displays the message "The document exists". Otherwise, if the XMLHttpRequest object's status property holds 404, the document does not exist, which the code indicates by displaying the message "The document does not exist".

Using a HEAD request means that you do not have to download the entire document in order to check if it exists — something that can use up considerable time if the document is long. HEAD requests are to recover data from the server on particular documents without having to download the entire document.

Check If a Document Exists

① Create a new page, exists.html, that includes a button with the caption "Check if google.html exists" and pass the getData function the name of the file you want to check on, google.html.

② Make a HEAD request for the required document, and check if the document exists.

If status returned is 200, the document exists.

110

③ Indicate in the target `<div>` element
If the status returned is 404.

A status of 404 means the document
is not accessible at the URL you
specified.

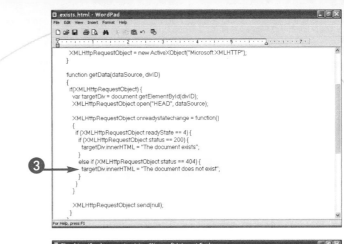

④ Open the new page in a browser and
click the button.

● The message "The document
exists" appears if google.html
exists in the same directory on
the server as exists.html.

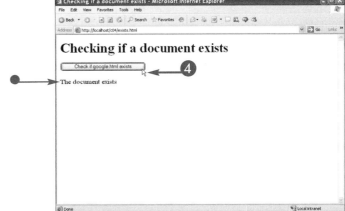

Apply It

If the Web resource, such as a PHP script, or a crucial document, is missing online and you cannot get access
to it, it is good to have a fallback plan. Chapter 2 discusses what to do if a browser does not support
JavaScript, but if the browser supports JavaScript and you cannot reach your required PHP script on the
server you should call a JavaScript function that can handle the problem, even if that just means alerting the
user to the issue. Here is some sample code that calls an alternate JavaScript function if you cannot use Ajax:

```
XMLHttpRequestObject.onreadystatechange = function()
{
  if (XMLHttpRequestObject.readyState == 4) {
    if (XMLHttpRequestObject.status == 200) {
      doAjaxWork;
    }
    else if (XMLHttpRequestObject.status == 404) {
      alternateJavaScriptFunction();
    }
  }
}
```

Use Two XMLHttpRequest Objects at the Same Time

You can encounter problems if you have several Ajax-enabled controls like buttons in your application and you only have one XMLHttpRequest object. Say, for example, that the user clicks one button, which connects that XMLHttpRequest object to the server and makes it wait for a response. While that object waits for a response, an impatient user may click the other button, which forces the same XMLHttpRequest object to connect to the server with a new request and makes it start waiting again. Then the server response from the first request comes back and is mixed up because the XMLHttpRequest object is waiting for the second response.

The simplest solution is to create two different XMLHttpRequest objects. Creating these two new objects is simple by using the JavaScript new operator. Be sure to give these two new XMLHttpRequest objects different names, such as XMLHttpRequestObject1 and

XMLHttpRequestObject2. You go through the same procedure to create the two new XMLHttpRequest objects, but you store them in different variables.

Then you can use two entirely different getData functions, one for each of two different buttons: function getData(dataSource) { } function getData2(dataSource, divID) { }. The getData function uses XMLHttpRequestObject, and the getData2 function uses XMLHttpRequestObject2. Doing things this way ensures that you keep the XMLHttpRequest objects separate as the user issues multiple requests. When the user clicks one button, one XMLHttpRequest object is used to download data from the server; when the user clicks the other button, the other XMLHttpRequest object is used, keeping the objects separate and making sure that no XMLHttpRequest object is expected to handle two requests simultaneously.

Use Two XMLHttpRequest Objects at the Same Time

① Use two buttons to connect to the getData and getData2 functions, which download the text in the data.txt and data2.txt files.

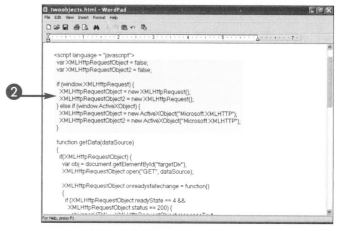

② Add the code needed to create two XMLHttpRequest objects, named XMLHttpRequestObject and XMLHttpRequestObject2.

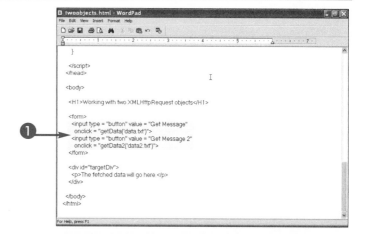

3 In addition to the `getData` function, which downloads data.txt, add the `getData2` function, which uses `XMLHttpRequestObject2` and downloads data2.txt.

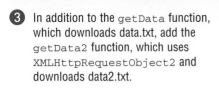

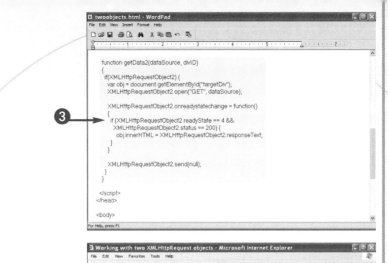

```
function getData2(dataSource, divID)
{
  if(XMLHttpRequestObject2) {
    var obj = document.getElementById("targetDiv");
    XMLHttpRequestObject2.open("GET", dataSource);

    XMLHttpRequestObject2.onreadystatechange = function()
    {
      if (XMLHttpRequestObject2.readyState == 4 &&
        XMLHttpRequestObject2.status == 200) {
          obj.innerHTML = XMLHttpRequestObject2.responseText;
        }
    }

    XMLHttpRequestObject2.send(null);
  }
}

    </script>
  </head>

  <body>
```

4 Open the Web page in a browser and click either button.

● The data in data.txt or data2.txt is downloaded and appears.

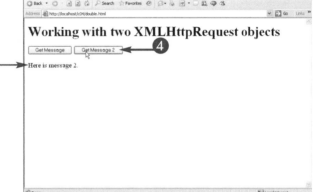

Working with two XMLHttpRequest objects

Here is message 2.

Extra

You must be careful when handling multiple `XMLHttpRequest` requests because it brings up issues of accessing and displaying the right data. If the user clicks one button and then another in this example, and the data comes in at different speeds, it is possible that the second message appears first and is overwritten by the first message. That is the opposite order from what the user expects, but depending on how the Internet responds — and how the server responds — that can happen.

A solution to the problem is to have each `XMLHttpRequest` request display its downloaded messages in different locations in the application's Web page. For example, if you have one `<div>` element named `targetDiv` and another named `targetDiv2`, the `getData` function can display its data in `targetDiv` and the `getData2` function can display its data in `targetDiv2`. In that way, you can keep the downloaded data from the two `XMLHttpRequest` objects separate.

Create an Array of XMLHttpRequest Objects

You can use an array of XMLHttpRequest objects to support simultaneous Ajax requests to a server. You can use two XMLHttpRequest objects to handle two buttons in an Ajax application. However, if you have a dozen buttons, not just two, you can store the XMLHttpRequest objects in an array and simply use one getData function.

To add new XMLHttpRequest objects to the array, you can use the built-in JavaScript push method like this:

```
var XMLHttpRequestObjects = new Array();
function getData(dataSource)
{ var index = 0; if (window.XMLHttpRequest)
{ XMLHttpRequestObjects.push(new
XMLHttpRequest()); }
else if (window.ActiveXObject)
{ XMLHttpRequestObjects.push(new
ActiveXObject("Microsoft.XMLHTTP")); }
```

Each time you use the push function, you add another XMLHttpRequest object to the array. In that way, you are guaranteed a fresh XMLHttpRequest object for each

request because a new XMLHttpRequest object is added to the array.

To determine where the most recently created XMLHttpRequest object is in the array, you use the array's length property, which returns the number of items in the array, and subtract 1 (because array indexes are zero-based). Therefore, the index of the most recent XMLHttpRequest object in the array is equal to XMLHttpRequestObjects.length - 1.

After loading a new XMLHttpRequest object into the array, you can refer to it easily as XMLHttpRequestObjects [XMLHttpRequestObjects.length - 1], which means you can now manage multiple XMLHttpRequest objects in your application. When you need a new XMLHttpRequest object, you just use the most recent one that was created, which makes sure that no XMLHttpRequest objects are used for more than one request. You have successfully stored your XMLHttpRequest objects in an array by using one at a time and keeping track of those XMLHttpRequest objects one by one.

Create an Array of XMLHttpRequest Objects

① Create a new Web page named requestarray.html.

Make sure there are two buttons, one of which calls the getData function to download data.txt; the other button calls getData to download data2.txt.

② Create a new array named XMLHttpRequestObjects and push a new XMLHttpRequest object into the array.

③ Add the JavaScript code to get the location in the array of the new XMLHttpRequest object and store that location in a variable named index.

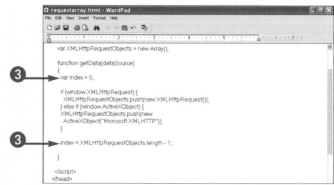

④ In the remainder of the `getData` function, **replace the** `XMLHttpRequestObject` **variable with the expression** `XMLHttpRequestObjects[index]`.

⑤ Open the Web page in a browser, and click either button.

- The browser downloads the data you want and displays it using multiple `XMLHttpRequest` objects in the array.

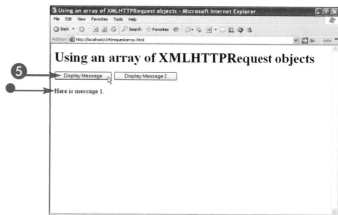

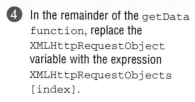

Apply It

Although this example works, you might not want to fill up an array with `XMLHttpRequest` objects if your user is going to use your application for a long time. The problem is that adding a new `XMLHttpRequest` object to your object array every time the user clicks a button is going to use up a lot of memory in the long run. To avoid this, you can create a new array named `arrayTracker` that holds data about each object in the `XMLHttpRequestObjects` array:

```
var arrayTracker = new Array();
```

When a new `XMLHttpRequest` object is added to the `XMLHttpRequestObjects` array, you can add the text "Not OK to overwrite" to the `arrayTracker` array as well:

```
arrayTracker.push("Not OK to overwrite");
```

In addition, when you are done with an object in the `XMLHttpRequestObjects` array, you can set that object's text in the `arrayTracker` array to "OK to overwrite":

```
arrayTracker[index] = "OK to overwrite";
```

Then when you need to find space in the `XMLHttpRequestObjects` array for a new `XMLHttpRequest` object, you simply find one whose entry in the `arrayTracker` array says "OK to overwrite", and store the new `XMLHttpRequest` object in the corresponding location in the `XMLHttpRequestObjects` array.

Handle Multiple XMLHttpRequest Requests at the Same Time

You can use multiple XMLHttpRequest objects to handle multiple requests to the server using JavaScript *inner functions*. An inner function is a function defined inside another function, and using them enables you to handle multiple XMLHttpRequest objects easily. You can handle multiple Ajax requests at the same time by using two XMLHttpRequest objects, or XMLHttpRequest objects stored in an array. However, the easiest way is to use inner functions.

When you define a function inside another function, the inner function has access to the data in the enclosing function, even after the call to the enclosing function is over. That is perfect here, because in the getData function, the function you connect to the XMLHttpRequest object's onreadystatechange property is an inner function. That means all you have to do is create a new XMLHttpRequest object each time you call the getData

function. Each time you call the getData function, a new XMLHttpRequest object is created and tied to a new copy of the inner function. When the inner function downloads the data and returns, the new XMLHttpRequest object is automatically destroyed.

Using inner functions, the only change you have to make to the code for the Ajax applications you write is to place the code to create the new XMLHttpRequest object inside the getData function, so a new XMLHttpRequest object is created each time the getData function is called.

To sum up, in order to let your Ajax applications handle multiple concurrent Ajax requests simultaneously, all you have to do is place the code for the creation of the XMLHttpRequest object inside the getData function so a new XMLHttpRequest object is created each time that function is called.

Handle Multiple XMLHttpRequest Requests at the Same Time

① Create a new Web page called multiple.html, and give it two buttons that are both connected to the getData function.

You can use one button to download data.txt and the other to download data2.txt.

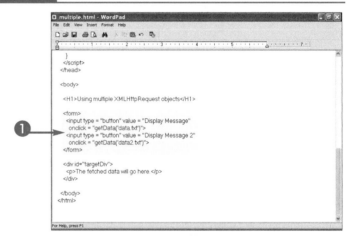

② Add the code to create a new XMLHttpRequest object inside the getData function.

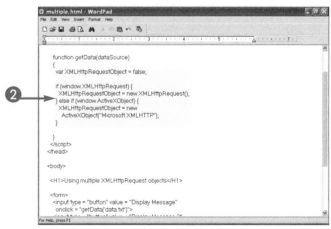

③ Add the rest of the code to make the XMLHttpRequest object connect to the server and download the requested file.

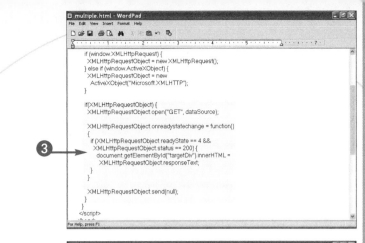

③

④ Open the Web page in your browser and click either button.

● The browser downloads the data you want and displays it using multiple XMLHttpRequest objects.

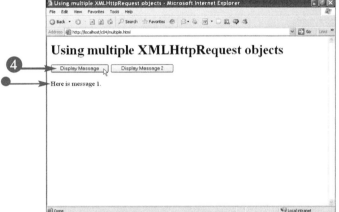

Apply It

Although the code in this task deletes the XMLHttpRequest object automatically, you can also delete that object yourself to make sure. To do that, you can use the JavaScript delete statement, and set the XMLHttpRequestObject variable to null this way:

```
XMLHttpRequestObject.onreadystatechange = function()
{
  if (XMLHttpRequestObject.readyState == 4 &&
    XMLHttpRequestObject.status == 200) {
      document.getElementById("targetDiv").innerHTML =
        XMLHttpRequestObject.responseText;
      delete XMLHttpRequestObject;
      XMLHttpRequestObject = null;
  }
}
```

Call a Different Domain Safely

You can access data on a different domain than the one your Web page is stored on if you know what you are doing. When an Ajax application in a browser tries to access a Web domain that it does not come from, such as Google, browsers become suspicious that your application is sending sensitive data somewhere it should not be going, and they display a warning dialog box that the user must click to dismiss.

That means that, in Ajax applications, you cannot access a different Web domain than your application is in unless you take special precautions. For example, if the googleSuggest application tries to access Google Suggest directly like this:

```
        function getGoogleSuggest()
{ if (input.value) { getData( "http://www.
google.com/complete/search?hl=en&js=true&qu
=" + input.value); }
```

then the user sees a warning dialog box. That is not what you want to happen, especially when you are using Ajax to provide the user with a smooth browsing experience.

To avoid that kind of dialog box, you can have an online script, such as a script named googleSuggest.php, to contact Google Suggest instead. Here is what that looks like: function getGoogleSuggest() { if (input. value) {getData("googleSuggest.php?query=" + input.value); }. The code in googleSuggest.php can contact the Google Suggest Web site for you, instead of having to contact that site directly from the browser, which is what causes the warning dialog box to appear.

As long as you use a script on the server side to contact a different domain, rather than using your Ajax application in the browser to contact that domain, the user does not see a warning dialog box. Using a server-side script to call another domain, rather than calling another domain from the browser, is the way to fix this problem.

Call a Different Domain Safely

① Contact Google Suggest directly.

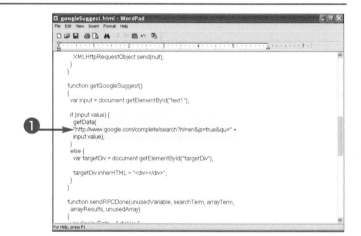

② Type a letter in the text field in googleSuggest.html.

The browser displays a warning dialog box.

③ Select an option in the dialog box.

If you click Yes, the character you type in the text field is sent to Google Select, and Google Select's suggestions appear in the Web page.

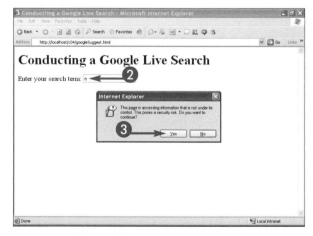

4 To avoid the warning dialog box, send the user's typed entry to googleSelect.php, which replays it to the Google Select Web site.

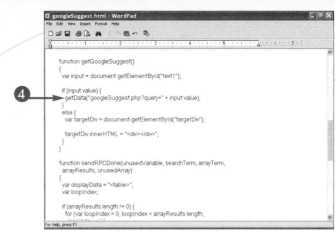

5 Type a character in the text field now, and you see Google Suggest's suggestions without a warning dialog box.

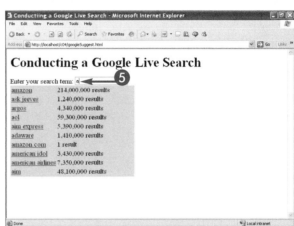

Extra

You may not want to have to route Ajax requests through an online script — for example, you may just want to use Google Suggest, but do not have access to a server where you can place a PHP script like googleSuggest.php. Another way to handle the security warning raised by the browser when your application attempts to send data to a different Web domain than the one it came from is to click the Yes button in the warning dialog box. This allows the data to be sent to the domain you want to send it. If you do not mind dealing with the warning dialog box, just click Yes to acknowledge the warning, and then continue.

You can also turn warnings like this off. For example, in Internet Explorer, choose Tools→ Options, click Advanced in the dialog box that appears, and deselect the "Warn if forms submittal is being redirected" check box to turn this warning dialog box off.

Debug Ajax Code

You can use the Firefox browser to debug Ajax scripts. The capabilities of Firefox here far exceed what is available in Internet Explorer. In particular, you can use a script in an extension to Firefox named Greasemonkey to debug Ajax scripts by watching Ajax requests as they are made by your application.

To install Greasemonkey, go to the page `http://greasemonkey.mozdev.org/`. To install Greasemonkey, just click the Install Greasemonkey link when you have that page open in Firefox. When you install Greasemonkey, you see a monkey face at the lower right in Firefox; to toggle Greasemonkey on and off, click that icon.

After you install Greasemonkey, you can get Julien Couvreur's XMLHTTPRequest debugger script at `http://blog.monstuff.com/archives/000252.html`. To install that script in Greasemonkey, just right-click the link to the script, and select the Install User Script menu item.

Doing so opens a dialog box, and you can select which URLs the script should be active for — that is, which Web pages to debug — by entering those URLs in the Included Pages box.

When you navigate to one of those URLs in Firefox, the Ajax debugger script becomes active automatically. When an Ajax request is sent to the server, a dialog box opens and displays the details of the request — where the request is sent; whether it is a GET, POST, or other type of request; what the status of the XMLHttpRequest object is when the request is complete; and so on.

You can also specify which pages should make the debugging script active by selecting the Manage User Scripts item in Firefox's Tools menu, which opens the dialog box that lists the scripts to track in the debugger.

Debug Ajax Code

① Navigate to `http://greasemonkey.mozdev.org/`.

② Right-click the Install Greasemonkey link to install.

Greasemonkey is installed.

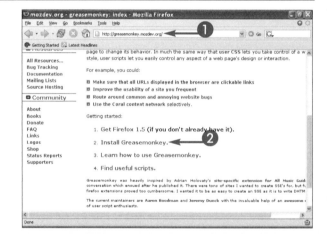

③ Navigate to `http://blog.monstuff.com/archives/000252.html`.

④ Right-click the link to the Ajax debugger, and click the Install User Script menu item.

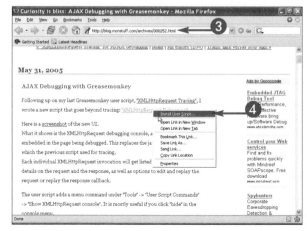

The Manage User Scripts dialog box appears.

⑤ Click Add.

⑥ Type the URL(s) you want to debug.

⑦ Click OK.

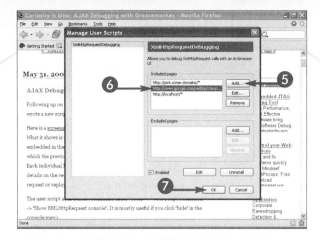

⑧ Navigate to one of the URLs you want to debug and perform an Ajax action, such as entering characters in the Google Suggest page.

● The debugger script displays information about the Ajax requests the page is making, and the results of those requests.

Extra

When it comes to debugging your Ajax applications, Firefox is far superior to Internet Explorer. The JavaScript debugging power of Internet Explorer is at best rudimentary. Whenever there is a problem in a script, Internet Explorer gives you a very basic error message — most often, "Object Expected", which simply means that it cannot make your JavaScript work and cannot create an object out of it. That message is practically useless compared to the Firefox JavaScript console, opened with Firefox's Tools → JavaScript Console menu item. The Firefox JavaScript console is full of error messages rich in information that pinpoints the problem in JavaScript scripts.

Greasemonkey is a powerful tool, giving you a window behind the scenes as a script executes. However, there can be security holes in Greasemonkey scripts that hackers may attack. Security issues were discovered in Greasemonkey version 0.3.4, for example, and as a result, that version is no longer distributed.

Convert Mouse Events into a Standard Format

Y ou can use the mouse in Ajax applications, and in fact, the mouse is often used in such applications to trigger events that cause the application to fetch data from the server behind the scenes. For example, when the user moves the mouse over an element in a Web page, such as an image in a navigation bar, and you want to fetch text to display in a drop-down menu connected to that image, you can use Ajax to fetch that data. On the other hand, you might have a shopping cart application where the user can drag an item to a shopping cart image on the Web page, and when the item is dropped, the server is notified of the purchase, using Ajax.

To make these common types of Ajax applications work, you must be able to handle the mouse. The problem is that different browsers use the mouse in entirely

different ways. In Internet Explorer, you use the `window.event` object to get data about mouse events. In Mozilla and Firefox, however, an event object is passed to event handler functions. In some browsers, you get the X location of the mouse with the event object's pageX property; in others, you get it with the clientX property.

In order to unify your JavaScript code, it is worthwhile to create a new JavaScript object with one set of properties. For example, this object may have properties named x and y to hold the X and Y location of the mouse in the Web page. You may store the target element of the mouse event in a property named target. For example, the target element may have just been clicked. Creating a new mouse event this way allows you to write the same JavaScript across the different browsers you may come across.

Convert Mouse Events into a Standard Format

① Connect the `onmousemove` event handler of the `<body>` tag to a function named `getMouseData`, passing the mouse event object as a parameter named `event`.

Mozilla and Firefox both pass an event object, but in Internet Explorer, this event object is null.

② Add two text fields to display the location of the mouse.

③ Create a function named `MouseEvent` that creates a new event object with x, y, and target properties.

The x and y properties hold the mouse's location in the Web page, and the target property holds the HTML element that containts the mouse pointer when the event occurs.

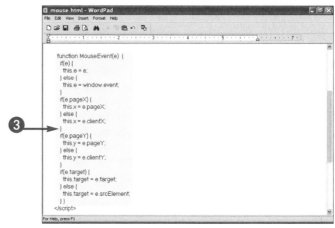

④ Add the `getMouseData` function, which is connected to the mouse move event.

This function displays the current x and y location of the mouse in the two text fields in the Web page.

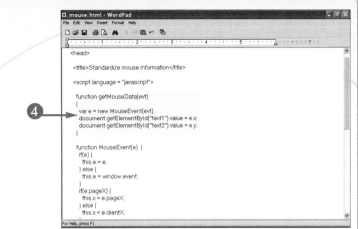

⑤ Open the Web page in a browser and move the mouse.

● The Web page displays the current x and y location of the mouse.

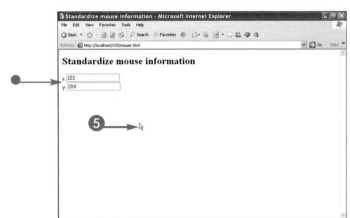

Apply It

You can use the target property of the mouse event object created in this task to determine which HTML element in the Web page receives the mouse event. For example, the mouse may move over an image, making the image the target of a `mouseover` event. You can use this code to determine if a particular HTML element is the target of the mouse event.

Example:
```
function getMouseData(evt)
{
  var e = new MouseEvent(evt);

  if(e.target === document.getElementById("text1")) {
    alert("The text1 text field was the target of the mouse event.");
  }
}
```

Note the use of the === (three equal signs) operator here, which you use in JavaScript when you want to compare two objects to see if they are the same object.

Handle Mouse Down and Mouse Up Events

Y ou can handle mouse down and mouse up events in JavaScript in Ajax applications. This is useful in case you want to handle the case where the user selects an item with the mouse in preparation for dragging that item in the Web page, or releases that item after dragging it. Being able to drag and drop items in a Web page is especially important in Ajax applications where you want to support a drag-and-drop shopping cart.

To handle mouse down events, where the user presses a mouse button, you use an HTML element's onmousedown JavaScript event handler. For example, you could connect a JavaScript function named getMouseDownData to an image's mouseDown event this way: <img onmousedown= getMouseDownData(event)>. Now when the mouse button is pressed when the mouse is over that image, the getMouseDownData is called. In Mozilla and Firefox, the

event parameter holds the mouse event object; in Internet Explorer, that object is null.

To handle mouse up events, you can use the onmouseup event attribute of HTML elements. For example, to connect a JavaScript function named getMouseUpData to an image's mouseUp event, you can use this HTML: <img onmouseup=getMouseUpData(event)>. When the user releases the mouse button over this image, the getMouseUpData function is called automatically. As with the onmousedown event attribute, in Mozilla and Firefox, the event parameter holds the mouse event object; in Internet Explorer, the object is null.

When you handle these events, the event object holds the location at which the mouse goes down or up, as well as the element that is the target of the mouse event. Using this event object, you can determine what is happening with the mouse in your JavaScript code.

Handle Mouse Down and Mouse Up Events

① Add code to connect the onmousedown event to a function named getMouseDownData and the onmouseup event to a function named getMouseUpData.

② Add the HTML to display two text fields and a <div> element that displays text.

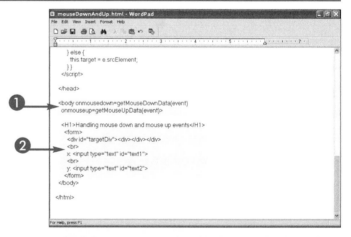

③ Add the getMouseDownData function after standardizing the mouse event for different browsers, and display the mouse location and the text "The mouse went down at:".

Note: See the section "Convert Mouse Events into a Standard Format" to learn how to standardize mouse events for different browsers.

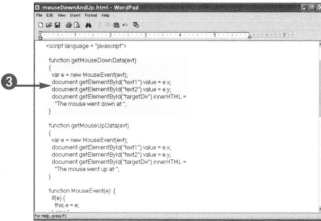

④ Add the `getMouseUpData` function after standardizing the mouse event for different browsers, and display the mouse location and the text "The mouse went up at:".

Note: See the section "Convert Mouse Events into a Standard Format" to learn how to standardize mouse events for different browsers.

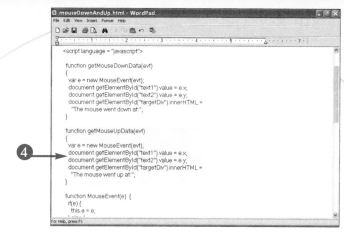

④

⑤ Open the Web page in your browser, and click the mouse button on the page.

● The Web page displays the text "The mouse went down at:" or "The mouse went up at:" and the mouse position.

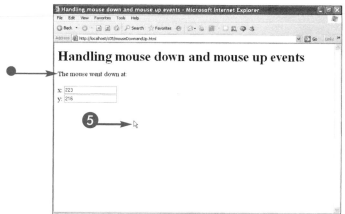

⑤

Handling mouse down and mouse up events

Extra

As you can see, standardizing mouse information saves you a great deal of code. If you do not create your own mouse event object with standard x and y properties, you must duplicate the code that tests which browser you are working with in both the `getMouseDownData` and `getMouseUpData` functions. You call the `MouseEvent` function to get a standard mouse event object with x and y properties to hold the mouse location no matter what browser you use.

If you want to handle mouse events in multiple HTML elements, you can connect a different function to each HTML element, or you can use just one function and use code to determine in which element the mouse event occurs.

Example:
```
if(e.target === document.getElementById
("img1")) {
    handleImagClick();
}
```

Handle Mouse Move Events

You can use the onmousemove event attribute in HTML elements to determine the current position of the mouse. Using this event attribute allows you to know where the mouse is at all times — when the mouse moves, this event occurs, and any function you choose is called with a mouse event that gives you the new location of the mouse. You can use the onmousemove event attribute to track the mouse as it is being dragged, which lets you move an HTML element as the user creates it in a Web page, for example.

You can watch the mouse as it is moved by the user by connecting the <body> element's onmousemove event attribute to a function such as getMouseData this way: <body onmousemove=getMouseData(event)>. In Mozilla and Firefox, the event parameter holds a mouse event object; in Internet Explorer, this parameter holds null.

As the user moves the mouse over your Web page, the mouse move event happens continuously. This event is not generated for every pixel over which the mouse travels — it only occurs a few times a second, but that allows you to track the mouse easily. You can even write Ajax applications that send the new location of the mouse to the server in real time, and if you use some fancy online programming, as is possible with the Java language, you can draw an image to match the user's mouse movements and send the image back to the browser. Doing so gives the appearance that the user is actually using the mouse to draw in the browser, but you need a very good connection to the server to be able to handle the quick flow of mouse events in this case.

Handle Mouse Move Events

① Connect the <body> element's onmousemove to the function getMouseData.

② Add two text fields that show the location of the mouse as it moves.

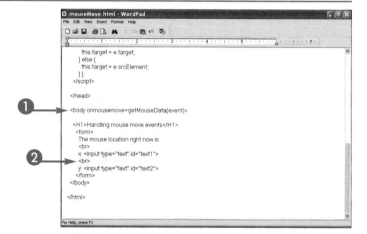

③ Create the getMouseData function, and standardize the mouse event.

Note: See the section "Convert Mouse Events into a Standard Format" to learn how to standardize mouse events.

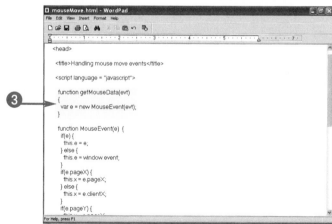

④ Add the code to display the x and y location of the mouse in the Web page.

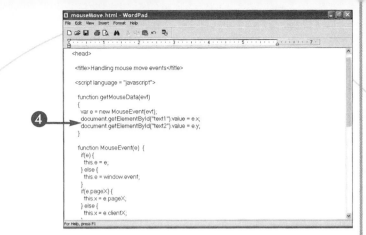

④

⑤ Open the Web page in a browser, and move the mouse.

- The current location of the mouse appears in the text fields.

⑤

Apply It

If you want to let the user move an HTML element with the mouse, you can use code like this, where `handleDown` and `handleMove` are connected to the `<body>` element's `onmousedown` and `onmousemove` attributes respectively.

Example:
```
function handleDown(e)
{
  var e = new MouseEvent(e);
  offsetX = e.x - parseInt(e.target.style.left);
  offsetY = e.y - parseInt(e.target.style.top);
}

function handleMove(e)
{
  var e = new MouseEvent(e);
  var x = e.x - offsetX;
  e.target.style.left = x + "px";
  var y = e.y - offsetY;
  e.target.style.top = y + "px";
}
```

Handle Mouse Click and Double-Click Events

You can handle mouse click and double-click events in Ajax applications. Handling these events in Ajax applications is a very powerful technique, because users are accustomed to making things happen in a Web page by clicking or double-clicking elements in the page. You already know that you can connect buttons to JavaScript code, but you can also connect HTML elements like images to JavaScript code as well — when the user clicks or double-clicks an image, for example, you can respond to that. When the user clicks an image map, for example, which displays all the restaurants along a route, you can use Ajax behind the scenes to download more information about a particular restaurant that is clicked and display it in an alert box or a floating `<div>` element.

You handle the click event with the `onclick` mouse event attribute. When you connect an HTML element's event attribute to a JavaScript function, the browser calls that function automatically when the user clicks that HTML element. That works not just for buttons, but also for any visible HTML element, such as images.

You can also use the `ondblclick` event attribute to handle double-click elements. When the user double-clicks an HTML element that has a JavaScript function connected to the `ondblclick` event attribute, the function is automatically called.

Both the `onclick` and `ondblclick` event handler functions are passed in an event object in Mozilla and Firefox. In Internet Explorer, that event object is null, and you use the `window.event` object instead. You have to provide for this difference in browsers in your JavaScript code, branching for Internet Explorer to use the `window.event` object, and in Mozilla and Firefox to use the passed event object.

Handle Mouse Click and Double-Click Events

1. Connect the `<body>` element's `onclick` event attribute to a JavaScript function named `getMouseClickData`, and the `ondblclick` event attribute to a function named `getMouseDoubleClickData`.

2. Add two text fields to display the location of the mouse and a `<div>` element to display text that indicates whether the page is clicked or double-clicked.

3. Add the code for the `getMouseClickData` function, standardizing the mouse event and displaying the x and y location of the mouse.

Note: See the section "Convert Mouse Events into a Standard Format" to learn how to standardize mouse events.

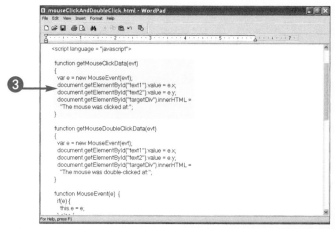

④ Add the code for the `getMouseDouble ClickData` function, standardizing the mouse event and displaying the x and y location of the mouse.

Note: See the section "Convert Mouse Events into a Standard Format" to learn how to standardize mouse events.

④

⑤ Open the Web page in a browser, and click or double-click the page.

● The Web page displays the location of the mouse as you click or double-click the page.

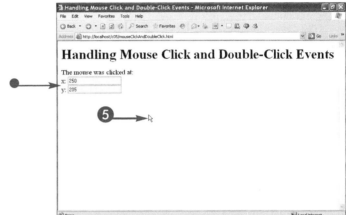

Extra

If you want to use the `onclick` or `ondblclick` events to create an image map — that is, a clickable image — that lets the user navigate to other locations, you can use JavaScript like this, which navigates the browser to www.usatoday.com:

```
navigator.go("http://www.usatoday.com")
```

Using the `onclick` event, you can make any HTML element, such as an image, look and act like a button. You can even change an image when it is clicked to a depressed version of the image, much as a button looks like when it is depressed as you click it, using code like this:

```
function changeImage(imageURL)
{
   document.getElementById("targetImg").
innerHTML =
      "<img src= " + imageURL + ">";
}
```

Handle Mouse Enter and Leave Events

You can use the mouse enter and leave events to determine when the mouse leaves or enters a particular HTML element. These events let your code react when the mouse enters the bounds of an image, for example, or leaves the image. This is useful, for example, if you want to use Ajax to fetch text for tool tips that you can display in a page. A tool tip is a small window that gives more information about the element the mouse is over, and you can display such a window using CSS. To show the tool tip, you can wait until the mouse enters the image's area on the screen; you can hide the tool tip when the mouse leaves the image's display area.

You handle mouse enter events with the `onmouseenter` event attribute. You can use this event attribute to tie the mouse enter event to a JavaScript function like this in the case of an image: `<img onmouseenter="showToolTip (event)">`. When the mouse pointer enters the image in the browser, the `showToolTip` function is called automatically.

You can handle mouse leave events with the `onmouseleave` event attribute. The `onmouseleave` attribute can connect a JavaScript function to the mouse leave event for an image, where you want to hide a tool tip when the mouse leaves the image: `<img onmouseleave="showToolTip(event)">`.

As with the other mouse events, you have access to a mouse event object when either the mouse enter or leave event occurs; this object is passed to the event handler functions in Mozilla and Firefox, but in Internet Explorer, the passed object is null, and you use the `window.event` object instead.

Handle Mouse Enter and Leave Events

① Connect the `onmouseenter` event attribute of an image to a function named `getMouseEnterData` and the `onmouseleave` event attribute of the image to a function named `getMouseLeaveData`.

② Add a `<div>` element to display text and two text fields to display the current location of the mouse.

③ Create the `getMouseEnterData` function, standardize the mouse event and display the location of the mouse.

Note: See the section "Convert Mouse Events into a Standard Format" to learn how to standardize mouse events.

④ Create the `getMouseLeaveData` function, standardize the mouse event, and display the location of the mouse.

Note: See the section "Convert Mouse Events into a Standard Format" to learn how to standardize mouse events.

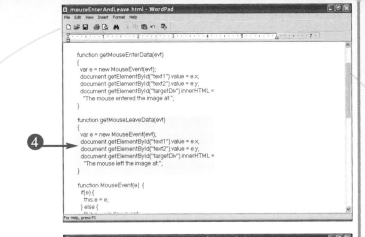

⑤ Open the Web page in your browser and move the mouse into and out of the image.

● The Web page reports the locations at which the mouse enters and leaves the image.

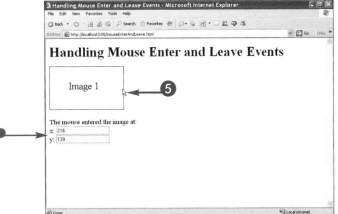

Extra

The onmouseenter and onmouseleave event attributes are good when you want to display tool tips, but not so good for other uses, like drop-down menus. The reason is that you can display a drop-down menu when the mouse enters an HTML element, but you cannot use the onmouseleave event attribute to hide the menu, because the user moves the mouse into the menu at that point and the menu is not hidden until the user makes a selection.

The onmouseenter and onmouseleave event attributes are useful when creating browser games. They let you track when the mouse enters a certain region in a Web browser without having to use the onmousemove event. The event attributes use a lot of if statements to see if the mouse is in the first region, then testing the second region the same way, and so on. Using onmouseenter and onmouseleave, you are automatically notified when the mouse enters specific parts of a Web page.

Create a Shopping Cart Application

Y ou can use Ajax to create shopping cart applications, which is one of the most exciting Ajax possibilities. By using an Ajax-driven shopping cart application, you can simply drag items you want to purchase to a shopping cart icon, and Ajax is used to send the information about the purchase to the server automatically. You do not have to navigate from page to page, as you do with most shopping cart systems now.

You can click a button that says, for example, Add item to cart to move to the shopping cart page. You can see your item in the shopping cart. Then you go back to browsing the shopping catalog to continue with other purchases. Ajax is designed to make that kind of experience easier by eliminating the need to navigate from page to page.

Using Ajax, you simply drag the item you want to purchase into the shopping cart. The application sends a notification to the server that your item is in the shopping cart, and no page refresh is needed. That notification can include a number or other data identifying the item in which you are interested, which the server can keep track of. After you drop the item in the shopping cart, a message from the server may appear that acknowledges the new item in the shopping cart.

Ajax way is a great technique to use to make purchases — because you do not have to navigate from page to page as part of the tedious process that makes Web shopping feel so difficult. This is one of the major uses of Ajax in Web applications.

Create a Shopping Cart Application

① Add a `targetDiv` `<div>` element that holds text the shopping cart receives from the server.

② Add a `<div>` element that stands for an MP3 player, and connect its `onmousedown` event attribute to a function named `handleDown`.

③ Add a `<div>` element that stands for the shopping cart.

④ Add styling for the MP3 player `<div>` element so that it appears in color.

⑤ Give it a large z-index property value, which allows it to move over other page elements when it is dragged.

⑥ Add styling for the shopping cart so that it appears in color.

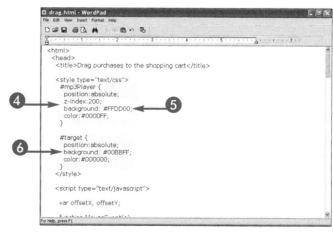

7 Add the `handleDown` method, standardize the mouse event so that it has the same properties across browsers, and display a message acknowledging that the mouse went down inside the MP3 player.

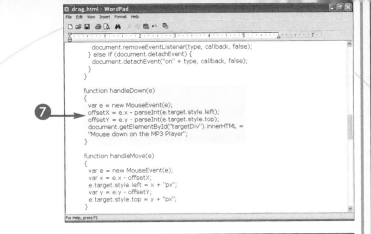

8 Open the Web page in your browser and click the mouse button inside the MP3 player area.

● The message "Mouse down on the MP3 Player" appears in the page.

Extra

Note the two lines that set the global variables offsetX and offsetY in the handleDown function:

```
function handleDown(e)
{
  var e = new MouseEvent(e);
  offsetX = e.x - parseInt
(e.target.style.left);
  offsetY = e.y - parseInt
(e.target.style.top);
  document.getElementById("targetDiv")
.innerHTML = "";
}
```

These lines record the location inside the MP3 player `<div>` element where the mouse goes down. It is not necessary to do this, but recording that location lets you drag the MP3 player while keeping the mouse at its original location inside the MP3 player `<div>` element.

You do not have to use `<div>` elements in your shopping cart application. In a finished application, you might want to use images of the MP3 player and of the shopping cart. To do that, just replace the `<div>` elements with `<img>` elements.

Drag an HTML Element in a Shopping Cart Application

You can use the `mousemove` event handler in a shopping cart application in order to support dragging of HTML elements to the shopping cart. You are responsible for moving the element that is being dragged, and you can do that using CSS styles.

There are a number of ways to support drag-and-drop operations in browsers, but you must be careful that your code works across different browsers. So far, you have only connected mouse move events to code using the `onmousemove` event handler in HTML like this: `<body onmousemove="handleMove(event)">`. However, you only want to make the item being purchased move when it is being dragged, not in response to all mouse movements at any time. You can add mouse listener functions to an HTML element at runtime using the document object's `addEventListener` method in Internet Explorer, and the document object's `attachEvent` method in Mozilla and Firefox.

To connect a function named `handleMove` to the `onmousemove` event attribute of the document object at runtime, you can use this expression in Internet Explorer: `document.addEventListener("onmousemove", handleMove, false)`. The argument of false at the end indicates that you want to catch events that bubble from an HTML element up to that element's containing element in case they are not handled by the element itself. In Mozilla and Firefox, you use the expression `document.attachEvent("onmousemove", handleMove, false)`.

Using the document object's `addEventListener` or `attachEvent` method, depending on the browser, allows you to capture mouse events when appropriate. In the case of a shopping cart application, you can start capturing mouse move events after the mouse button is pressed when the mouse pointer is over an item to purchase so that you can move the item when the user starts moving the mouse.

Drag an HTML Element in a Shopping Cart Application

① When the mouse goes down in a shopping cart application, call a new function named `addListener`, passing that function the name of the two mouse events to capture — `mouseMove` and `mouseUp`, and the function that will handle those events — `handleMove` and `handleUp`.

② In the `addListener` function, add the JavaScript to connect the requested event to the requested event handler.

The `handleMove` function moves the item you purchase.

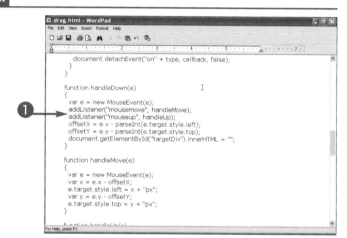

③ In the `handleMove` function, standardize the mouse event across browsers, then adjust the x location of the mouse to preserve its location inside the item being dragged.

④ Set the dragged item's x location using the style property `e.target.style.left`.

⑤ Adjust the y location of the mouse to preserve its location inside the dragged item, and set the item's y location using the style property `e.target.style.top`.

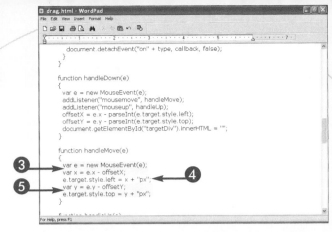

⑥ Open the Web page in a browser and click and drag the item.

The dragged item follows the mouse.

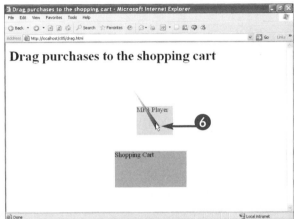

Extra

Note the code in the `handleMove` event that moves the item the user is dragging:

```
var x = e.x - offsetX;
e.target.style.left = x + "px";
var y = e.y - offsetY;
e.target.style.top = y + "px";
```

The `"px"` here refers to pixels, which means that the measurements you make here are in pixels. You can also use other units of measure, such as inches, if you use the abbreviation "in", as in this code:

```
var x = e.x - offsetX;
e.target.style.left = x + "in";
var y = e.y - offsetY;
e.target.style.top = y + "in";
```

There is discussion going on at the World Wide Web Consortium (W3C) at www.w3.org, the group that standardizes HTML, on changing the way you attach event handlers to events at runtime in browsers. However, even if changes are made at some point in the future, the technique used in this task will still work for a long time to come.

Drop an HTML Element in a Shopping Cart Application

You can use the `onmouseup` event to handle the case where you release the mouse button to drop an item you are dragging into a shopping cart. When you drag an item into the shopping cart and release that item, an `onmouseup` event occurs. In the `onmouseup` event handler, you can disconnect any event listeners from the `onmousemove` and `onmouseup` events, because the drag-and-drop operation is now over. Then test if the item is dropped in the shopping cart.

After the dragged item is dropped, disconnect the `onmousemove` and `onmouseup` events from your JavaScript code because the drag-and-drop operation is over. To disconnect a function named `handleMove` from the `onmousemove` event of the document object at runtime, you can use this expression in Internet Explorer: `document.removeEventListener("onmousemove",`

`handleMove, false)`. The argument of false at the end indicates that you also want to disconnect from events that bubble from an HTML element up to that element's containing element in case they are not handled by the element itself. In Mozilla and Firefox, use the expression `document.detachEvent("onmousemove", handleMove, false)`.

After you disconnect your code from the `onmousemove` and `onmouseup` events, check if the dragged item is dropped in the shopping cart. To check that, you need the location at which the item is dropped and the coordinates of the shopping cart. You can use styles to get that information. For example, here is how you get the x location of the cart: `x = parseInt(cart.style.left)`. The JavaScript `parseInt` function converts the text in the `style.left` property into a number.

Drop an HTML Element in a Shopping Cart Application

① When you release the mouse button, stop dragging the item you are moving to the shopping cart.

You can do that by calling a new function named `removeListener`.

```
        e.target.style.top = y + "px";

    function handleUp(e)
    {
      var e = new MouseEvent(e);
      removeListener("mousemove", handleMove);
      removeListener("mouseup", handleUp);

      var target = document.getElementById("target");
      var x = parseInt(target.style.left);
      var y = parseInt(target.style.top);
      var width = parseInt(target.style.width);
      var height = parseInt(target.style.height);

      if(e.x > x && e.x < x + width &&
        e.y > y && e.y < y + height){
          document.getElementById("targetDiv").innerHTML =
            "You dropped the item on the shopping cart.";
      }
    }
```

② In the `removeListener` function, disconnect your code from the `onmousemove` and `onmouseup` events to stop dragging the dragged item.

```
    function addListener(type, callback)
    {
      if (document.addEventListener) {
        document.addEventListener(type, callback, false);
      } else if (document.attachEvent) {
        document.attachEvent("on"+type, callback, false);
      }
    }

    function removeListener (type, callback)
    {
      if (document.removeEventListener) {
        document.removeEventListener(type, callback, false);
      } else if (document.detachEvent) {
        document.detachEvent("on" + type, callback, false);
      }
    }

    function handleDown(e)
    {
      var e = new MouseEvent(e);
      addListener("mousemove", handleMove);
      addListener("mouseup", handleUp);
```

3 Get the coordinates of the shopping cart in the browser.

4 Check to see if the dragged item is dropped inside the shopping cart.

If the dragged item is dropped inside the shopping cart, display the message "You dropped the item on the shopping cart."

5 Open the Web page in your browser and click and drag an item into the shopping cart.

● The message "You dropped the item on the shopping cart." appears.

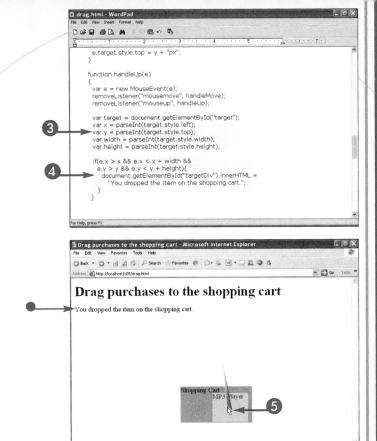

Apply It

You may have multiple items on the page that the user can drag. To determine which item the user has dragged, you can use the target property of the mouse event object, e. Here is how you could compare e.target to various draggable items, using the JavaScript === operator, which you use to compare objects:

```
function handleUp(e)
{
  var e = new MouseEvent(e);
  removeListener("mousemove", handleMove);
  removeListener("mouseup", handleUp);
  if(e.target === document.getElementById("image1")){
    //handle image1 dropped
  }
  if(e.target === document.getElementById("image2")){
    //handle image2 dropped
  }
}
```

Update a Shopping Cart on the Server

O nce you drop a dragged item into the shopping cart in your shopping cart application, notify the server of the new selection. Using Ajax, you can notify the server behind the scenes, without causing a page refresh.

That is the whole point of Ajax applications — you can notify the server behind the scenes. In the case of an Ajax-driven shopping cart system, you can notify the server that the user made a selection, and fetch data from the server in response.

You can notify the server that the user dragged an item into the shopping cart using the XMLHttpRequest object's open method like this: XMLHttpRequestObject.open("GET", "purchase.txt"). In this case, you simply fetch the text in the file puchase.txt from the server. That works if

you just want to fetch a generic acknowledgment from the server indicating that it has been notified that the user made a selection.

On the other hand, if you want to pass the ID of the item the user selects to the server, use an online program. For example, you might want to pass the ID of the dropped item to an online script named purchase.php, and if you use the GET method, you can do that with URL encoding like this: XMLHttpRequestObject.open("GET", "purchase.php?ID=49393"). This expression prepares the XMLHttpRequest object to send the ID number of the dropped item to the purchase.php server-side script.

When you notify the server-side script of the ID of the item that the user has purchased, the server-side script can add that item to its internal shopping cart for the user.

Update a Shopping Cart on the Server

① When the user drops an item in a shopping cart application, check to see if the item is dropped in the shopping cart.

```
function handleUp(e)
{
  var e = new MouseEvent(e);
  removeListener("mousemove", handleMove);
  removeListener("mouseup", handleUp);

  var target = document.getElementById("target");
  var x = parseInt(target.style.left);
  var y = parseInt(target.style.top);
  var width = parseInt(target.style.width);
  var height = parseInt(target.style.height);

  if(e.x > x && e.x < x + width &&
    e.y > y && e.y < y + height){
    var XMLHttpRequestObject = false;

    if (window.XMLHttpRequest) {
      XMLHttpRequestObject = new XMLHttpRequest();
    } else if (window.ActiveXObject) {
      XMLHttpRequestObject = new
      ActiveXObject("Microsoft.XMLHTTP");
    }
```

② If the dragged item is dropped inside the shopping cart, use Ajax to fetch the file purchase.txt from the server.

The purchase.txt file contains the text "You just bought a fine MP3 player."

```
    if(e.x > x && e.x < x + width &&
      e.y > y && e.y < y + height){
      var XMLHttpRequestObject = false;

      if (window.XMLHttpRequest) {
        XMLHttpRequestObject = new XMLHttpRequest();
      } else if (window.ActiveXObject) {
        XMLHttpRequestObject = new
        ActiveXObject("Microsoft.XMLHTTP");
      }

      if(XMLHttpRequestObject) {
        XMLHttpRequestObject.open("GET", "purchase.txt");

        XMLHttpRequestObject.onreadystatechange = function()
        {
          if (XMLHttpRequestObject.readyState == 4 &&
            XMLHttpRequestObject.status == 200) {
            document.getElementById("targetDiv").innerHTML =
              XMLHttpRequestObject.responseText;
            delete XMLHttpRequestObject;
            XMLHttpRequestObject = null;
```

③ Use the `responseText` property to recover and display the text in the `purchase.txt` file in the Web page.

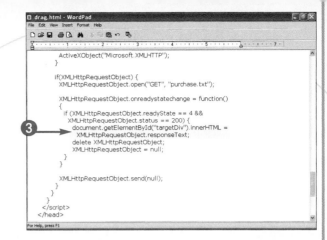

④ Open the Web page in your browser, and click and drag an item into the shopping cart.

● The message "You just bought a fine MP3 player." fetched from the server appears.

Apply It

You can also send data to the server, such as the ID of the item dragged to the shopping cart, using URL encoding with the GET method, or the send method with the POST method. Here is how you can send an ID value of 49393 using POST.

Send an ID Value
```
if(XMLHttpRequestObject) {
    XMLHttpRequestObject.open("POST", "purchase.php");
    XMLHttpRequestObject.setRequestHeader('Content-Type',
     'application/x-www-form-urlencoded');

    XMLHttpRequestObject.onreadystatechange = function()
    {
        if (XMLHttpRequestObject.readyState == 4 &&
            XMLHttpRequestObject.status == 200) {
                document.getElementById("targetDiv").innerHTML =
                    XMLHttpRequestObject.responseText;
        }
    }
    XMLHttpRequestObject.send("ID=49393");
}
```

Download Image Names Using Ajax

You can use Ajax to download images and other binary objects in Web pages. Ajax is text based. The data you send back and forth to the server using Ajax must also be text-based, which includes data stored in XML format. Currently, there is no way to use XML to encode binary data and store it in XML documents — it all has to be text.

It seems that you are stuck here — that you can download only text with Ajax. That is only partly true, however. You can use Ajax together with dynamic HTML to do much more. Dynamic HTML allows you to download new items in a Web page at runtime, and if you use Ajax to get the text corresponding to the item you are supposed to download, you are all set.

To see how that works, look at the standard HTML `<img>` element. This element has a `src` attribute that holds the URL of the image that the element is supposed to display. For example, the `<img>` element `<img src="http://www.nourl.com/images/image.jpg">` displays the image at `www.nourl.com/images/image.jpg`.

If you want to change that image at runtime, you can use dynamic HTML to rewrite the HTML of the `<img>` element so that the `src` attribute points to a different URL. The browser notices that the `<img>` element has changed and downloads the new image for you automatically, which gives the impression that you have been able to download images using Ajax. In fact, all you have to do is to download the name of an image or its URL, rewrite the `<img>` element, and dynamic HTML does the rest.

Download Image Names Using Ajax

① Add three buttons to a Web page and connect them to the getData function, which downloads the files `imageName.txt`, `imageName2.txt`, and `imageName3.txt`.

`imageName.txt` holds the image file name Image01.jpg, `imageName2.txt` holds the name Image02.jpg, and so on.

② Add the code to download the requested image name file, using Ajax in the `getData` function.

③ Display the name of the requested image to confirm that you are able to read that name.

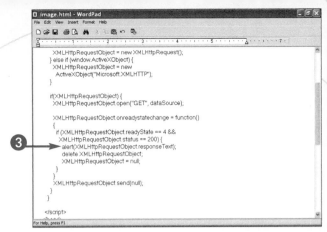

```
    XMLHttpRequestObject = new XMLHttpRequest();
  } else if (window.ActiveXObject) {
    XMLHttpRequestObject = new
    ActiveXObject("Microsoft.XMLHTTP");
  }

  if(XMLHttpRequestObject) {
    XMLHttpRequestObject.open("GET", dataSource);

    XMLHttpRequestObject.onreadystatechange = function()
    {
      if (XMLHttpRequestObject.readyState == 4 &&
        XMLHttpRequestObject.status == 200) {
        alert(XMLHttpRequestObject.responseText);
        delete XMLHttpRequestObject;
        XMLHttpRequestObject = null;
      }
    }
    XMLHttpRequestObject.send(null);
  }
}

</script>
```

④ Open the new page in a browser and click a button.

● The corresponding image name is displayed in an alert box.

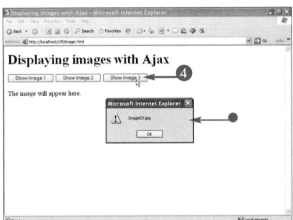

Extra

Besides the name or URL of the image, you can download more data about the image as well. For example, you can download the height and width of the image so that you are able to write a new <img> element complete with height and width attributes like this: <img src="Image03.jp" height="120" width="205">. Using the height and width elements lets the browser know how much space to allow for the image in the Web page, and if you do not give the browser that information, the image appears to jump in size as it is downloaded and displayed. If you want to download height and width information as well as the image's name or URL, you have two choices. You can store all that information in a single file, which means a single Ajax access to the server, but you must use the JavaScript string functions to extract the image name/URL, width, and height from the data you have downloaded. Alternatively, you can use three files for these three data items, which means three Ajax accesses to the server.

Another attribute whose value you might consider downloading from the server is the value of the alt attribute, which holds alternate text that the browser displays if the image cannot be shown. The alt attribute is theoretically required, but most browsers do not insist on it.

Display Images Using Ajax and Dynamic HTML

After you use Ajax to download the names of images to display in a Web page, you can use dynamic HTML in a browser to display those images. For example, say that you have an image element with the ID targetImage, like this: `<img id="targetImage">`. At runtime, you can change the image displayed in this `<img>` element using dynamic HTML. All you have to do is to change the HTML of the `<img>` element such that the src attribute holds the URL of the new image you want to display.

For example, if you store the URL of the new image you want to display in a variable named newImageName, you can rewrite the `<img>` element to display that new image like this in JavaScript: `document.getElementById("targetImage").innerHTML = "<img src= " + newImageName + ">"`. The browser writes the new HTML to the `<img>` element, and then downloads the image whose URL to which you have set the src

attribute. You simply create the HTML to display the image you want at runtime.

After you download the name or the URL of the image to display, all you have to do is to use JavaScript to rewrite the `<img>` element, setting the src attribute to that name or URL. For example, if you fetch the name of the image file to use using an object named XMLHttpRequestObject, here is how you can display that image file using dynamic HTML:

```
document.getElementById("targetDiv").innerH
TML = "<img src= " + XMLHttpRequestObject
.responseText + ">"
```

After you execute that JavaScript, the browser automatically downloads and displays the new image whose name or URL is in the XMLHttpRequestObject object's responseText property.

Display Images Using Ajax and Dynamic HTML

1 Add a `<div>` element to display downloaded images.

You can also use an empty `<img>` element.

2 Create an object corresponding to the `<div>` element.

③ Assign the `<div>` element the new HTML to display the image whose name or URL you downloaded using Ajax.

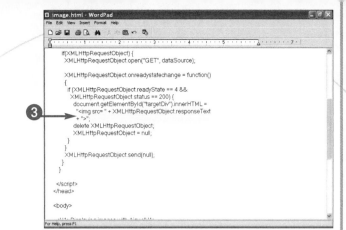

④ Open the new page in a browser and click a button.

● The corresponding image is downloaded and displayed.

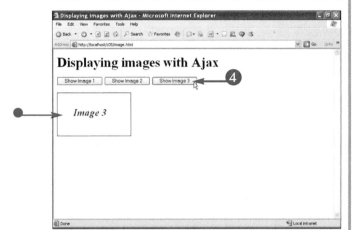

Apply It

You can download other types of binary objects besides images using Ajax and dynamic HTML. For example, you can use the HTML `<object>` element to download any kind of binary object, using Ajax code.

Example:
```
XMLHttpRequestObject.onreadystatechange = function()
{
    if (XMLHttpRequestObject.readyState == 4) {
        if (XMLHttpRequestObject.status == 200) {
            document.getElementById("targetDiv").innerHTML =
                "<object codebase = " +
                XMLHttpRequestObject.responseText + ">";
        }
        else if (XMLHttpRequestObject.status == 404) {
            alternateJavaScriptFunction();
        }
    }
}
```

Create an Ajax-Driven Menu System

Y ou can create interactive menus in Web pages using Ajax, and doing so is a common Ajax technique. When the user moves the mouse over a certain section of a Web page, you can use Ajax to access the server, downloading the menu items to display. Using Ajax, you can make your menus interactive, displaying different items at different times as appropriate.

For example, if you want to let users select the size or color of an item they want to purchase, you can use Ajax to check with the server to see what size and colors of the item are currently available. Then you can use JavaScript and CSS styles to display a drop-down menu from which the user can select. In that way, the user does not end up selecting a color or size of an item that is not available.

You can create a menu system using JavaScript and CSS styles in a Web page. For example, you might display the menu names using images in a menu bar. You can use CSS styles to position the menu as needed in your Web page: `<img id = "menu1" src="menu1.jpg" style= "left:30; top:50; width:200; height:40;">`. Just below that menu's image in the Web page, you can place a `<div>` element that displays the menu items. To start, that `<div>` element should be invisible: `<div id = "menuDiv1" style="left:30; top:100; width:100; height: 70; visibility:hidden;"><div></div> </div>`.

When the user moves the mouse over the menu's image, you can download the names of the items that should appear in that menu and display them in the `<div>` element. When users click a menu item, you can respond to their selections using JavaScript.

Create an Ajax-Driven Menu System

① Add the `<img>` elements to display two menus and two `<div>` elements that display the menu items fetched using Ajax.

menu1.jpg holds an image displaying the menu name Color and menu2.jpg holds an image displaying the menu name Size.

② Connect the `<body>` element's `onmousemove` event attribute to a function named check.

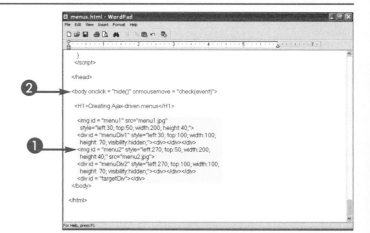

③ Add the JavaScript code to the check function to check if the mouse is over the first menu, and if so, call `getData(1)`.

④ Add the JavaScript code to the check function to check if the mouse is over the second menu, and if so, call `getData(2)`.

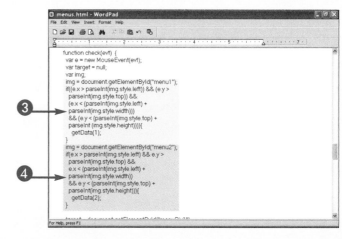

5 In the `getData` function, add the code to display the number of the menu that the user selected in an alert box.

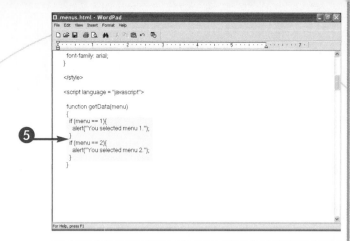

6 Open the Web page in a browser, and move the mouse over either menu.

- The browser displays the menu you selected in an alert box.

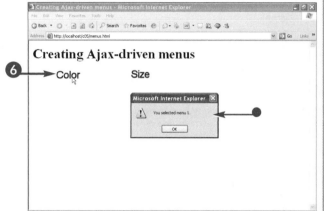

Apply It

Another good way of displaying interactive menu items is to use an HTML `<select>` control to display a list box in a Web page. For example, say you have this `<select>` control:

```
<select name="select1">
   <option>Red</option>
   <option>White</option>
</select>
```

You can change the items in the `<select>` control this way in JavaScript:

```
document.form1.select1.options[0].text = "1";
document.form1.select1.options[1].text = "2";
```

If you want to create new items in the `<select>` control at runtime, you can do this in Mozilla and Firefox:

```
var option1 = document.createElement("OPTION");
document.form1.select1.add(option1, null);
option1.innerHTML = "3";
```

And this in Internet Explorer:

```
var option1 = document.createElement("OPTION");
document.form1.select1.options.add(option1);
option1.innerHTML = "3";
```

Display a Menu Using Cascading Styles

You can use Cascading Style Sheets (CSS) to display a menu in an Ajax-driven application. One common way of doing that is to use a `<div>` element to display the menu items in the menu and to use an HTML table inside the `<div>` element so that each menu item has its own cell in the table.

The reason this is a good way of displaying the menu items in a menu is that you can connect JavaScript code to each table cell's `onclick` event attribute so that when a menu item is clicked, the correct JavaScript code for that item is called.

For example, say that using Ajax, you download the text for a menu's items like this: `"Small, Medium, Large"`. You can break that text up into an array of three items, `"Small"`, `"Medium"`, and `"Large"` using the built-in JavaScript string function split this way: `split(" ,")`.

After creating the array holding the menu items, you can loop over that array, creating the HTML table that holds the menu items. You can also connect each menu item's `onclick` event attribute to a function that takes the appropriate action when that menu item is clicked. After creating the HTML table, assign it to the `<div>` element's `innherHTML` property to load the table into the `<div>` element.

After you use Ajax to download the items for the menu, create an HTML table containing those items where each cell is connected to the JavaScript function that responds when the item is clicked, and load that table into the `<div>` element, you can make that `<div>` element visible by setting its visibility style property to "visible", displaying the menu.

Display a Menu Using Cascading Styles

1 Style the `<div>` elements that display your menus, being sure to give them a background color so they are visible when displayed.

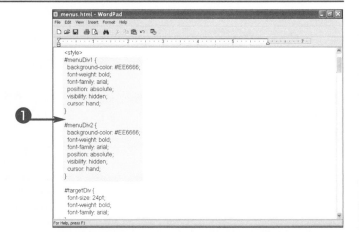

2 To show the request menu in a function named show, split the string holding the menu items downloaded from the server into an array.

3 Loop over the array, assembling the HTML that will create the table holding the menu items. Connect each menu item to a function named display that will display the user's menu selection.

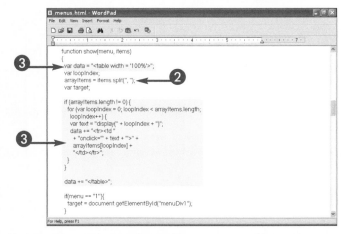

④ Get an object corresponding to the `<div>` element that displays the menu items.

⑤ Place the HTML to display the menu items in the `<div>` element, and make that `<div>` element visible.

```
                      + "onclick='" + text + "'>" +
                        arrayItems[loopIndex] +
                      "</td></tr>";
              }
          }

          data += "</table>";

          if(menu == "1"){
④           target = document.getElementById("menuDiv1");
          }

          if(menu == "2"){
              target = document.getElementById("menuDiv2");
          }

          if(target.style.visibility == "hidden"){
⑤           target.innerHTML = data;
              target.style.visibility = "visible";
          }
      }

      function hide()
```

⑥ Open the Web page in your browser and move the mouse over a menu.

The browser displays the menu items fetched using Ajax.

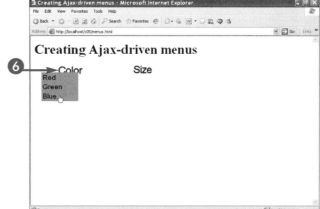

Extra

When you want to display a menu or any free-floating element using cascading styles, do not forget to set the element's position style to absolute this way: `"position: absolute;"`. Setting the element's position property to absolute means that you can specify its location in the Web page in absolute terms, using pixel measurements. The other option is to use relative positioning, where you position an element with respect to its default position in a page. When you want to display drop-down menus, absolute positioning is best.

When displaying a menu, you can set the cursor style property for the menu `<div>` element to "hand" to turn the mouse cursor to a hand when the mouse is over the menu. That makes your menu look more like a menu, because otherwise, the mouse cursor looks like the standard mouse pointer. If the mouse cursor looks like a hand, that gives it the appearance of being able to select items in a menu. Unfortunately, turning the mouse cursor into a hand icon only works in Internet Explorer.

Hide a Menu Using CSS

You can close Ajax-driven menus by hiding them using CSS. When you open a menu by displaying it using an HTML element such as a `<div>` element, you set the `<div>` element's visibility property to "visible". That displays the `<div>` element that contains the menu. If you have already set the `<div>` element's left, top, width, and height style properties, and set its position style property to "absolute", that makes the menu appear at the location you specify.

On the other hand, when the user moves the mouse away from the menu, that menu should close. Because you use a `<div>` element to display the items in the menu, that menu does not automatically close — you must make it close by yourself.

The idea here is that you must watch the mouse, using the `onmousemove` event attribute, for example. When the mouse moves, you can check if it moves away from the

open menu, and if it has, you close that menu. You can check the mouse's location in your Web page by taking a look at the event object in Mozilla and Firefox, and the `window.event` object in Internet Explorer — see the section "Convert Mouse Events into a Standard Format" for more details.

You can check if a menu is open by checking the visibility property of the `<div>` element that contains that menu. If that property is "visible", the menu is open. You can check if a menu is open using this JavaScript: `if (menuDiv1.style.visibility == "visible"){...}`.

If the menu is open, you can close it by simply hiding the `<div>` element that contains the menu. To hide that element, all you have to do is to set its visibility style to "hidden" this way:

`menuDiv1.style.visibility = "hidden"`.

Hide a Menu Using CSS

① When the mouse is outside the menu area, call a function named `hide` to hide the menu.

② Add the code to hide the menu, if it is open.

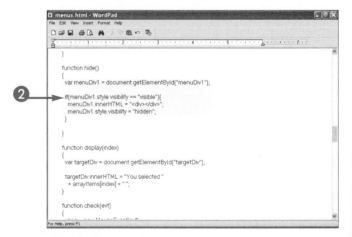

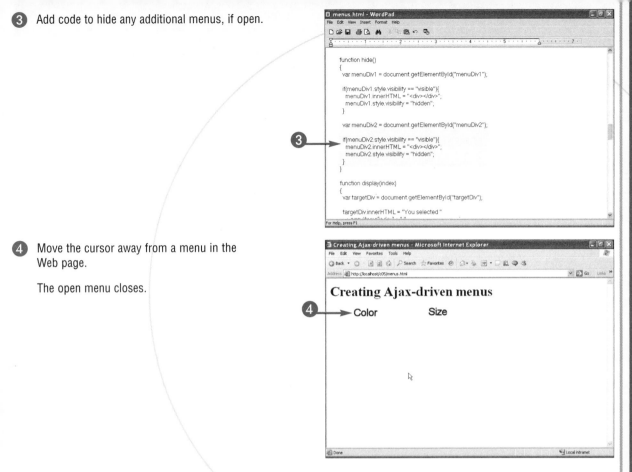

③ Add code to hide any additional menus, if open.

④ Move the cursor away from a menu in the Web page.

The open menu closes.

Extra

The example in this task uses the function hide to close both menus. That is fine for example code to keep the example simple, but in a real-world application, you probably want to use separate hide functions, one for each menu you have. After checking if a menu is open, you can call the appropriate hide function, such as hideMenu1, if a particular menu is open. The code works either way, but using separate hide functions and avoiding executing extra code speeds up the response of your application.

When you close a menu, you may want to erase its contents because the next time the menu opens, you may want to update its contents using data fetched from the server, using Ajax. To erase the contents of a menu, you can set the innerHTML property of the enclosing <div> element to some empty HTML like this: "<div></div>". If you set the HTML of the enclosing <div> element to an empty string, " ", some browsers will not let you rewrite the inner HTML of that element afterward.

Read Ajax-Driven Menu Selections

You can make Ajax-driven menus you create on the fly respond to mouse clicks. The usual way to create menus using Cascading Style Sheets is to display an HTML table inside a `<div>` element. That way, each table cell can correspond to a different menu item, which very neatly gives each menu item its own line in the menu. It is also a good choice to use an HTML table to display the items in a menu because each table cell has an `onclick` event, which you can use to handle mouse clicks as the user selects items from your menu.

Here is how it works. Say that when the user clicks a menu item, you want a function named display called with the number of the menu item — the top item in the menu is item 0, the next is item 1, and so on. When you loop over the items in a menu, for example, they are held

in an array named `arrayItems`, adding them to the HTML table that displays the menu items. You can create the JavaScript that is used to call the display function this way: `var text = "display(" + loopIndex + ")"`, where `loopIndex` is the loop index of the loop that iterates over the menu items.

To actually create the table cell that displays the menu item, you can use this expression: `"<tr><td " + "onclick='" + text + "'>" + arrayItems [loopIndex] + "</td></tr>"`. That connects the current table cell element's `onclick` event attribute to the display function. When the user clicks this menu item, the display function is called, and the browser automatically passes the display function to the index of the menu item that the user clicks.

Read Ajax-Driven Menu Selections

1 Add the JavaScript code to make menu items call the display function when they are clicked.

2 In the display function, add the JavaScript to display the selected menu item in a `<div>` element.

③ Style the `<div>` element so that the selection the user makes is visible in the Web page.

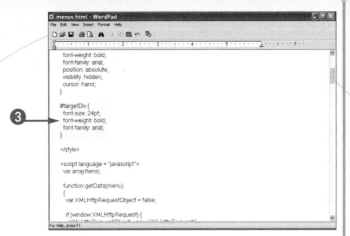

④ Select a menu item in the Web page by clicking it.

● The Web page displays the menu item you selected.

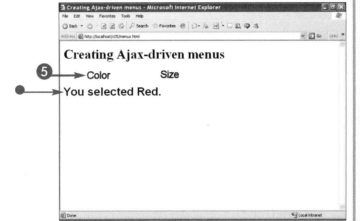

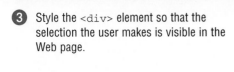

Apply It

You may want to send the user's menu selection to the server, as opposed to simply displaying that selection in a Web page. For example, if you connect the menu items in the Size menu to this function, the size selection made by the user automatically sends the setSize.php script on the server.

Example:
```
function sendSizeToServer(index) {
  if(XMLHttpRequestObject) {
    XMLHttpRequestObject.open("POST", "setSize.php");
    XMLHttpRequestObject.setRequestHeader('Content-Type',
      'application/x-www-form-urlencoded');
    XMLHttpRequestObject.onreadystatechange = function() {
      if (XMLHttpRequestObject.readyState == 4 &&
        XMLHttpRequestObject.status == 200) {
          document.getElementById("targetDiv").innerHTML =
            XMLHttpRequestObject.responseText;
      }
    }
    XMLHttpRequestObject.send("size=" + index);
  }
}
```

Using Ajax Frameworks

You can use Ajax *frameworks,* many of which are available on the Internet free, to simplify your Ajax development. An Ajax framework is made up of prewritten Ajax code that you can use so you do not have to write the same code yourself from scratch. Ajax usually involves a limited number of well-defined tasks:

GET or POST

You can use the GET method to download text from the server, or you can use the GET method to download XML from the server. Alternatively, you can use the POST method to send data to the server and download text or XML. Those four operations make up the great bulk of Ajax work — although, of course, there are other possibilities, such as sending HEAD requests to the server. If you can get and use some prewritten code to perform those common operations, you can save yourself a great deal of time.

Code Reuse

The idea behind Ajax frameworks is one of *code reuse.* Once you develop the code needed to perform the common Ajax tasks, you can put that code into your own Ajax framework, which can be as simple as a simple JavaScript file. That code is usually in the form of functions that you can call as needed. You can reuse your code over and over, simply by calling those functions, without having to rewrite that code from scratch. This process is made even easier if you use a prewritten Ajax framework that someone else has developed. All you have to do is to install the code in your application and call the functions you need. You do not even have to know how those functions do what they do.

Free for Downloading

Because Ajax has become so popular, many Ajax frameworks have appeared, and many of them are free to download. In general, all you have to do is download the framework you want to work with, install it, and use it. It is important to install the framework properly — in particular, make sure that you have all the necessary files and that you place them where they are required.

You usually install an Ajax framework on the server. The most simple of Ajax frameworks are simply JavaScript files that end with the extension .js, which you place in the same directory on the server as your Web page. To allow your Web page access to the JavaScript in the Ajax framework, you can use the HTML <script> element, thereby using that element's src attribute to hold the URL of the JavaScript file you want to access.

For example, this chapter develops its own simple Ajax framework, named ajaxframework.js. This framework is a JavaScript file that contains the JavaScript functions you need to perform the four central Ajax tasks by using GET to download text or XML from the server, or using POST to download text or XML from the server. Each such task is supported by a function, such as readTextWithGet, which lets you download text from the server using the GET method with Ajax.

Install a Framework

To install this Ajax framework, store the JavaScript file for the framework, ajaxframework.js, in the same directory as the Web page in which you want to use the framework. Then use the HTML `<script>` element this way to make the functions in the framework accessible to your code in the Web page: `<script src="ajaxframework.js">`. That includes the JavaScript in ajaxframework.js in your Web page so you can call the functions in it.

After you install the framework and make its code available to your own code in your Web page, you can call functions like `readTextWithGet`, which contacts the server, gets the data you want, and returns it to you.

Ajax frameworks are helpful because not only do they perform Ajax tasks for you, they also may have good Ajax programming practices built in, such as being able to work with multiple `XMLHttpRequest` objects in case an impatient user clicks a number of Ajax-enabled buttons in quick success, error handling, and so on.

Server-Side Frameworks

The more advanced Ajax frameworks execute primarily on the server. These frameworks are often considerably more powerful than the simple Ajax frameworks. Not only do they allow you to execute code on the server, but they can actually generate JavaScript that will be executed in the browser. With some of the advanced frameworks, all you have to do is specify what code you want to execute on the server, and the framework will create the JavaScript for you that will allow you to connect to your code on the server using Ajax. These server-side frameworks often come with extra power built in, such as new controls that let you perform Ajax drag-and-drop operations simply in your applications.

To use one of the more advanced server-side Ajax frameworks, you need to be able to run programs on your server. The most common type of server-side Ajax framework is written in PHP, so you will need a server that supports PHP. All you have to do is install the framework on your server, write the code you want executed on the server, and use the framework to interact with that code from inside your Web page as that page is executed by the browser. For more on the advanced type of Ajax frameworks, see Chapter 8.

Two Kinds of Frameworks

There are two different types of Ajax frameworks — those that execute in the browser, and those that execute on the server and in the browser. The simple Ajax frameworks are all of the former kind. They are JavaScript files that you can include in your Web page, accessing the prewritten code in the framework simply by calling JavaScript functions. These frameworks are written in pure JavaScript, and they execute in your browser.

Finding Frameworks

For a good list of the available Ajax frameworks, look at `http://ajaxpatterns.org/Ajax_Frameworks`. This page gives you the URLs of many Ajax frameworks, most of which are free. Look at the framework before you decide to download it. You should determine if it is free. For example, some Ajax frameworks are part of larger programming packages, and those can be very expensive. Make sure that any framework you are interested in comes with the right price — and is free, most of the time. Next, check if you are getting the right kind of Ajax framework. Some frameworks are designed for use in your Web pages along with your JavaScript code. These frameworks are the easiest to work with. All you have to do is to include the code for the framework, and you are set. On the other hand, some Ajax frameworks take considerable installation on the server to get them started, and involve the use of a scripting language to make them work. To use these frameworks, you will need support on the server for the scripting language the Ajax framework requires, and quite possibly, you may have to configure the framework correctly. That can involve considerable work and time. If that is not what you want, use one of the simpler, JavaScript-based Ajax frameworks instead. The decision is up to you.

Create the
readTextWithGet Function

You can create your own Ajax framework if you write the code that will access the server using Ajax to perform common tasks. To read text from the server using Ajax and the GET method, you can write a function named readTextWithGet, and place it in your Ajax framework, which will be called ajaxframework.js in the code for this book.

You pass two parameters to this function, readTextWithGet. The first parameter is the URL you want to access to get text from the server. For example, that URL could be data.txt if that file is in the same directory as your Web page that the user opens in the browser, or you can use a full URL, such as http://www.notanisp.com/data.txt. Because this function uses the GET method, you can also send URL-encoded data by adding that data to the end of the URL, like this: http://www.notanisp.com/data

.txt?text=hello. You do not have to fetch just the contents of a text file on the server — the URL can point to a server-side script, such as http://www.notanisp.com/data.php. You can pass data to that server-side script using URL encoding, like this: http://www.notanisp.com/data.php?text=hello.

The second parameter lets the readTextWithGet pass the data it gets from the server back to your code. To send the text it downloads from the server back to your code, you pass this function a *callback* function. A callback function is simply a function that you can call when you have data that you have downloaded from the server. When readTextWithGet reads the required text from the server, it will pass that text to the callback function you have specified, which is how the downloaded text is passed to your JavaScript.

Create the readTextWithGet Function

① Create the readTextWithGet function in the ajaxframework.js file.

This function is passed to the URL to contact on the server and to a callback function to pass the downloaded text to.

② Create a new XMLHttpRequest object.

Because a new XMLHttpRequest object is called each time this function is called, this function can handle multiple XMLHttpRequest requests at the same time.

③ Use the XMLHttpRequest object's open method to configure the object to call the requested URL.

④ Connect an anonymous function to the XMLHttpRequest object's onreadystatechange property.

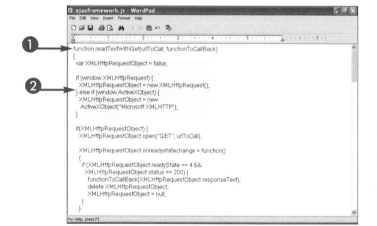

5 Use the `send` method to send the `XMLHttpRequest` request to the server.

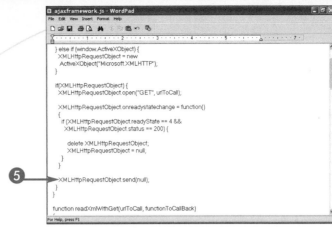

6 When the required text is downloaded from the server, pass it to the callback function so that you make that text available to the code that called the `readTextWithGet` function.

Note: To install and test this code, see the section "Get Text with the readTextWithGet Function."

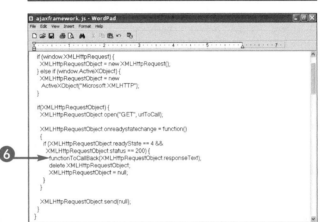

Extra

Some Ajax frameworks do not use a callback function to return the text they have downloaded from the server. Instead, they place that text in a global JavaScript variable, which means that you can get access to the downloaded text by reading the value of that global variable. That works, but is not necessarily good programming practice. If the framework code uses a global variable that you also use in your code, the value in your variable may be overwritten by mistake, or the value in the framework's variable may be overwritten by mistake. To use a framework that passes data back using global variables, you have to know all the variables it places data in. It is usually a better idea to pass data back to the calling code with a callback function.

You can also send data to the server using URL encoding. Because this code uses the GET method, you have to use URL encoding to send data to the server. You cannot send data as a simple text string as you can with the POST method.

Get Text with the readTextWithGet Function

Y ou can use the readTextWithGet function in the ajaxframework.js sample Ajax framework to read text from the server using the GET method. See the section "Create the readTextWithGet Function" to create the readTextWithGet function in the ajaxframework.js file, which is available in the downloadable code for this book.

The readTextWithGet function is part of the sample Ajax framework ajaxframework.js, which means that it will fetch data for you from the server using Ajax techniques. You do not have to write the code for this function yourself because it has already been written for you. Call this function from your own code to download text from the server. In order to use this function, you place ajaxframework.js in the same directory on the server as your Web page, and you include the ajaxframework.js Ajax framework in your Web page using this HTML: <script src="ajaxframework.js">. That makes the functions in ajaxframework.js available to your own code.

After including ajaxframework.js, you can call the readTextWithGet function, passing it the URL of the text you want to download, and the name of your JavaScript function that you want to be called with the downloaded text.

After the text you request is downloaded, that text is automatically passed to your callback function. If you name your callback function, say, dataHandler(data), then the text passed to this function is passed as the data parameter. Inside the dataHandler function, you can refer to the text downloaded from the server using the data variable.

To use the readTextWithGet function, simply pass it the URL of the data you want to fetch using Ajax and the callback function that should be called when the text has been downloaded. When the text is ready, the callback function is passed to that text, making it available to your code.

Get Text with the readTextWithGet Function

① Add two buttons to a Web page, and connect each one to the readTextWithGet function, using the first button to download data.txt, and the second button to download data2.txt, using the callback functions callback1 and callback2.

This Web page, ajaxframework.js, data.txt, and data2.txt, must all be in the same directory on the server.

data.txt holds the text "This text was fetched using Ajax.", and data2.txt holds the text "This text was also fetched using Ajax."

② Add a <div> element with the ID targetDiv to display the downloaded text.

③ Include the ajaxframework.js file.

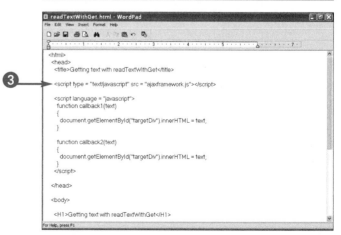

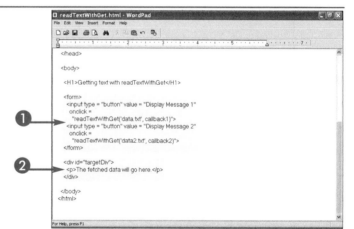

④ Create the callback functions `callback1` and `callback2`, and make those functions display the text they are passed in the `targetDiv` `<div>` element in the Web page.

⑤ Open the Web page in your browser and click either button.

The Web page displays the text downloaded using Ajax in the `readTextWithGet` function.

Apply It

You can use the `readTextWithGet` function in the `ajaxframework.js` sample Ajax framework to get text from the server. If you want to send data to the server, you can URL-encode that data like this:

```
<form>
  <input type = "button" value = "Display Message 1"
    onclick =
      "readTextWithGet('http://www.noisp/data.php?value=1',
        callback1)">
  <input type = "button" value = "Display Message 2"
    onclick =
      "readTextWithGet('http://www.noisp/data.php?value=2',
        callback2)">
</form>
```

Create the readXmlWithGet Function

You can create a function named readXmlWithGet in the ajaxframework.js sample Ajax framework to read XML from the server. When you create functions like readXmlWithGet in an Ajax framework, you make those functions available for later reuse. You can use those functions over and over, simply by including the framework's code in your Web page and then calling those functions as needed.

The readXmlWithGet function accesses a given URL, using the GET method, and reads the data sent back from the server as XML. You pass this function to the URL to fetch data from, as well as the name of, a callback function.

The readXmlWithGet function will access the URL you pass to it, download the XML data, and pass that XML to the callback function. In the callback function, you can use that XML data as you like. For example, if you pass

the URL data.xml to the readXmlWithGet function, this function attempts to download data.xml from the same directory as the Web page from which you have called the readXmlWithGet function. If you pass the URL http://www.noisp.com/data.xml to the readXmlWithGet function, it will attempt to download data.xml from that URL — just remember that, as always with Ajax, if you attempt to access a Web domain other than the one the Web page that uses Ajax comes from, the browser displays a warning dialog box.

The XML you download using the readXmlWithGet function need not be from an XML file, of course. You can also access server-side programs using this function as well. For example, you might access a URL like data.php, or http://www.noisp.com/data.php, which would return XML data. You could use that XML data just as if it came from an XML file on the server.

Create the readXmlWithGet Function

① Create the readXmlWithGet function so that you can pass it the URL to fetch and the function to call back when the XML data is downloaded.

② Create the XMLHttpRequest object to use downloading data.

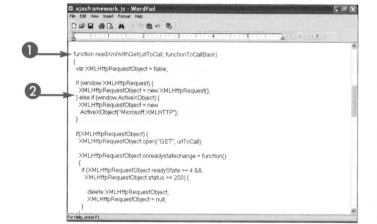

③ Configure the XMLHttpRequest object to access the requested URL on the server.

④ Connect an anonymous function to the XMLHttpRequest object's onreadystatechange property as usual in Ajax code.

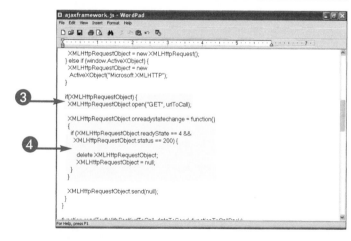

⑤ Use the `XMLHttpRequest` object's
`send` method to connect to the
server and download the requested
XML data.

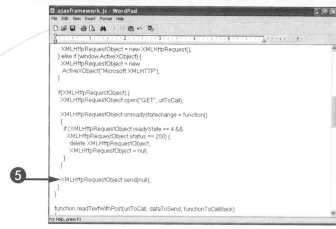

⑥ Call the `callback` function,
passing it the downloaded XML data.

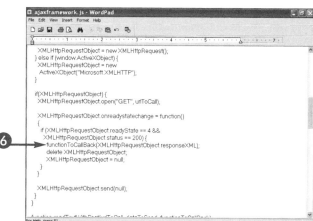

Extra

Because the `readXmlWithGet` function uses the
GET method to communicate with the server, you
can send data to the server using URL encoding.
Because this function uses the GET method, not the
POST method, you cannot send data as a simple
text string, but must URL-encode it.

A number of Ajax frameworks use global variables
instead of callback functions to pass data back to
you. After you call a function in such a framework,
you can check the value in the global variable, which
holds the data you requested after it is downloaded.
That technique works adequately, but it has a
fundamental drawback — using global variables.
When you use an Ajax framework that writes data
to global variables, you have to be careful that you
are not already using global variables with the same
name in your code. If you are, the framework code
could overwrite the value in your global variable by
mistake, or you could overwrite the data in its
global variable. For that reason, it is usually safer to
use callback functions — such functions are not
called until the data has been downloaded, and
there is no possibility of confusion with global
variables.

Get XML with the readXmlWithGet Function

You can use the `readXmlWithGet` function in the `ajaxframework.js` sample Ajax framework that comes in the downloadable code for this book to read XML from the server using the GET method. See the section "Create the readTextWithGet Function" to create the `readTextWithGet` function in the `ajaxframework.js` file.

This function, `readXmlWithGet`, is in the sample Ajax framework `ajaxframework.js`, and it is designed to fetch XML date from the server for you. Because this function is available in this framework, you merely have to include the framework in your Web page, making the functions in the framework available to your code. To use `readXml WithGet`, you only need to include the `ajaxframework.js` file in a `<script>` element this way: `<script src="ajaxframework.js">`. That makes the functions in `ajaxframework.js` available to your own code.

After you have included `ajaxframework.js` in your Web page, you can use the `readXmlWithGet` function,

passing it the URL of the XML data you want to fetch, as well as a callback function to call when the data has been downloaded. When the XML data has been fetched from the server, `readXmlWithGet` passes that data to the callback function you have specified. For example, if your callback function is named `XmlCallback(data)`, then the data parameter passed to this callback function holds the XML data you requested. Bear in mind that the XML data will be a JavaScript XML document object and that you are responsible for extracting the actual data you want from it yourself.

The XML data you download can come from an XML document, such as `data.xml`. The XML data you download can also come from a program on the server, such as `data.php`. In either case, the `readTextWithGet` function will download the XML you have requested and pass those contents to your callback function.

Get XML with the readXmlWithGet Function

① Connect two buttons to the `readXmlWithGet` function, making one button download `data.xml` with the callback function `callback1`, and the second download `data2.xml` with the callback function `callback2`.

The `data.xml` document contains this XML: `<?xml version = "1.0" ?><data>This text was fetched using Ajax.</data>`, and the `data2.xml` document contains this XML: `<?xml version = "1.0" ?><data>This text was also fetched using Ajax.</data>`.

② Add a `<div>` element with the ID `targetDiv` to display text.

③ Include the `ajaxframework.js` file.

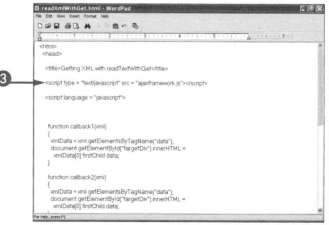

160

④ Create the callback functions `callback1` and `callback2`, and make those functions display the XML data they are passed in the `targetDiv` `<div>` element in the Web page.

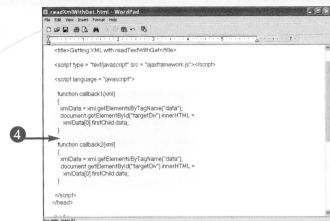

⑤ Open the Web page in your browser and click either button.

The Web page displays the XML data downloaded using Ajax in the `readXmlWithGet` function.

Apply It

It is not difficult to use the `readXmlWithGet` function in the `ajaxframework.js` sample Ajax framework to download XML data from the server. You can also send data to the server if you URL-encode that data like this:

```
<form>
  <input type = "button" value = "Display Message 1"
    onclick =
      "readXmlWithGet('http://www.noisp/data.php?value=1',
        callback1)">
  <input type = "button" value = "Display Message 2"
    onclick =
      "readXmlWithGet('http://www.noisp/data.php?value=2',
        callback2)">
</form>
```

Create the readTextWithPost Function

Y ou can create your own function to read text from the server using the POST method. Using POST allows you to send data to the server easily. You can create a function named readTextWithPost that you can add to the Ajax framework ajaxframework.js that lets you download text from the server using the POST method.

If you use the GET method, you can write a function to get text from the server, passing it only to the URL to access, and a callback function. The function contacts the URL you pass to it and downloads the text the server sends back. After the text is downloaded, the function calls the callback method you specify, passing that function to the text you download.

On the other hand, using POST is different from using GET. When you use the GET method, you can URL-encode

any data you want to send to the server, adding that data to the end of the URL you access on the server. When you use POST, you can explicitly send data to the server using the XMLHttpRequest object's send method.

To work with the readTextWithPost function, you pass it not two data items, but three — the URL to access, the callback function to pass any downloaded data to, and the data you want to send to the server. The data to send to the server is in string form, where you assign parameters values, like this "message=Hello there!", which you can also pass as "message=Hello+there!" — the server-side script converts the + to a space. Your server-side code can extract data from that string by looking for the text connected to the passed parameters.

Create the readTextWithPost Function

① Create the readTextWithPost function, giving it the parameters urlToCall, dataToSend, and functionToCallBack.

② Create an XMLHttpRequest object.

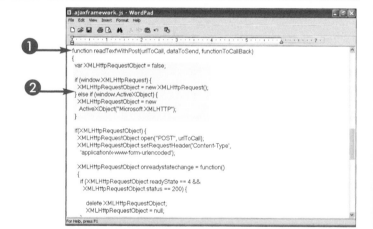

③ Configure the XMLHttpRequest object to use the POST method.

④ Set the Content-Type header to 'application/x-www-form-urlencoded' to support the POST method.

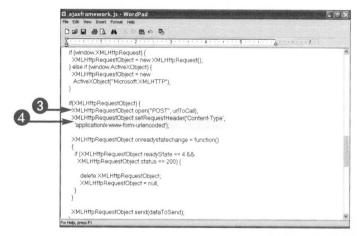

162

5 Connect the XMLHttpRequest object's onreadystatechange property to an anonymous function.

6 Send the downloaded text data to the callback function.

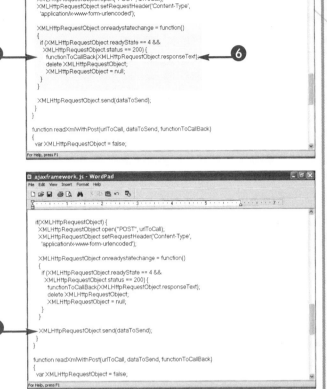

7 Send the data to the server using the XMLHttpRequest object's send method.

Extra

Sending data to the server with POST is more secure than sending data URL-encoded with the GET method, because the data is not added publicly to the end of the URL you access. The data you send to the server is stored inside the HTTP headers sent to the server, which means that they are not as visible as URL-encoded data. For that reason, many programmers use the SEND method whenever they want to send data to the server.

When you use the POST method, do not forget to set the XMLHttpRequest object's 'Content-Type' header to 'application/x-www-form-urlencoded' using the setRequestHeader method, as shown in the code for this task. When Ajax programmers use the POST method, forgetting to set that header properly is the biggest cause of errors, and it can be a hard thing to debug. If your data is not arriving in your server-side program correctly, check to make sure you have set this header properly.

Get Text with the readTextWithPost Function

Y ou can use the readTextWithPost function to read text from the server after using the POST method to send text to the server. See the section "Create the readTextWithPost Function" to create the readTextWith Get function in the ajaxframework.js file.

You use readTextWithPost to read text from the server after explicitly passing data to the server; if you do not want to send data to the server, you can use the readTextWithGet function instead. See the section "Create the readTextWithGet Function" for more details.

The PostreadTextWithPost function is part of the sample Ajax framework ajaxframework.js that you can get in the downloadable code for this book. Because this function is built into that framework, you only have to include the ajaxframework.js file in your Web page to use that function and gain full access to Ajax code. You include the

ajaxframework.js file using the HTML <script> element like this: <script src="ajaxframework.js">. After you include that file in your Web page, you can use the readTextWithGet function.

You pass three parameters to the PostreadTextWithPost function — the URL you want to access, the data you want to send to the server, and the name of a callback function. The readTextWithPost function will contact the URL you pass to it, sending the data you pass to this function to the server. When the server sends back text, the readTextWithPost function passes that text to the callback function, making that text accessible to your code. For example, if you name your callback function callback1(data), then the PostreadTextWithPost function passes the text it downloads from the server to that callback function, and you can access the downloaded text as the parameter named data in your code.

Get Text With the readTextWithPost Function

1 Add a button to your Web page that, when clicked, calls the readTextWithPost function, make that function call the URL echoText.php, send the data 'message=It works!', and give the callback function's name as display.

The echoText.php script is a very simple one, and only echoes the text associated with a parameter named message back to the browser: <? echo ($_POST["message"]);?>.

2 Add a <div> with the ID targetDiv that holds the text fetched from the server.

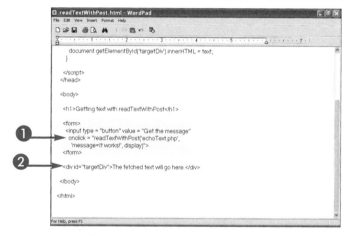

3 Include the ajaxframework.js Ajax framework in your code to make the readTextWithGet function accessible.

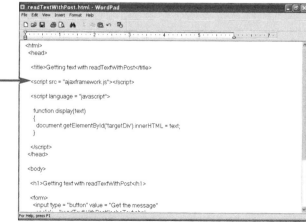

④ Add the display function, which simply displays the text passed to it in the `targetDiv` `<div>` element.

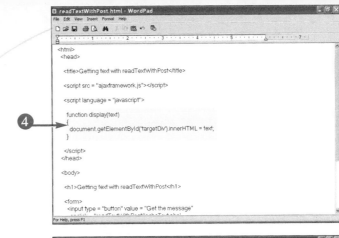

④

```
<html>
  <head>

    <title>Getting text with readTextWithPost</title>

    <script src = "ajaxframework.js"></script>

    <script language = "javascript">

    function display(text)
    {
      document.getElementById('targetDiv').innerHTML = text;
    }

    </script>
  </head>

  <body>

    <h1>Getting text with readTextWithPost</h1>

    <form>
      <input type = "button" value = "Get the message"
```

⑤ Open the Web page in your browser and click the button.

The text data is passed to the `echoText.php` script, which sends the text back to the Web page where the text displays.

⑤

Getting text with readTextWithPost

Get the message

It works!

Apply It

This example only passes a single parameter message, with the text "It works!" to the server. If you want to pass multiple parameters, separate them with an ampersand (&), as you see here, where this code passes the parameters message and greeting to the server-side script `echoText.php`:

```
<h1>Getting text with readTextWithPost</h1>

<form>
  <input type = "button" value = "Get the message"
    onclick = "readTextWithPost('echoText.php',
      'greeting=Hello there&message=It works!', display)">
</form>

<div id="targetDiv">The fetched text will go here.</div>
```

The text `"greeting=Hello there&message=It works!"` can also be passed as
`"greeting=Hello+there&message=It+works!"`, as in normal URL encoding; the + will be converted to a space.

Create the
readXmlWithPost Function

You can create a readXmlWithPost function that will read XML from a server after you send data to that server, and add that function to the sample Ajax framework ajaxframework.js available in the downloadable code for this book. When you add this function to that framework, you can reuse that function throughout your applications, calling that function every time you need to send data to the server and read XML data sent in reply. The readXmlWithPost function handles all the details, saving you the trouble of writing the Ajax code over and over.

You can write a function to get XML data from the server while sending data using the GET method — see the section "Create the readXmlWithGet Function." But to use the GET method to send data to the server, append

that data to the end of the URL you are accessing. That makes the data you send to the server very public.

To avoid that, you can use the POST method instead. When you use POST, however, you explicitly send data to the server using the XMLHttpRequest object's send method. When you use the POST method, the data you send to the server is stored in the request's headers, and not attached to the end of the URL you are accessing.

When you use the readXmlWithPost function, you pass it not just two parameters as you would when you use the GET method, but three parameters: the URL you want to access on the server, the data to send to the server, and the callback function to call when the XML data you have requested has been downloaded. The readXmlWithPost function will pass the downloaded XML data to your callback function.

Create the readXmlWithPost Function

① Create the function readXmlWithPost now, giving it three parameters: urlToCall, dataToSend, and functionToCallBack.

② Create a new XMLHttpRequest object.

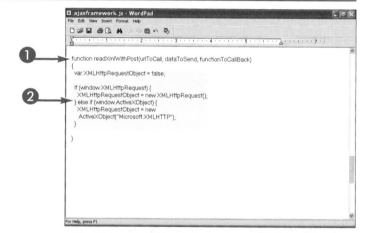

③ Configure the XMLHttpRequest object to use the POST method to send data, and set the 'Content-Type' header to 'application/x-www-form-urlencoded'.

④ Connect an anonymous function to the XMLHttpRequest object's onreadystateproperty to handle the Ajax download.

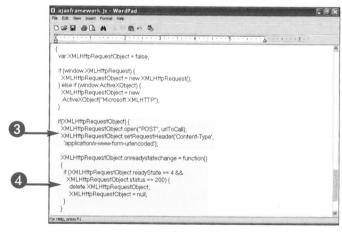

5 Pass the downloaded XML data to the callback function.

6 Send the data passed to the readXmlWithPost function with the XMLHttpRequest object's send method.

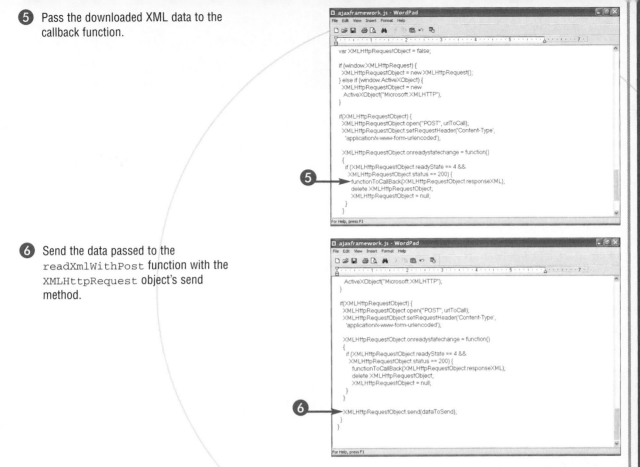

Extra

When the XML data you request from the server is sent back to you, that data is in JavaScript XML document form, which means that you must extract that data yourself. You typically do that with the XML document object's getElementsByTagName method, which returns an array of XML elements. You can extract the data in each element with the element's firstChild property, which returns the text node in the element, and the data property of the text node, which holds the text in that node.

When you use the POST method to send your data to the server, that data is more secure than simply sending data appended to the end of a URL, as you do with the GET method. When you send data using the POST method, that data is not as publicly exposed as it is with the GET method, because it is stored in the headers for the POST method's request. Because of that, many programmers use the SEND method to send data to the server.

Get XML with the readXmlWithPost Function

You can read XML data from the server using the readXmlWithPost function. This function is part of the sample Ajax framework ajaxframework.js in the sample code for this book. See the section "Create the readXmlWithPost Function" for more on this function.

To use the readXmlWithPost function, first add ajaxframework.js to your Web page using the HTML <script> element this way: <script src="ajax framework.js">. That assumes that ajaxframework.js is in the same directory on the server as the Web page in which you are using it is. If you store ajaxframework.js in another directory, or on another server, give the full URL to that file in the <script> element something like this: <script src="http://www.noisp.com/user/ajaxframework.js">.

You pass the readXmlWithPost function three parameters — the URL to fetch XML data from, the data

you want to send to that URL, and the callback function to pass the fetched XML data. The data you send to the URL must be in the standard format for POST requests; for example, to pass the text "No worries." to the server as the value of a parameter named message, you could pass the text string "message=No worries.". You could also convert the space to a plus sign (+) this way: "message=No+worries.", and the plus sign is automatically converted back to a space in the server-side script.

After the XML data has been fetched from the server, the readXmlWithPost function passes that data to the callback function, giving you access to that data in your code. Bear in mind that the XML data will be in JavaScript XML document object form, and it is up to you to extract the data you want from that object, using code in the callback function.

Get XML with the readXmlWithPost Function

1 Add a button to your Web page that calls the readXmlWithPost function, passing it the URL to send data to, echoXml.php; the data to send, "message=It works!"; and the callback function, which is named display.

The echoXml.php script simply echoes the message you send it in an XML element named <data>.

2 Add a <div> element to display the downloaded data.

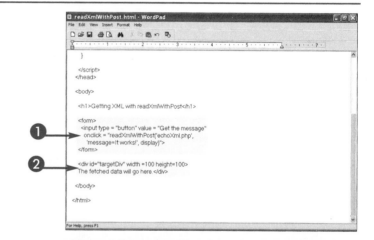

3 Include ajaxframework.js to make the readXmlWithPost function available to your code.

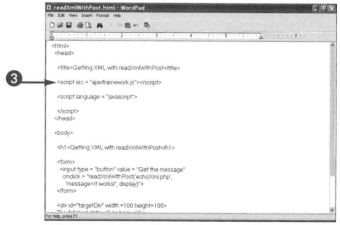

④ Add the display function to display the data in the XML downloaded from the server.

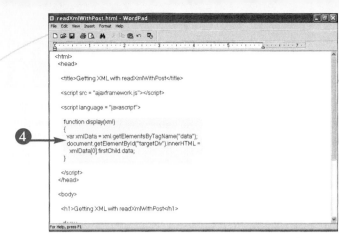

⑤ Open the Web page in your browser and click the button.

You should see the message "It works!", which is sent to the server and sent back to the browser as XML.

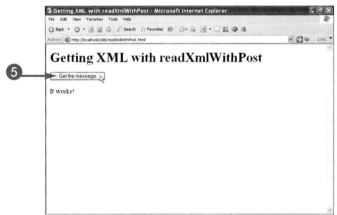

Apply It

This task's code downloads a single XML element named `<data>` and extracts the text inside that element. If the XML you download has multiple XML elements, you might extract the data from them using a loop. For example, if you download multiple `<data>` elements and want to add the text in them to a `<select>` control, you could use code like this:

```
function display(xml)
{
  var xmlData = xml.getElementsByTagName("data");
  for (loopIndex = 0; loopIndex < options.length;
    loopIndex++ )
  {
    selectControl.options[loopIndex] = new
      Option(xmlData[loopIndex].firstChild.data);
  }
}
```

Install AJAXLib

You can use the `AJAXLib` Ajax framework to save you some programming effort when you create Ajax applications. An Ajax framework like the `AJAXLib` framework contains prewritten code to use Ajax to download data from the server, using Ajax techniques.

`AJAXLib` is one of the simpler Ajax frameworks. This framework is made up simply of a JavaScript file, `ajaxlib.js`. You use this JavaScript file by placing it in the same directory as the Web page in which you want to use it, and include the code in `ajaxlib.js` in your Web page using the HTML script element, like this: `<script src="ajaxlib.js">`. Alternately, if `ajaxlib.js` is in another directory or at a totally different URL, you must give that URL in the value assigned to the `src` element, such as in this example: `<script src="http://www.noisp.com/user/ajaxlib.js">`.

Because `AJAXLib` consists of only one JavaScript file, installing this Ajax framework is very easy — after you

download `ajaxlib.js` and include it in your Web page using the `<script>` element, you are done. There is no more installation required.

You can get `AJAXLib` at `http://karaszewski.com/tools/ajaxlib/`. Downloading is free. Navigate to that site and download `ajaxlib.js`. When you install `AJAXLib`, you have access in JavaScript to its single function — `loadXMLDoc`. The `loadXMLDoc` function downloads the XML data you request — you simply pass this function the URL that points to that data, the name of a callback function, and a third parameter that, if set to true, lets you remove indentation white space in the downloaded XML.

The callback function is not passed the XML data directly, however. Instead, you read that data from a global variable named `resultXML`, using the code in the callback function.

Install AJAXLib

① Navigate to `http://karaszewski.com/tools/ajaxlib/`.

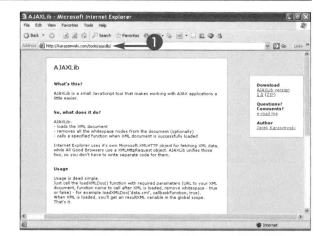

② Right-click the AJAXLib Version 1.0 link, and in the menu that opens, select Save Target As and save `ajaxlib.js` where it is accessible from the Web page in which you want to use it.

If you use Mozilla or Firefox, select Save Link As in the menu that opens.

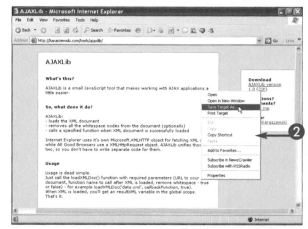

③ Include `ajaxlib.js` in your Web page using an HTML `<script>` element.

④ Call the `loadXMLDoc` function as needed to download the XML data you require.

Extra

The AJAXLib Ajax framework depends on the use of a global JavaScript variable, which can cause some issues you should know about. Some Ajax frameworks call your callback function with the data you request, but some store that data in a global JavaScript variable. Because AJAXLib stores the data you have downloaded in a global variable named `resultXML`, you should not use that name for any of your own variables or you may have a conflict with the `resultXML` variable. Such a conflict could mean that you overwrite the value in `resultXML` after AJAXLib stores a value in it, or that AJAXLib overwrites a value you have stored in it.

AJAXLib is a simple framework, and it uses the GET method to contact the server, which explains why there is no third parameter in the `loadXMLDoc` that you can use to pass data to the server with. If you want to pass data to the server, use URL encoding when working with AJAXLib.

Access the Server With AJAXLib

After installing AJAXLib's ajaxlib.js so that it is accessible, you can use AJAXLib to use Ajax techniques to access XML from the server. AJAXLib is an Ajax framework, and it is available free from the Internet. See the section "Install AJAXLib" for more information.

Using AJAXLib to download data is not difficult. AJAXLib supports only a publicly accessible function — loadXMLDoc, which is the function you use to download XML data from the server. AJAXLib is not written to download simple text; it downloads only XML and uses an XMLHttpRequest object's responseXML property to retrieve the downloaded data and passes that data to your code.

To use AJAXLib, pass the loadXMLDoc function the URL of the XML data you want to download, the name of a callback function, and a true/false parameter that indicates if you want to strip out indentation text from the XML data.

The URL you pass to the loadXMLDoc function can point to either a file, such as data.xml, or a server-side program such as data.php. Either way, this online source must return data in a format that the browser recognizes as XML.

AJAXLib calls the callback function when the data you want has been downloaded. However, that data is not passed to the callback function; instead, you access that data using a global variable named resultXML. That variable holds the retrieved XML data in JavaScript XML document object form.

The third parameter you pass to the loadXMLDoc function is interesting. It indicates if you want to strip out "whitespace" data from the XML data. Often, XML documents are indented with spaces, tabs, newline and/or return characters, and AJAXLib can remove all those from your XML data automatically if you make the third argument you pass to the loadXMLDoc function true.

Access the Server With AJAXLib

① Pass that function that name of an XML document, data.xml; a callback function named handleXML, and a value of false so that AJAXLib does not strip whitespace.

The data.xml document in the downloadable code for this book holds
```
<?xml version = "1.0"
?><data>This text was fetched
using Ajax.</data>.
```

② Add a <div> element with the ID targetDiv to display text data in.

③ Include the `ajaxlib.js` file in your Web page.

④ Create the `handleXML` function that AJAXLib will call when your data downloads.

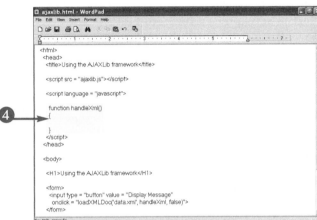

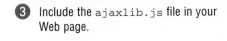

Apply It

You can remove whitespace from your XML data by making the third parameter you pass to AJAXLib's `loadXMLDoc` function true:

```
<input type = "button" value = "Display Message"
  onclick = "loadXMLDoc('data.xml', handleXml, true)">
```

You do not need to remove whitespace if you explicitly extract XML elements from the downloaded XML data, as this example does with the `getElementsByTagName` function. However, if you plan to use code to move from element to element inside your XML, removing whitespace text can be very useful. Look at this example:

```
<?xml version = "1.0" ?>
<document>
  <data>
  This text was fetched using Ajax.
  </data>
</document>
```

Here, the whitespace text between the `<document>` tag and the `<data>` tag, and the whitespace text between the `</data>` tag and the `<document>` tag is considered XML text nodes, which you would have to navigate over in code if you did not remove them.

Download Data With AJAXLib

After you have contacted the server using the AJAXLib function loadXMLDoc — see the section "Access the Server With AJAXLib" — you can handle the XML data that AJAXLib downloads for you. To download the XML data in a document named data.xml, you can call the AJAXLib function loadXMLDoc this way: loadXMLDoc('data.xml', handleXml, false). This expression requests loadXMLDoc to download data.xml, which is found in the same directory on the server as the Web page the user is viewing in the browser, and call a callback function in your code named handleXML when the download is complete. The third parameter is set to false to indicate that you do not want AJAXLib to strip whitespace from your XML data; setting that parameter to true makes AJAXLib strip whitespace nodes — that is, text nodes whose content is entirely whitespace, such as tabs, spaces, return characters, or line feeds, from that data.

AJAXLib downloads your XML data, places it in a global variable named resultXML, and calls the callback function you specify. When your callback function is called, your data is accessible in the resultXML variable. That data will be in JavaScript XML document object form, which means that you use JavaScript methods to extract your data from that object. See Chapter 9 for more on XML, and how to handle XML data in Ajax.

For example, to extract the data in XML elements named <data>, you can use this line of code: var xmlData = resultXML.getElementsByTagName("data");, which removes the <data> elements and stores them in an array named xmlData.

To extract the text from the first <data> element, you can refer to that element as xmlData[0]. You can access the text node inside the <data> element as xmlData[0].firstChild. To get the text content of that node, you can use the expression xmlData[0].firstChild.data.

Download Data With AJAXLib

1 Connect a button to the AJAXLib loadXMLDoc function, passing that function the name of an XML document, data.xml; a callback function named handleXML; and a value of false so that AJAXLib does not strip whitespace.

The data.xml document in the downloadable code for this book holds <?xml version = "1.0" ?><data>This text was fetched using Ajax.</data>

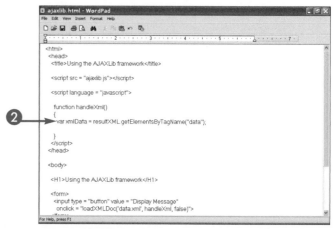

2 In the handleXML function, extract all <data> elements into an array named xmlData.

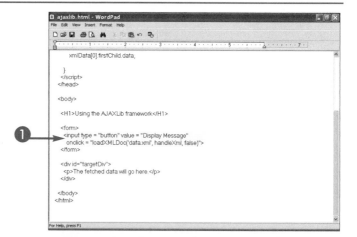

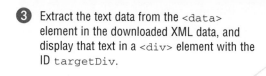

3 Extract the text data from the `<data>` element in the downloaded XML data, and display that text in a `<div>` element with the ID `targetDiv`.

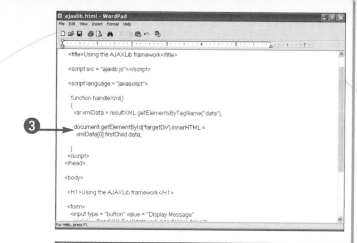

4 Open the new page in a browser and click the button.

The data in the `data.xml` document is downloaded and displayed.

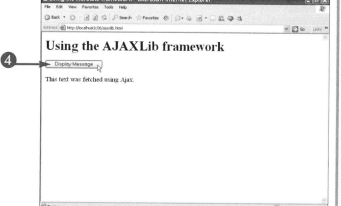

Extra

While useful, AJAXLib has no error handling built in. That means that if your requested XML data cannot be downloaded correctly, your callback function is never called. To rectify this issue, you can either add code to the AJAXLib loadXMLDoc function to handle errors, or add code to your own JavaScript to handle the case where your callback function is never called with any data.

AJAXLib uses a global variable, resultXML, to return XML data to your code. Most Ajax frameworks will pass downloaded data to your callback function directly as a function parameter. However, AJAXLib uses a global variable to pass that data to your code instead. That means that to use AJAXLib, you must avoid using the name resultXML as the name for a variable in your own code in order to avoid conflicts with the global variable of the same name that is filled with data by AJAXLib. Alternately, if your code uses the name resultXML and you do not want to change that name, you can edit the code in AJAXLib's ajaxlib.js directly to change the name of the global variable that AJAXLib uses to pass data to your code.

Install libXmlRequest

You can use the Ajax `libXmlRequest` framework to download XML data using either the GET or POST method and Ajax techniques. This Ajax framework also supports pooling of `XMLHttpRequest` objects, which means that the code will not generate too many of those objects, no matter how many accesses to the server you request. Every time a request is completed, the `XMLHttpRequest` object for that request is placed back in the pool of such objects, where it can be reused the next time another such object is needed.

You can get the `libXmlRequest` Ajax framework free at www.whitefrost.com/reference/2003/06/17/libXmlRequest.html. Just navigate to that page, right-click the `libXmlRequest.js` link, and download that file. Doing so means that you will not have to write your own Ajax code to use Ajax. All you have to do is call the functions in this framework.

The `libXmlRequest.js` is a JavaScript file, as with many of the Ajax frameworks. To make that file work, include it in your Web page using the HTML `<script>` element so that the code in `libXmlRequest.js` is accessible from your own JavaScript code. You include `libXmlRequest.js` using the `<script>` element like this: `<script src="libXmlRequest.js">`.

There are two main methods in the `libXmlRequest` Ajax framework: the `getXML` and `postXML` methods, which use the GET and POST methods, respectively, to retrieve XML from the server. You can use these functions in either a synchronous way, which waits for data to come from the server before the function returns; or an asynchronous way, which is the Ajax way, where the function returns before your data is downloaded, and a callback function is called after that data is downloaded.

Install libXmlRequest

① Navigate to the Web page www.whitefrost.com/reference/2003/06/17/libXmlRequest.html.

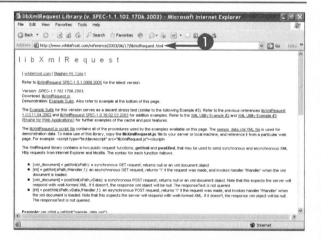

② Download `libXmlRequest.js` by right-clicking the link and selecting Save Target As in Internet Explorer or Save Link As in Mozilla or Firefox, and saving `libXmlRequest.js` where it is accessible from the Web page in which you want to use it.

③ Use a `<script>` element to include `libXmlRequest.js` in your Web page.

④ Call the `libXmlRequest` framework's `getXML` or `postXML` method, as required.

When you call the `getXML` or `postXML` method, you must preface it with `org.cote.js.xml` like this: `org.cote.js.xml.getXml`.

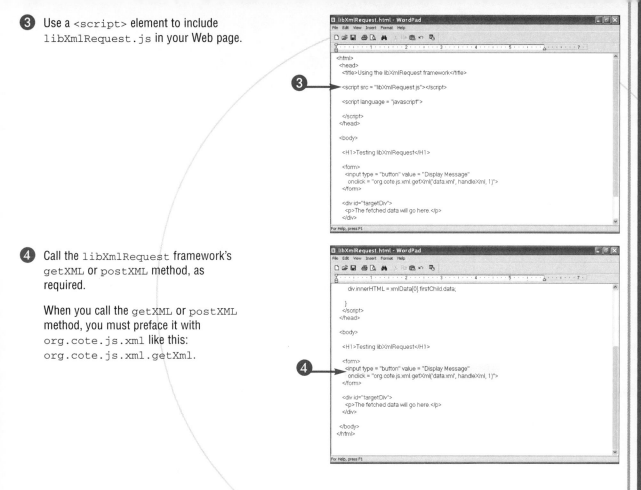

Apply It

One of the aspects of Ajax that bears a little more discussion is that if you access the same URL over and over on a server, your browser may cache that data. That means that even if the data you access changes, your browser will pass the same cached data to you over and over again. To avoid that when using the Ajax `libXmlRequest` framework, you can pass a value of false to its `setCacheEnabled` method:

```
<script language = "javascript">
  org.cote.js.xml.setCacheEnabled(false)
</script>
```

You can also clear the cache so fresh data is downloaded if you call the `clearCache` method like this:

```
<script language = "javascript">
  org.cote.js.xml.clearCache()
</script>
```

Access the Server with libXmlRequest

Y ou can use the getXml and postXml functions in the libXmlRequest framework to download XML data. There are two forms of these functions: one that downloads data synchronously, and one that downloads data asynchronously. When you download data synchronously by calling a function, that function will not return until the data has been downloaded this risks bringing your code to a halt. The Ajax way of doing things is to download data asynchronously; when you call a function to download your data, and that function returns immediately, your code does not come to a halt. Instead, a callback function is called when your data is downloaded.

The libXmlRequest getXML function executes synchronous or asynchronous requests to the server using the GET method. For synchronous requests, you simply pass the URL you want to fetch XML data from the server, and this function returns null if it is not

successful, or it returns a JavaScript XML document object if successful. For asynchronous requests — the kind you use in Ajax — you pass the URL the name of a callback function, and a value you want returned if getXml makes the request successfully. For example, getXml(Url, handleXml,1) accesses Url on the server, calls the callback function handleXml with the downloaded data, and returns "1" if the request to the server was made successfully.

The libXmlRequest postXML function executes synchronous or asynchronous POST requests to the server. For synchronous requests, you call this function the same way as getXml except that you also pass the text data you want to send to the server this way: postXml(URL, data). For asynchronous requests, you call this function as you do getXml, except that you also pass the data to send to the server like this: postXml(Url, data, handleXml,1).

Access the Server With libXmlRequest

① Connect a libXmlRequest function, such as getXml to a button so that it downloads data.xml, makes the callback function handleXml, and returns a value of "1" if it sends its request to the server successfully.

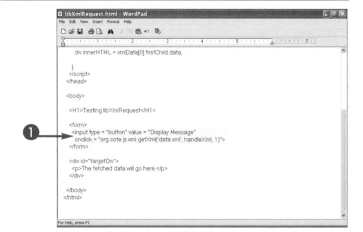

② Use a <script> element to include the libXmlRequest.js file.

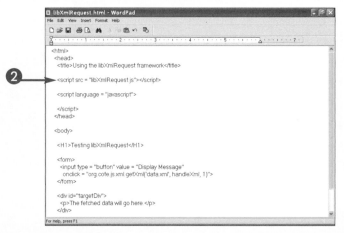

③ Add the `handleXml` callback function.

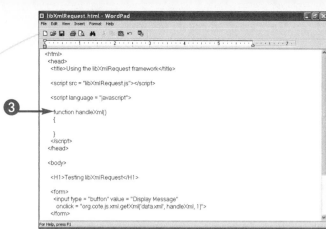

④ Give the `handleXml` callback function two parameters.

The second parameter holds the JavaScript XML document object that contains your downloaded data.

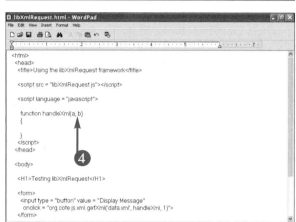

Apply It

When you use the `libXmlRequest` framework, you can use `XMLHttpRequest` object pooling, which means that instead of creating new `XMLHttpRequest` objects for new requests, you can direct the `libXmlRequest` framework to use a previously created `XMLHttpRequest` object if any are available. To enable `XMLHttpRequest` object pooling, call the `setPoolEnabled` method, passing it a value of true:

```
<script language = "javascript">
  org.cote.js.xml.setPoolEnabled(true)
</script>
```

To check if `XMLHttpRequest` object pooling is enabled, you can use the `getPoolEnabled` method this way:

```
<script language = "javascript">
  if(org.cote.js.xml.getPoolEnabled()){
    alert("Pooling is enabled.");
  }
</script>
```

Download Data with libXmlRequest

You can download XML data using the libXmlRequest Ajax framework. There are two ways of doing that: the getXml or the postXml method. You can use both of these methods either synchronously, where they try to fetch data immediately and will not return until they can get that data; or asynchronously, where they will return at once and call a callback function when your data has been downloaded.

You can call getXml(url), passing it the URL of the XML data you want to download. This method uses the GET method to access the server. Doing so makes the call a synchronous one, and this function returns a value of null if it cannot fetch the data you want, or a JavaScript XML document object holding that data if successful. If you call this method like this, getXml(url, callback, 1), then this function accesses the server asynchronously and

returns without waiting for a response from the server. When this function returns, it returns "1" if it is able to request the data you wanted from the server. When that data is downloaded, the callback function is called with two parameters, and the second of these is your XML data in JavaScript XML document object form.

The postXml function, which accesses the server using the POST method, works the same way as getXml, except that you also pass any text data you want to the server, so the ways you call postXml are: postXml(url, data), and postXml(url, data, callback, 1). The data you pass to the server is the usual text string you use with the POST method, such as "message=hello". Like the getXml, postXml also calls the callback function you have specified, and the second parameter passed to that function contains your XML data.

Download Data with libXmlRequest

① In the callback function that the libXmlRequest framework passes your data to, use the getElementsByTagName method to get an array holding the XML elements you want.

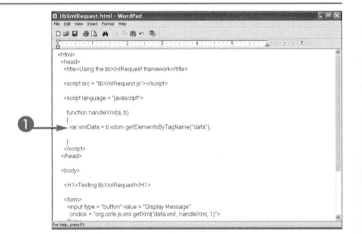

② To display the downloaded data, start by creating an object corresponding to a `<div>` element in your Web page.

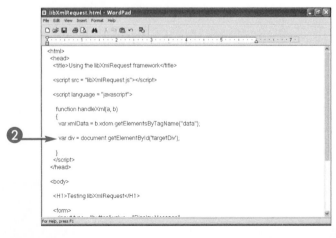

3 Extract the data you want and display it in the `<div>` element.

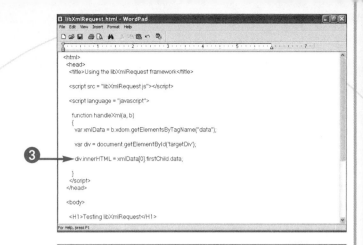

4 Open the Web page in a browser and download your requested data.

The downloaded data appears in the `<div>` element.

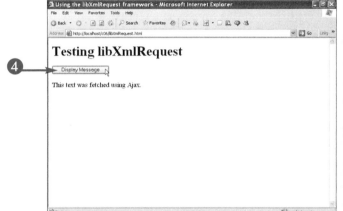

Apply It

The `libXmlRequest` framework has a method you can call to check whether it is able to create an `XMLHttpRequest` object — the `org.cote.js.xml.testXmlHttpObject` method. To use that method, you can call a function when the user clicks a button:

```
<input type = "button" value = "Display Message"
  onclick = "getData('data.xml')">
</form>
```

In the called function, you can check if the `libXmlRequest` framework will be able to create an `XMLHttpRequest` object before using the methods of that framework, such as `getXml`:

```
function getData(data)
{
  if org.cote.js.xml.testXmlHttpObject() {
     org.cote.js.xml.getXml(data, handleXml, 1);
  }
}
```

You can use the XHConn Ajax framework to connect to servers and download data using Ajax techniques. You can get this popular Ajax framework free online at `http://xkr.us/code/javascript/XHConn/`. All you have to do is right-click the link to XHConn.js and save it. Because XHConn is written entirely in JavaScript, installation is straightforward — all you have to do is download XHConn.js and store it where your Web page can access the JavaScript inside it.

XHConn differs from the Ajax frameworks you have already seen in a number of respects. When you want to use it, you create a new XHConn object in JavaScript using the JavaScript new operator, and then work with the method of that object, such as the connect method to connect to the server and download data. That is a switch from the usual JavaScript framework, where you simply call JavaScript functions without creating any objects.

After creating an XHConn object and using the connect method, XHConn downloads the data you have requested — you can use GET or POST with XHConn. You specify which method you want when you call the XHConn connect method. After your data has been downloaded, XHConn makes that data accessible to your code, but here again there is a rather unique twist — XHConn does not just pass you your data. It actually passes the entire XMLHttpRequest object to your callback function.

When you have the XMLHttpRequest object, you can use that object's responseText or responseXML properties to read your data. As you can see, XHConn is more object-oriented than other Ajax frameworks — you start by creating an object and XHConn passes you an object. If you are comfortable with object-oriented programming, this framework may be a good match for you.

Install XHConn

① Navigate to the XHConn home page at `http://xkr.us/code/javascript/XHConn/`.

② Right-click the link to XHConn.js

③ In the menu that opens, select Save Target As in Internet Explorer, or Save Link As in Mozilla or Firefox, and save XHConn.js where it is accessible from the Web page in which you want to use it.

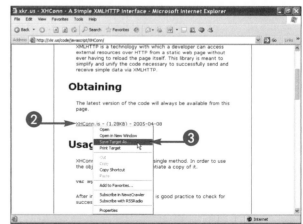

4 Include the XHConn.js file in your Web page with the HTML <script> element.

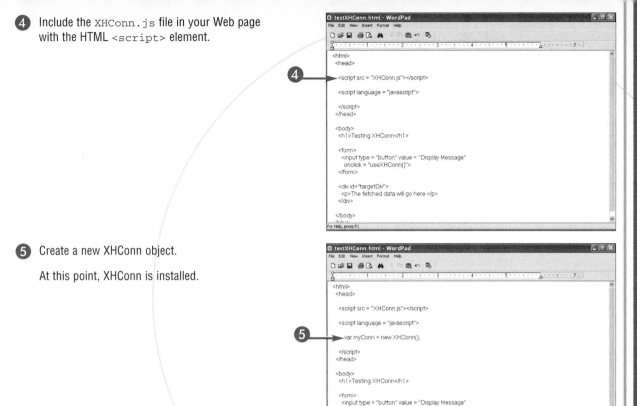

5 Create a new XHConn object.

At this point, XHConn is installed.

Apply It

The XHConn documentation says you should check to make sure that when you try to create an XHConn object that you check to make sure that the object is in fact created. Here is some code you can use to do that:

Example:

```
<script src = "XHConn.js"></script>

<script language = "javascript">

    var myConn = new XHConn();

    if (!myConn) {
      alert("XHConn creation failed.");
    }

</script>
```

Access the Server with XHConn

You can use the XHConn Ajax framework to access the server using either the GET or POST method. To use the XHConn framework, first create an XHConn object using the JavaScript new operator like this: `var myConn = new XHConn()`. Then you can use the connect method of the new XHConn object to connect to the server.

The connect method takes four parameters. The first parameter is the URL you want to contact; this can be the URL of a file online or a Web program. As usual, if you want to access a domain other than the one your Web page comes from, you should use a program online in your same domain to access the other domain, or the browser will display a warning. Either the second parameter is `"GET"` or `"POST"`, to indicate the HTTP method you want

to use to access the server. The third parameter holds a text string of data to send to the server in the usual `"parameter1=data1&parameter2=data2..."` form. You pass data to the server this way when you use the POST method; if you want to use the GET method, URL-encode your data and append it to the end of the URL you are accessing. The fourth parameter you pass to the connect method is the name of the callback function you want to use. XHConn passes the callback function the XMLHttpRequest object used to access the server, and you are free to recover your data using the responseText or responseXML properties of that object. The XMLHttpRequest object is the only parameter passed to the callback function. To install the XHConn Ajax framework, see the section "Install XHConn."

Access the Server with XHConn

① Add a button to a Web page, and connect that button to a JavaScript function named useXHConn.

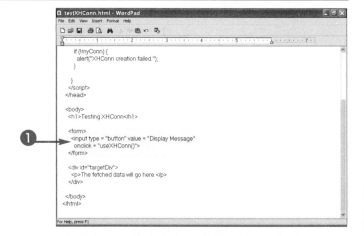

② Include the XHConn.js file.

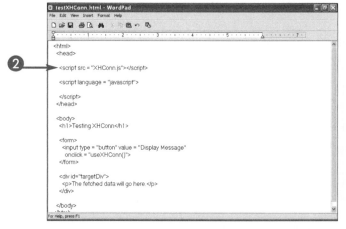

③ In the `useXHConn` function, create a new `XHConn` object.

④ Use the `XHConn` object's `connect` function to connect to a file on the server named `xhconn.txt`, using the GET method with no data to send to the server, and a callback function simply named `callback`.

The `xhconn.txt` file holds the text "This data was downloaded with the XHConn Ajax framework."

When the connect function executes, you have connected to the server.

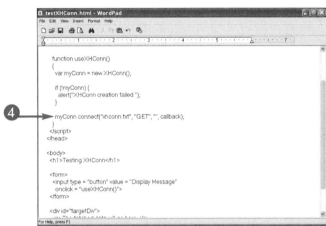

Apply It

You can access the server using the GET method in XHConn's connect method:

```
var myConn = new XHConn();
if (!myConn) {
  alert("XHConn creation failed.");
}
myConn.connect("xhconn.txt", "GET", "", callback);
```

However, you can also use the POST method with XHConn. You do that by passing "POST" to the connect method instead of "GET". When you use the POST method, you can also pass data to the server, as in this code, which connects the text Hello to a parameter named message:

```
var myConn = new XHConn();
if (!myConn) {
  alert("XHConn creation failed.");
}
myConn.connect("data.php", "POST", "message=Hello", callback);
```

185

Download Data with XHConn

You can download data from the server using the XHConn framework after you connect to the server and request that data. After you create an XHConn object, you use the connect method to connect to the server like this: `myConn.connect("xhconn.txt", "GET", "", callback)`. You specify the URL you want to access, the HTTP method to use — you can use `"GET"` or `"POST"` — the data to send to the server, and a callback function. When you execute this function, the XHConn framework connects to the URL you request on the server, passing it any data you specify. After the data you request is downloaded, the XHConn framework calls your callback function.

The callback function is the function that handles the data downloaded from the server. This function is passed only one parameter — an XMLHttpRequest object containing the data you have requested. It is up to you to extract the data you want from the XMLHttpRequest object. That is a significant difference from other Ajax frameworks, which pass you the data you request to your callback function. If you request text data, that data is usually passed to your callback function. Alternatively, if you request XML data, that data is passed to your callback function.

However, the story is different with XHConn. When you use this framework, the entire XMLHttpRequest object is passed to your callback function. In fact, that is the only item passed to the callback function. In the callback function, you access your data using the responseText property if you request text data, or the responseXml property if you request XML data. For more information on accessing the server using XHConn, see the section "Access the Server with XHConn."

Download Data with XHConn

① Include the XHConn.js file in your Web page using a `<script>` element.

② In a function named useXHConn connected to a button in a Web page, create an XHConn object and use it to connect to the server, downloading a file named xhconn.txt and using a callback function named callback.

The xhconn.txt file holds the text "This data was downloaded with the XHConn Ajax framework."

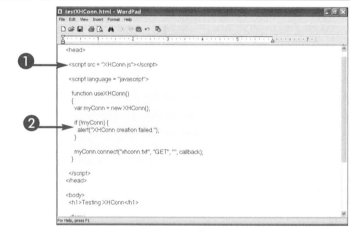

③ Create the callback function, giving it one parameter, an XMLHttpRequest object.

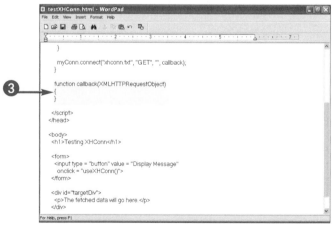

186

④ Use the `XMLHttpRequest` object's responseText property to recover the text downloaded from the server, and display that text in the Web page.

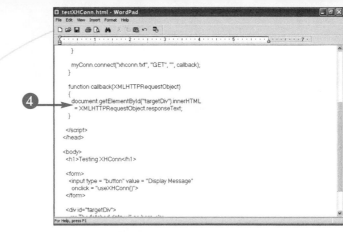

⑤ Open the Web page and click the button.

The XHConn framework downloads the data you requested and the data appears in the Web page.

Extra

Note that the XHConn framework does not include any error handling. If you want to handle errors, you must edit the XHConn framework's code directly, taking care of the case where the requested data is not downloaded as expected. In such a case, you can pass an error code to the callback function, or a value of null. You can also display an alert box if you prefer.

The XHConn framework handles multiple calls to the connect method without problem. That is, you can call the connect method a number of times and XHConn handles the `XMLHttpRequest` objects needed automatically. Note that you should use different callback functions to handle multiple concurrent `XMLHttpRequest` requests.

Although the XHConn framework works, there really is no reason to pass the full `XMLHttpRequest` object to the callback function. Part of the entire reason for Ajax frameworks in the first place is to save you programming effort so that you do not have to deal with extracting data from the `XMLHttpRequest` object directly.

Install
SACK

You can use the popular SACK Ajax framework to execute Ajax techniques and work with servers. The SACK framework is free, and it stands for Simple AJAX Code Kit. You can get Sack free at `http://twilightuniverse.com/resources/code/sack/`.

The SACK framework is powerful, even though, as with many other Ajax frameworks, it is built using JavaScript. This framework can even handle the automatic display of text downloaded from the server in specific HTML elements. For example, if you download text from the server, you can tell SACK to display that text in a `<div>` element by giving SACK the ID of that `<div>` element.

You can use SACK to download text data or XML data from the server by using the GET or POST method to do it. In all, SACK is one of the most versatile and proven of the JavaScript-based Ajax frameworks.

To get SACK, navigate to `http://twilightuniverse.com/resources/code/sack/` and right-click the link with the text "the full zip distribution", saving the Zip file `tw-sack.zip`. When you unzip that file, you get SACK demo files, including a PHP file, and `tw-sack.js`.

The `tw-sack.js` file is the SACK framework itself. Copy the file to a location accessible to the Web page in which you want to use the SACK framework. In the Web page where you want to use SACK, include `tw-sack.js` with an HTML `<script>` element like this: `<script src="tw-sack.js">`. If you are placing `tw-sack.js` in a different directory from the one that contains the Web page that will use SACK, include the URL to `tw-sack.js` like this: `<script src="http://www.noisp.com/user/tw-sack.js">`. After you install SACK, you can create a SACK object and configure it to access the server.

Install SACK

① Navigate to `http://twilightuniverse.com/resources/code/sack/`.

② Right-click the full zip distribution link.

③ In the menu that opens, select Save Target As in Internet Explorer, or Save Link As in Mozilla or Firefox, and save `tw-sack.zip` to your hard drive.

④ Unzip `tw-sack.zip` and store the Sack framework `tw-sack.js` where it is accessible from the Web page in which you want to use it.

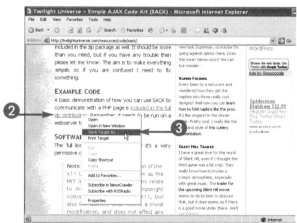

⑤ Include `tw-sack.js` in a `<script>` element in your Web page to make the SACK framework available to your code.

⑥ Create a new SACK object using the JavaScript new operator.

Sack is now installed.

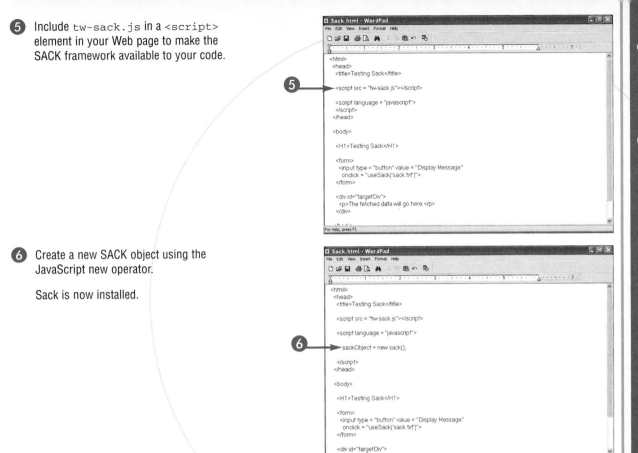

Apply It

This task created a SACK object, but it is a good idea also to notify the user if creating that object did not go as planned. Here is some JavaScript code that alerts the user if there is a problem getting SACK started by displaying the message "Sack creation failed." in an alert box:

```
<script src = "tw-sack.js"></script>

<script language = "javascript">

    var sackObject = new Sack();

    if (!sackObject) {
      alert("Sack creation failed.");
    }

</script>
```

Access the Server with SACK

Y ou can access the server using the SACK Ajax framework. After you install the SACK framework and create a `Sack` object, you can configure it to perform the Ajax operations you want. To work with SACK, you must create a `Sack` object, which you can do with the JavaScript new operator like this: `var sackObject = new Sack()`. You can also pass the file you want to access on the server to `Sack()` when you create a new `Sack` object, like this: `var sackObject = new Sack("data.txt")`.

When you create a `Sack` object, you can configure it to work with Ajax. To configure a `Sack` object, you can set a variety of properties of that object. For example, the `Sack` object's `requestFile` property lets you set the file that the `XMLHttpRequest` should be sent to. To send a request for the file `data.txt`, for example, set the

`requestFile` property this way: `sackObject.requestFile = "data.txt"`.

To set the method used to access the server, set the `Sack` object's method property to any valid HTTP method, including `"GET"` or `"POST"`. If you do not supply a method, the `"POST"` method is the default method.

You can also use the element property of the `Sack` object to pass to Sack the HTML element in which you want to display the downloaded text. Do not use this property with downloaded XML, but if you are downloading simple text, SACK gives you a real timesaver here by letting you indicate directly which HTML element should display the text that SACK downloads, because SACK displays that text in the element directly. After you configure the `Sack` object, you simply call the `runAJAX` method to access the server.

Access the Server with SACK

① Include `tw-sack.js` in your Web page, using a `<script>` element.

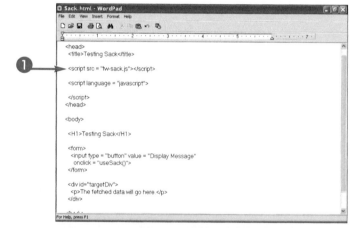

② Create a new `Sack` object.

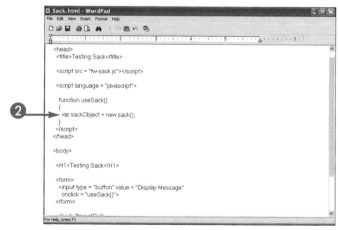

3 Configure your `Sack` object.

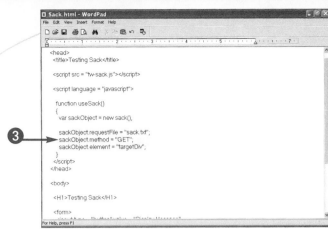

4 Use the `runAJAX` method to access the server.

If you pass data to the `runAJAX` method, that data is sent to the server, so make sure you use the standard `"parameter1=data1& parameter2=data2...."` format.

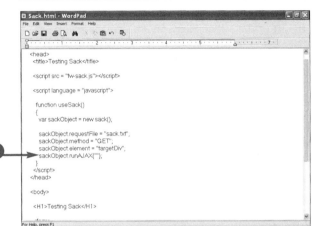

Extra

Besides the element property of the `Sack` object, you can also use the execute property, which treats the downloaded text as if it were JavaScript, and executes it. The execute property is another useful, timesaving property of the `Sack` object — if you are downloading JavaScript and want to execute it, you can have that JavaScript executed automatically by SACK simply by using the execute property. Just set this property to true — the default is false — to execute the downloaded text as JavaScript.

The `Sack` object's `responseStatus` property gives you the response status returned from the server. This property holds an array — the element at index 0 holds the response code, and the element at index 1 holds the text description of that code. This property is useful to determine what error occurs if there is a problem.

The `Sack` object's `AjaxFailedAlert` property holds a text-warning message that SACK displays if the user's browser does not support `XMLHttpRequest` objects. To turn off this warning, set this property to null.

Download Data with SACK

Y ou can download data in a number of ways with the SACK Ajax framework. After creating and configuring a `Sack` object, you can access the server with that object. When the data you request is downloaded, you can access that data in several ways.

If you want SACK to display the downloaded data as text in an HTML element, you can use the `Sack` object's element property. If you use this property, SACK displays the downloaded text in the corresponding HTML element — all you have to do is assign this property the ID of the HTML element you want to use. For example, if you have a `<div>` element with the ID `"targetDiv"`, you can assign the `Sack` object's element property that ID like this: `sackObject.element = "targetDiv"`. Doing so makes SACK display any downloaded text in that element, using the element's `innerHTML` property.

Besides the `element` property, you can also use the `Sack` object's `execute` property. Assigning a value of true to that property makes SACK treat the downloaded text as JavaScript and executes it.

Finally, you can assign the name of a callback function to the `Sack` object's `onCompletion` property, and SACK calls that callback function when your data is downloaded. In the callback function, you can use the `Sack` object's `response` property to read any downloaded text, or the `responseXML` property to read any downloaded XML. The XML is in JavaScript XML document object form. No parameters are passed to the callback function, so if you want to access the `Sack` object from inside the callback function, make that object a global JavaScript object.

To install the SACK Ajax framework, see the section "Install SACK." To access the server with SACK, see the section "Access the Server with SACK."

Download Data with SACK

① Add a button to your Web page and connect it to a function named `useSack`.

② Add a `<div>` element to display results in, giving that element the ID `"targetDiv"`.

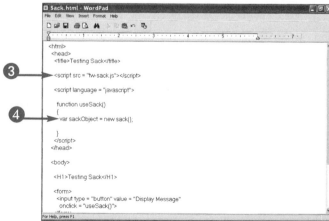

③ Include the SACK Ajax framework in your Web page.

④ In a function named `useSack`, create a new `Sack` object using the JavaScript `new` operator.

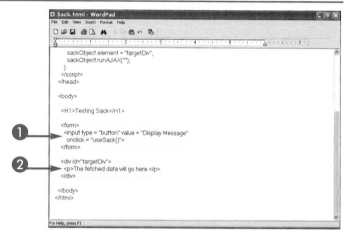

5 Configure the Sack object to download the file sack.txt and display the file's text in the targetDiv element.

The sack.txt file contains the text "This data was downloaded with the Sack Ajax framework."

6 Call the Sack method runAJAX to download your data.

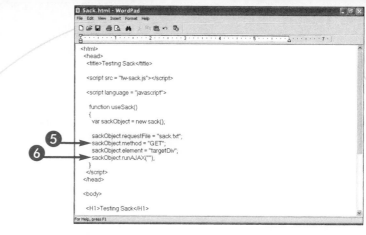

7 Open the Web page in your browser and click the button.

The file sack.txt is downloaded and its text appears in the Web page.

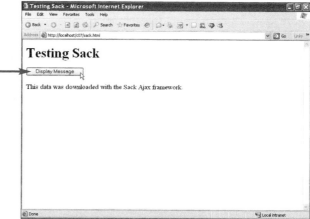

Apply It

This code performs the same operation as the SACK example in this task, except that it uses a more traditional callback function:

```javascript
var sackObject;
function useSack()
{
  sackObject = new sack();
  sackObject.requestFile = "sack.txt";
  sackObject.method = "GET";
  sackObject.onCompletion = callback;
  sackObject.runAJAX("");
}

function callback()
{
  document.getElementById("targetDiv").innerHTML =
  sackObject.response;
}
```

Install
Sarissa

Y ou can download and work with XML easily using the Sarissa Ajax framework, which you can get free from http://sourceforge.net/projects/ sarissa. The Sarissa framework is a JavaScript library that specializes in handling XML in Ajax applications.

Sarissa is a large package that lets you create XML documents from scratch, download XML documents from the server, work with the data inside them, and more. You can use XPath in XML to search through your XML documents and extract data from them. See Chapter 9 for more on XML. You can even use Extensible Stylesheet Language Transformation (XSLT) to transform XML into other types of documents, like HTML documents. In fact, Sarissa is designed mostly to let you work with XML in JavaScript, but it also lets you download XML using Ajax.

To use Ajax, you create a Sarissa DomDocument object, using the Sarissa getDomDocument method. You then set

the DomDocument object's async property to true, which means that any XML documents loaded into this object are loaded asynchronously, as you expect with Ajax. You then connect a callback function to the DomDocument object's onreadystatechange property, just as you would with an XMLHttpRequest object. Then you download your XML data with the DomDocument object's load method.

After your XML data is downloaded using Ajax and is stored in the Sarissa DomDocument object, you can use various Sarissa methods to access and work with that data. For example, you can use the Sarissa selectSingleNode method to access a single node of data in your XML document. You can also use Sarissa to extract the data from the XML nodes you recover from the document. Overall, Sarissa is a very handy package if you are going to use a lot of XML manipulation.

Install Sarissa

① Navigate to the Sarissa download page, http:// sourceforge.net/project/showfiles. php?group_id=75155 and click Download.

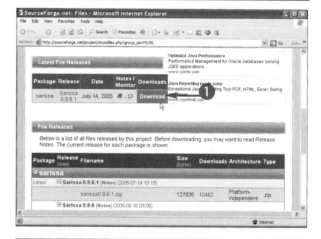

② Click the link to the Sarissa Zip file that appears, such as sarissa0.9.6.1.zip.

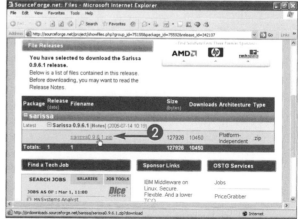

③ Select a download mirror close to you, and download `Sarissa.zip`.

Unzip `Sarissa.zip` and place the `Sarissa.js` files in the same directory as the Web page you plan to use them in.

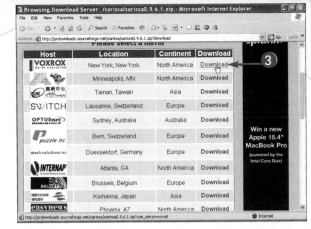

④ Include `sarissa.js` in your Web page. If you want to use Sarissa's XPath capabilities, include `sarissa_ieemu_xpath.js` as well.

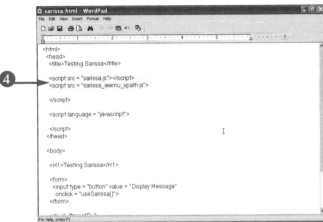

Extra

Sarissa is an interesting and powerful framework; however, it is extensive enough that you may sometimes wonder if the extra work is worth it. If you are going to do a lot of XML work, Sarissa is worth looking at in detail. Otherwise, you may find yourself performing usual Ajax operations using Sarissa's syntax and differences. For example, you have to assign a function to a Sarissa DomDocument's `onreadystatechange` property. Because you have to do this with an `XMLHttpRequest` object and then check the DomDocument's `readystate` property to see when the download is complete, Sarissa does not save you a great deal of time when it comes to writing the code for downloading XML.

Although Sarissa methods like `selectSingleNode` to extract data from XML objects can be useful, you can often write code to do the same thing using already available JavaScript methods like `getElementsByTagName`.

Access the Server with Sarissa

You can access the server with the Sarissa framework, which specializes in working with XML. To work with Sarissa, you first must include the Sarissa JavaScript files you want to use, starting with `sarissa.js`. If you want to let Sarissa use Xpath to extract text data from your XML data, you should also include `sarissa_ieemu_xpath.js`.

To get started, create a Sarissa `DomDocument` object, using the Sarissa method `getDomDocument` like this: `var domDocument = Sarissa.getDomDocument();`. That object is the basis of the work you can do with Sarissa. To set up the `DomDocument` object to access the server asynchronously, set the object's `async` property to true, like this: `domDocument.async = true;`. That means that when you call the Sarissa load method to read XML documents from the server, Sarissa will use asynchronous access to read that XML, as you would expect in an Ajax application.

You should also connect the `DomDocument` object's `onreadystatechange` property to a callback function. That function is called back when Sarissa contacts the server, and you can check the `DomDocument` object's `readyState` property to see if your data is ready after being downloaded.

If your data is ready, you can extract that data from the `DomDocument` object in the callback function using the methods and properties of the `DomDocument` object. For example, to extract an element named `<data>`, you can use the Sarissa `DomDocument` object's `selectSingleNode` method.

After you configure the `DomDocument` object as you want it and connect a callback function to it, you can download the XML data you want by using the Sarissa load method. To install the Sarissa framework, see the section "Install Sarissa."

Access the Server with Sarissa

① Create a new Sarissa `DomDocument` object.

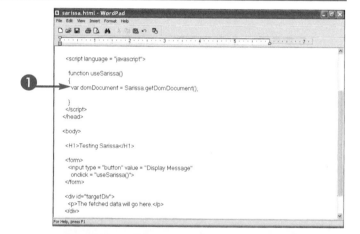

② Set the `DomDocument` object's `async` property to true to support asynchronous downloads.

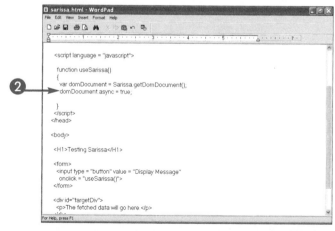

196

③ Connect a function to the `DomDocument` object's `onreadystatechange` property to handle the download when it arrives.

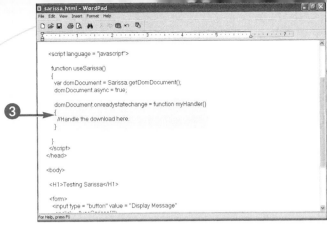

④ Connect to the server and start downloading data with a call to the `DomDocument` object's `load` method, which is downloading a document named `sarissa.xml` in this example.

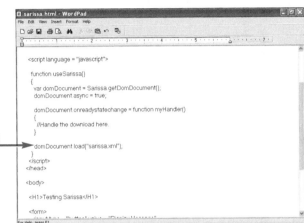

Apply It

You can also use Sarissa to load XML documents in a synchronous way, which will pause your code until the XML document has been downloaded. This example code lets you download a document named `sarissa.xml` synchronously:

```
function useSarissa()
{
    var domDocument = Sarissa.getDomDocument();

    domDocument.async = false;

    domDocument.load("sarissa.xml");

    //Handle the download here.
}
```

This works as long as `sarissa.xml` is available immediately. However, if it takes some time to find and download that document, your code will stop and wait until it is fully downloaded.

Download Data with Sarissa

Y ou can use the Sarissa framework to download XML data from a server. In order to download data with Sarissa, you must first create a DomDocument object, using the Sarissa method getDomDocument. You can make that DomDocument object download data in an asynchronous manner by setting its async property to true.

You should connect a callback function to the DomDocument object's onreadystatechange property. This function is called when the DomDocument object's readystate property changes, and when that property holds a value of 4, your data has been downloaded.

When all your data is downloaded, you can use Sarissa's methods to manipulate and work with that XML. For example, if you want to extract the text in an XML element named <data>, first extract that element from your XML data, which you can do with the Sarissa

DomDocument method selectSingleNode. To extract the <data> element, you can pass that method the XPath expression "//data", which finds the <data> element no matter where it is in the document — the XPath "//" means "start searching at the beginning of the document and keep searching every element until you find the one requested."

After you find the <data> element you want, you can extract the text from that element using the Sarissa method serialize. All you do is pass the element you have extracted from your data to the serialize method this way: serialize(element), and the serialize method will return the text from inside the element, saving you the trouble of extracting that text yourself.

To install the Sarissa framework, see the section "Install Sarissa." Also, see the section "Access the Server with Sarissa" for more on accessing the server with Sarissa.

Download Data with Sarissa

① Add a button to a Web page and connect that button to a function named useSarissa.

② Add a <div> element with the ID targetDiv in which to display downloaded data.

③ Attach a function to the DomDocument object's onreadystatechange property, and check if the readystate property equals 4, indicating that your XML data has been downloaded.

The XML document sarissa.xml contains the XML <?xml version="1.0" ?><ajax> <response> <data>This data was downloaded with the Sarissa Ajax framework.</data> </response> </ajax>.

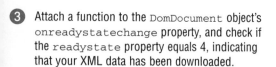

④ To handle the downloaded data use the method `selectSingleNode`, passing it the XPath expression `"//data"` to find the first `<data>` element anywhere in the XML data, and use the Sarissa serialize method to extract the text in the `<data>` element.

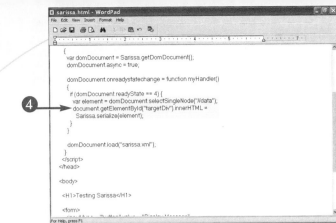

⑤ Open the Web page and click the button.

Sarissa downloads `sarissa.xml` and displays the text inside the `<data>` element in the Web page.

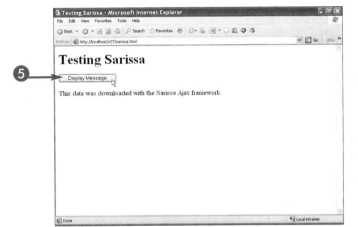

Apply It

You can also work with the element objects that Sarissa creates using standard JavaScript methods and properties, such as the `firstChild` property. Here is what that looks like in this task's example code:

```
function useSarissa()
{
  var domDocument = Sarissa.getDomDocument();
  domDocument.async = true;

  domDocument.onreadystatechange = function myHandler()
  {
    if (domDocument.readyState == 4) {
      var element = domDocument.selectSingleNode("//data");
      document.getElementById("targetDiv").innerHTML =
        element.firstChild.data;
    }
  }
}
```

Install Interactive Website Framework

Y ou can use the Interactive Website Framework (IWF) to work with Ajax techniques and download XML data. The IWF is available free at http://sourceforge.net/projects/iwf/. The IWF is a JavaScript-based Ajax framework that has a great deal of support built in for creating entire Web sites using JavaScript, Ajax, XML, HTML, and CSS. There is a great deal in this framework, and it can take a significant time investment to get everything working. However, once you invest that time and learn how this framework works, developing entire Web sites can become much easier.

The IWF centers around four JavaScript files: iwfcore.js, iwfgui.js, iwfxml.js, and iwfajax.js files, and you should include all four in your Web page to use the IWF. To do that, use multiple <script> elements.

The IWF solves a common problem that Ajax developers run into: browser caching. The problem is that browsers

like Internet Explorer read text or XML data from an URL for you, but they also store that data in an internal cache. The next time you try to read data from the same URL, the browser passes you the same data from its cache instead of trying to fetch that data from the server. That is a problem if your data changes, because your application is supplied cached data, not updated data.

The way Ajax applications usually solve this issue if they run into it is to append nonsense data to the end of the URL. For example, if you keep trying to access the URL www.noisp/data.php, you may get cached data over and over. However, if you access www.noisp/data. php?t=1, then www.noisp/data.php?t=2, and so on, those are unique URLs, and the browser does not give you cached data. Using URLs like that, the IWF makes sure that you do not get browser-cached data in your Ajax application.

Install Interactive Website Framework

① Navigate to the IWF download page, http://
sourceforge.net/project/showfiles.
php?group_id=140835 and click Download.

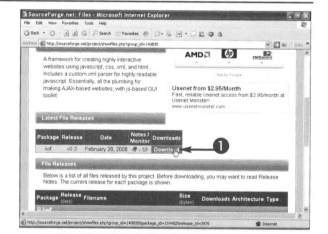

② Click the link to the IWF Zip file.

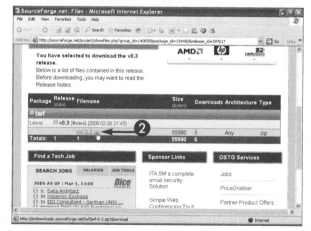

③ Click the Download button for a mirror near you, and unzip the IWF file after it is downloaded.

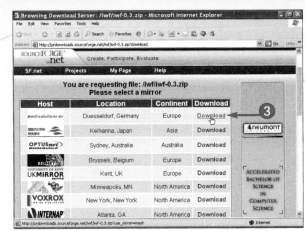

④ Include the `iwfcore.js`, `iwfgui.js`, `iwfxml.js`, and `iwfajax.js` files in your Web page.

Installation of IWF is complete.

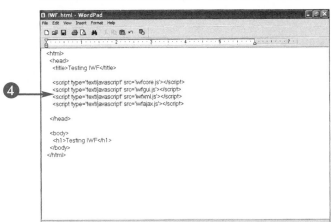

Extra

IWF gives you many built-in capabilities as well as working with Ajax, such as a number of functions that let you move elements around in a Web page. Using those functions, you can support drag-and-drop operations, for example. There are also a number of functions for formatting Web pages. IWF was built to provide a complete Web framework, allowing you to construct full-fledged Web applications, not just use Ajax in Web pages.

IWF supports functions that let you acquire XML data and insert that into HTML elements in a Web page automatically. IWF specializes in making XML easier to work with in your JavaScript. The normal way of working with XML in JavaScript is a little involved (see Chapter 9 for details), and once you get used to the techniques used in IWF for handling XML, your code can be much easier to write. If you are doing a lot of XML work, look at what IWF has to offer.

Connecting to the Server with the Interactive Website Framework

You can use the Interactive Website Framework (IWF) to connect to the server and access data or programs on that server. To use IWF, you have to include IWF scripts in your Web page: iwfcore.js, iwfgui.js, iwfxml.js, and iwfajax.js. You do that with the HTML <script> element like this:
<script src='iwfcore.js'></script>
<script src='iwfgui.js'></script> <script src='iwfxml.js'></script> and <script src='iwfajax.js'></script>

To interact with data on the server, you can use the IWF method named iwfRequest, which sends a request to the server for the XML data you want. IWF only works with XML data. To download a document named iwf.xml, you call iwfRequest("iwf.xml").

To work with IWF, your XML has to be in a specific format, starting with an XML declaration, followed by a document element named <response>, which encloses

an <action> element that contains your data. For example, if you want to store some HTML text in the iwf.xml document, you can do that like this:
<?xml version="1.0" ?> <response> <action type='html'>   This data downloaded using the IWF Ajax framework.</action> </response>

Note in particular the <action> element's type attribute, which specifies the type of your data, such as HTML, XML, JavaScript, and so on. In this case, the type of the data is given as HTML, which means you can display it directly in your Web page. One easy way of displaying that data is to set up a <div> element with the ID iwfContent like this: <div id='iwfContent'>, and IWF displays your data in that <div> element automatically using the element's innerHTML property. For information on how to install the Interactive Website Framework, see the section "Install Interactive Website Framework."

Connecting to the Server with the Interactive Website Framework

① Include the IWF iwfcore.js, iwfgui.js, iwfxml.js, and iwfajax.js files in your Web page.

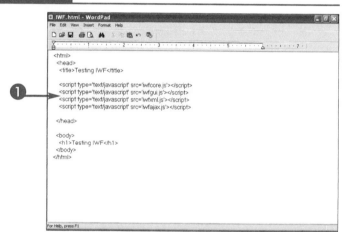

② Add a button connected to the IWF iwfRequest method.

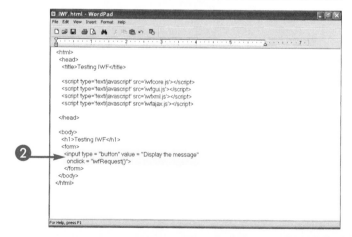

③ Create a new XML document named `iwf.xml` formatted as IWF expects it.

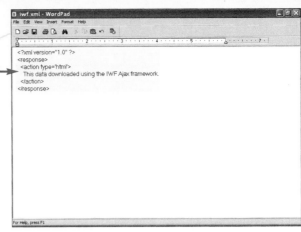

④ Pass the name of the XML document, `iwf.xml`, to the IWF `iwfRequest` method.

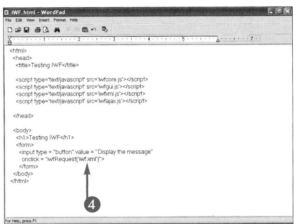

Extra

If you use HTML with IWF, it must actually be Extensible Hypertext Markup Language (XHTML). XHTML is the XML version of HTML that looks like normal HTML, but is actually XML. Go to `http://www.w3.org/TR/xhtml1/` for more on XHTML.

If you set the type attribute to `"javascript"`, IWF treats the downloaded data as JavaScript and executes it.

If the `<action>` element in the XML data from the server has a nonempty value assigned to the `errorCode` attribute, IWF calls a function named `iwfOnRequestError` in your JavaScript, passing that function the error message you specify:

```
<?xml version="1.0" ?>
<response>
  <action type='html' target='divResponse'
    errorCode='1' errorMessage='Internal error' >
    <h1>There has been an error.</h1>
    Sorry, the internal data was faulty.
    Please try your request again.
  </action>
</response>
```

Download Data with the Interactive Website Framework

You can use the Interactive Website Framework to download data from the server. To use IWF to download data from the server, first include the IWF scripts in your Web page `iwfcore.js`, `iwfgui.js`, `iwfxml.js`, and `iwfajax.js`. The HTML `<script>` element like this:

```
<script src='iwfcore.js'></script>
<script src='iwfgui.js'></script> <script src='iwfxml.js'></script> and <script src='iwfajax.js'></script>
```

To contact the server, you can use the IWF method named `iwfRequest`, which is responsible for sending a request to the server for the XML data you want to download. For example, to download a document named `iwf.xml`, you call `iwfRequest("iwf.xml")`.

Where that data goes when it is downloaded depends on how you want your data treated. If you set the XML data's `<action>` element's type attribute to `"javascript"`, your data is treated as JavaScript when it is downloaded, and IWF executes it. If you set the type attribute to `"xml"`, an `iwfXmlNode` object is passed to the callback function that you passed to the `iwfRequest` function.

If you set the type attribute to `"html"`, then your downloaded data is displayed in a `<div>` element with the ID `"iwfContent"`. You can also specify the ID of the `<div>` element you want your HTML to appear in yourself when you call the `iwfRequest` method. For example, `iwfRequest("iwf.xml", "targetDiv")` downloads the HTML data in `iwf.xml` and displays that data in a `<div>` element with the ID `targetDiv`, using the `<div>` element's `innerHTML` property. To see how to install the Interactive Website Framework, see the section "Install Interactive Website Framework." To see how to access the server with Interactive Website Framework, see the section "Connecting to the Server with the Interactive Website Framework."

Download Data With the Interactive Website Framework

① Include the IWF scripts in your Web page.

② Add a button that calls the IWF `iwfRequest` function to download the XML document `iwf.xml`.

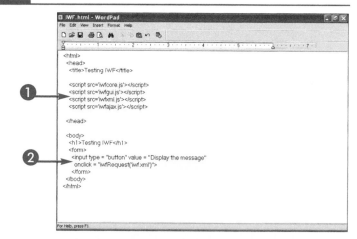

③ Create the `iwf.xml` XML document, placing some HTML text in it.

Note: For more on the XML format that you can use with IWF, see the section "Connecting the Server with the Interactive Website Framework."

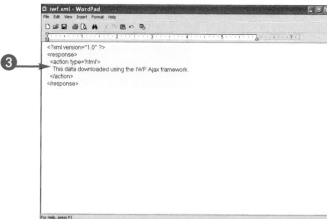

④ Add a `<div>` element with the ID `iwfContent` in which to display the downloaded data.

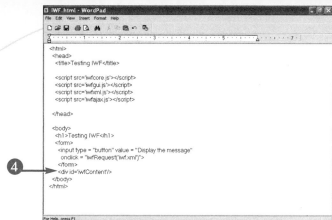

⑤ Open the Web page in a browser and click the button.

The HTML data in `iwf.xml` is downloaded and displayed.

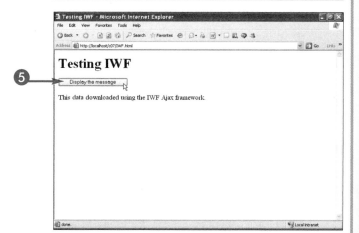

Extra

IWF also supports multiple `XMLHttpRequest` requests at the same time, so you do not have to worry about the user clicking too many Ajax-enabled buttons — no matter how many requests the user issues at once, IWF can handle them. IWF also prevents browser caching, which means that data sent from the server is not cached. You can access the same URL over and over, and the data from that URL is downloaded each time, not passed to you from the browser cache.

You can use IWF to parse XML data. For example, if you have XML data like this: `<data><date time="3PM"></data>`, you can access the time attribute using IWF like this:

```
var time = doc.data.date[0].time;
```

instead of something like this if you are using standard JavaScript methods:

```
var time = doc.documentElement.firstChild.
getAttribute("time");
```

As you can see, the IWF way of handling XML can save you a great deal of coding.

Install
RICO

Y ou can perform Ajax operations with the RICO framework, which you can download for free from http://openrico.org/rico/home.page. RICO is a very popular JavaScript framework that also supports Ajax. It offers a number of very nice visual effects, such as drag and drop, which are supported with RICO manipulation of HTML elements.

RICO also supports its own custom controls, such as a "LiveGrid" control, which can display data in a table format, and sort that data as well. You can also make Web page elements fade in and out of view, use an "accordion" control that displays data using text panes that you can slide open or closed, and more.

To get RICO for use with Ajax, download RICO. You will get both JavaScript files needed for RICO: `rico.js` and `prototype.js`. Add those two scripts to your Web page using the HTML `<script>` element this way: `<script src="prototype.js"></script>` and

`<script src="rico.js"></script>`. After you install these scripts, you are ready to use RICO.

You need to tailor your XML to fit the way RICO wants to read it. For example, if you use the XML `<?xml version = "1.0" ?> <ajax-response> <response type= "element" id="targetDiv"> <span>This data downloaded using the RICO framework.</span> </response> </ajax-response>`, then RICO knows you want to display the text "This data downloaded using the RICO framework" inside the HTML element in your Web page with the ID `targetDiv`.

To download data using Ajax techniques, you must create a RICO request with the `ajaxEngine.registerRequest` method. Then you can use the `ajaxEngine.sendRequest` method to send that request to the server. The RICO framework will download your XML data and display it or pass it to a callback function, as you direct.

Install RICO

① Navigate to http://openrico.org/rico/home.page and click the Downloads link.

② Right-click the link to rico.js, select Save Target As in Internet Explorer, or Save Link As in Mozilla or Firefox, and then save `rico.js` where it is accessible from the Web page in which you want to use it.

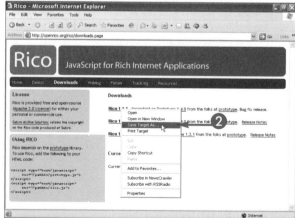

③ Right-click the link to `prototype.js`, and in the menu that opens, select Save Target As in Internet Explorer, or Save Link As in Mozilla or Firefox, and save `prototype.js` where it is accessible from the Web page in which you want to use it.

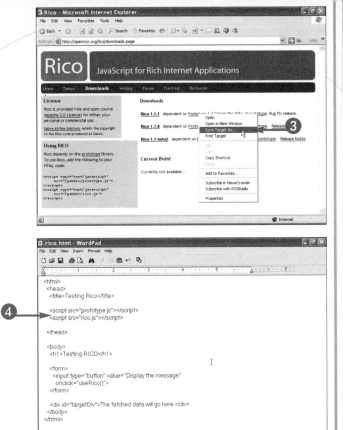

④ Include `rico.js` and `prototype.js` in your Web page using `<script>` elements.

Extra

RICO is very good at supporting drag and drop. You can see an example on the RICO demonstration page at http://openrico.org/rico/demos.page?demo=ricoDragAndDropSimple.html. RICO drag and drop is active in the sense that the elements you drop on a target can be Ajax-enabled to download data from the server. The drag-and-drop operation is smooth and can give your Web page a very professional feel.

The custom RICO controls like the LiveGrid control are also very popular. You can see a Rico LiveGrid control at http://openrico.org/rico/livegrid.page. This demo displays a table of titles of movies. When you click a column header, the LiveGrid control will re-sort itself automatically as the user watches. Connecting a LiveGrid control to server-side programming that connects to a database is a good option for displaying your data.

There is an accordion control, which lets you slide panes of text around, letting you stack a great deal of data in a small space. Take a look at the demo at http://openrico.org/rico/demos.page?demo=rico_accordion. Using this control, you can maximize the small amount of screen space available to you in a browser.

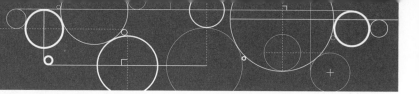

Access the Server with RICO

Y ou can access the server using the RICO JavaScript framework. To use RICO, you must first include the two necessary JavaScript files, `rico.js` and `prototype.js`, which you can do with HTML `<script>` elements this way: `<script src="prototype.js"> </script>` and `<script src="rico.js"></script>`.

The first step to connect to the server is to use the RICO `registerRequest` method to register a RICO request with the RICO Ajax engine, which is named ajaxEngine. That means the full name of this method is `ajaxEngine.registerRequest`. For example, if you want to download the data in a document named `rico.xml`, you can create a RICO request named `xmlRequest` this way: `ajaxEngine.registerRequest ("xmlRequest", "rico.xml")`.

When you register a request this way with the RICO Ajax engine, you can use that request to download data. To do that, you can refer to your new request, `xmlRequest`,

by name in your JavaScript code, like this: `ajaxEngine.sendRequest("xmlRequest", "")`. This expression contacts the server with your request. You pass the name of the request as the first parameter to the `ajaxEngine.sendRequest` method, and the data you want to pass to the server as the second parameter. Since there is no data to pass in this case, the second parameter is an empty string, `""`.

If you want RICO to display the downloaded data in an HTML element, you can register elements with the RICO Ajax engine like this: `ajaxEngine. registerAjaxElement("targetDiv")`. This registers the `<div>` element with the ID `targetDiv` with the Ajax engine. Then RICO knows about that element and can display your data in it when that data is downloaded. To install the RICO framework, see the section "Install RICO."

Access the Server with RICO

① Include the RICO JavaScript files using HTML `<script>` elements.

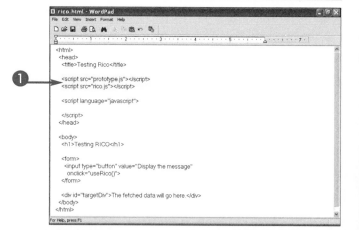

② Register a request for your XML document on the server with the RICO Ajax engine.

③ Register an HTML element with the RICO Ajax engine in which you want to display your downloaded data.

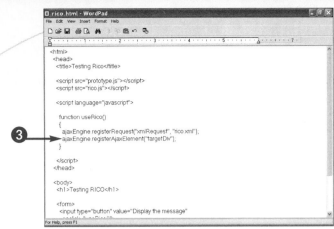

④ Send your request to the server using the Ajax engine's `sendRequest` method.

If you have any additional data to send to the server, include that data as the second parameter in the call to `sendRequest`.

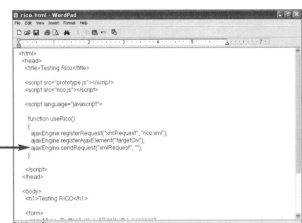

Apply It

The format you use to pass data to the RICO Ajax engine is worth noting. For example, say that you have registered a request named `xmlRequest` like this:

```
function registerAjaxInfo() {
    ajaxEngine.registerRequest("xmlRequest", "data.xml");
    ajaxEngine.registerAjaxElement("targetDiv");
}
```

Now you can pass multiple parameters to the server this way:

```
ajaxEngine.sendRequest("xmlRequest",
  "sandwich=" + sandwichType,
  "drink=" + drinkType);
```

RICO is usually used with larger Web frameworks like Struts, which means that the RICO requests will be sent to Struts action servlets which have the extension `.do` (see http://struts.apache.org/):

```
function registerAjaxInfo() {
    ajaxEngine.registerRequest("xmlRequest", "data.do");
    ajaxEngine.registerAjaxElement("targetDiv");
}
```

Download Data with RICO

ou can download XML data using download data from the server using the RICO framework. To use the RICO framework, you first must include the two RICO scripts, `prototype.js` and `rico.js`, which you can do with `<script>` elements like this: `<script src="prototype.js"></script>` and `<script src="rico.js"></script>`. After you add those scripts to your Web page, you can use RICO to download data from the server.

To download data, create a request and name it, as with this call: `ajaxEngine.registerRequest ("xmlRequest", "rico.xml")`, which names the request for `rico.xml` xmlRequest. You can also register an HTML element to display the data you download: `ajaxEngine.registerAjaxElement("targetDiv")`, which means that RICO displays the downloaded data in a `<div>` element named `targetDiv`. To send the request

to the server, use the `sendRequest` method like this: `ajaxEngine.sendRequest("xmlRequest", "");` if you have data to send to the server, you can pass that data as the second parameter in the `sendRequest` call.

The RICO framework requires that you format your XML data in a certain way. An XML document that you fetch from the server should start with an XML declaration such as `<?xml version = "1.0" ?>`, and the document element should be `<ajax-response>`. Inside the document element, you use `<response>` elements to indicate how RICO should handle your response to the browser. For example, `<response type="element" id="targetDiv">` means that you want to display the downloaded data in an HTML element with the ID `targetDiv` in the browser. Inside the `<response>` element, you can store the actual data that RICO downloads.

Download Data with RICO

1 Add a button to a Web page that calls a JavaScript function named `useRico`.

2 Add a `<div>` element with the ID `targetDiv` that displays the downloaded data.

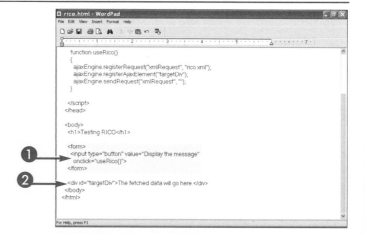

3 Include the RICO scripts in your Web page.

4 Add the `useRico` function, creating a RICO request to download an XML document named `rico.xml`.

⑤ Create `rico.xml`, storing the text "This data downloaded using the RICO framework." in it.

⑥ Open the Web page in a browser and click the button.

The downloaded data appears in the `<div>` element.

Apply It

Much of the Ajax functionality in RICO comes from the prototype JavaScript library, `prototype.js`. You can use the prototype library yourself directly if you include it in a Web page:

```
<script src="prototype.js">
```

To make an Ajax request, use the `Ajax.Request` method, setting the URL to contact, the HTTP method to use, any data you want to send, and you specify the callback function, which is just named callback here:

```
var myAjax = new Ajax.Request(
    url,
    {method: 'post',
      parameters: data,
      onComplete: callback}
);
```

After you make the Ajax request, you can get your downloaded data by using the `responseText` or `responseXml` property of the object passed to your callback function:

```
function callback(object)
{
    alert(object.responseText);
}
```

Install
SAJAX

You can use the SAJAX server-side Ajax framework to work with Ajax from the server. Like other server-side Ajax frameworks, SAJAX lets you create the JavaScript needed in an Ajax application on the server. All you need is server-side code, which can be in the ASP, ColdFusion, Io, Lua, Perl, PHP, Python, or Ruby languages on the server. SAJAX works with all of them.

You can get SAJAX free at www.modernmethod.com/sajax/. All you have to do is download the latest version of SAJAX and place it on your server — note that SAJAX does not work with IIS servers. SAJAX comes with examples, ready to use.

Here is how SAJAX works: You use it to create JavaScript functions in your Web pages. SAJAX can connect those JavaScript functions to code you write for server-side programs. The JavaScript that SAJAX creates for you

takes the data entered in the Web page and sends it to your server-side code to be processed, as you direct.

In other words, when the user navigates to a PHP-based Web page that uses SAJAX, SAJAX creates that Web page on the server and creates all the JavaScript needed to connect what the user does in the Web page to code on the server. For example, if you have a PHP function named add on the server, SAJAX can create the JavaScript needed to pass the data the user enters in a Web page to that function on the server.

Because SAJAX creates the JavaScript for your application, you only need to write a little JavaScript yourself. SAJAX handles the connection between the Web page and the code on the server by itself, sending the data to the server-side code and reading the results that the code passes back to the browser.

Install SAJAX

① Navigate to the SAJAX home page at www.modernmethod.com/sajax/, and click Download.

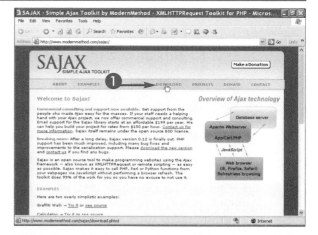

② In the menu that opens, right-click the link to the latest version of SAJAX, select Save Target As in Internet Explorer or Save Link As in Mozilla or Firefox, and save the ZIP file.

③ Unzip that file where SAJAX is accessible from the Web page in which you want to use it on a PHP-enabled server.

④ Open the `example_multiply.php` example in the SAJAX PHP directory to test if your installation was successful.

This example, which multiplies two numbers has sample numbers already entered for you by SAJAX.

⑤ Click the Calculate button.

You should see the result of the multiplication appear in the Web page, indicating that SAJAX is properly installed.

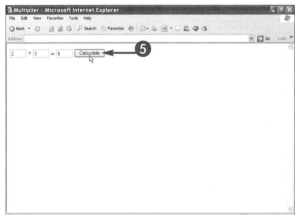

Extra

SAJAX supports multiple concurrent `XMLHttpRequest` requests. After all, if each button in your Web page is tied to separate `XMLHttpRequest` requests, you end up with multiple concurrent requests as users click multiple buttons before waiting for the response to their first button clicks to appear.

SAJAX performs well with multiple concurrent `XMLHttpRequest` requests in practice. Each request is handled individually, and the results appear from the server predictably. On the other hand, the SAJAX frequently asked question (FAQ) list at www.modernmethod.com/sajax/faq.phtml has a disquieting note that says, "At one point, multiple concurrent requests performed strangely. This may be fixed." So far, SAJAX seems to handle multiple concurrent `XMLHttpRequest` requests without issue.

As of version 0.10, SAJAX supports the `POST` method in addition to the default `GET` method when you use SAJAX with PHP on your server. As of the same version of SAJAX, you can now also send data to another URL besides your own domain without errors.

Write Server-Side Code with SAJAX

You can write server-side code with the SAJAX Ajax framework, and SAJAX automatically writes the JavaScript that lets you connect to that server-side code from a browser. To use SAJAX, you must write server-side code. The most common server-side language to use with SAJAX is PHP.

For example, to use SAJAX and PHP, you might begin a PHP file with the usual PHP markup, `<?`, and then include SAJAX support by including `Sajax.php` this way: `require("Sajax.php");`. For more on how to program using PHP, see Chapter 11.

After you include `Sajax.php` in your PHP file, you can write the PHP function you want to use to handle data sent from the browser. For example, if you write a function to add two numbers named `adder`, you would place the PHP code for the `adder` function in the PHP file: `function adder($operand1, $operand2) { return $operand1 + $operand2; }`. Now you

can use the `adder` function from the Web page that appears in the browser.

To complete the PHP, you must call the `Sajax` function `sajax_init()`, then export the `adder` function to make it available to JavaScript in the browser with this expression: `sajax_export("adder")`, and finally, you call the Sajax function `sajax_handle_client_request()`.

That completes the PHP code you need to write — all you do is include the `Sajax.php` support file, write the PHP code you want to call from JavaScript in the browser, and call three SAJAX functions to make the Web page complete. You end your PHP code with the markup `?>`.

SAJAX writes the JavaScript needed in your Web page for you, as long as you place the PHP code `<? sajax_show_javascript(); ?>` inside the HTML `<script>` element of your page. That completes the server-side code for a Web page.

Write Server-Side Code with SAJAX

① Include the SAJAX support file `Sajax.php` in your PHP server-side file.

In order to create an example that adds two numbers supplied by the user, name this file `add.php`.

② Create a PHP function named `adder`, which adds two numbers passed to it and returns their sum.

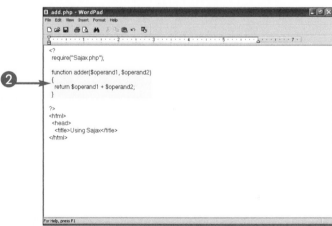

③ Add calls to `sajax_init()`, `sajax_export("adder")`, and `sajax_handle_client_request()` to complete the SAJAX support.

④ Place the PHP `<? sajax_show_javascript(); ?>` inside the HTML `<script>` element in the Web page to allow SAJAX to create the JavaScript needed to connect code in the Web page to the `adder` function on the server.

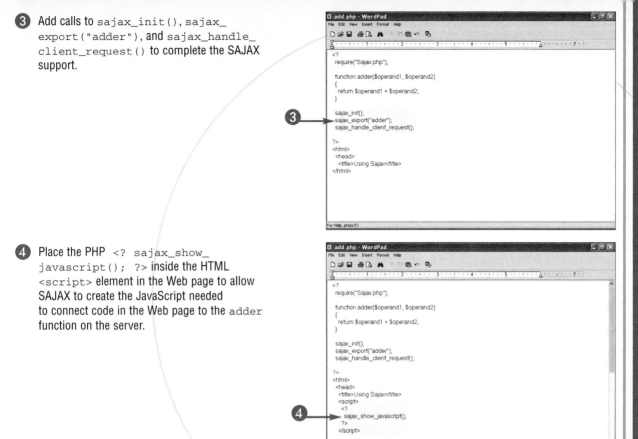

Apply It

This task exports only one PHP function, so you can connect to it with browser-side code, but you can export multiple functions this way:

Example:
```
<?
  require("Sajax.php");
  function adder($operand1, $operand2)
  {
    return $operand1 + $operand2;
  }
  function subtracter($operand1, $operand2)
  {
    return $operand1 - $operand2;
  }
  sajax_init();
  sajax_export("adder", "subtracter");
  sajax_handle_client_request();
?>
```

Write Browser-Side Code with SAJAX

You can write browser-side code to interact with server-side code using the SAJAX Ajax framework. For example, say you have a server-side function named adder that you want to pass two numbers, supplied by the user, and get the result back from the server. Doing that with SAJAX is no problem.

SAJAX specializes in letting you connect to server-side code. If you write the adder function on the server and use SAJAX to export that function — see the section "Write Server-Side Code with SAJAX" for more details — you can call the adder function from code in your Web page. Specifically, if the adder function is on the server in your SAJAX-supported code, and you export that function, you can call that function in your JavaScript in the browser by referring to that function as x_adder.

In other words, say you define the function adder this way in PHP: function adder($operand1,

$operand2) { return $operand1 + $operand2; }, and export it to make it available in the browser. Then you can call that function in the browser using this JavaScript: x_adder(operand1, operand2, display). Here, operand1 and operand2 are the two values you want to add, and the display function is a callback function that SAJAX passes the sum of the two numbers to.

The display function is written in browser-side JavaScript code. For example, if you want to display the result of adding two numbers in a text field with the ID result, you can do that like this in the display function: function display(result) { document.getElement ById("result").value = result; }.

That is how you connect to server-side code using SAJAX: You refer to a function that you have exported with SAJAX by prefixing it with "x_", pass the data to that function, and a callback function.

Write Browser-Side Code with SAJAX

① Add two text fields to a Web page to accept two numbers to add from the user.

② Add a text field with the ID result to display the sum of the two numbers.

③ Add a button connected to a function named addValues that adds the two values using server-side code.

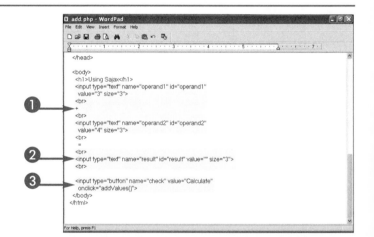

④ Add a function named addValues that adds the two numbers the user enters by passing them to the function x_adder, which connects to the adder PHP function on the server, which adds the two numbers. Also pass the name of a callback function, display, to the x_adder function, so that display is called with the results of the addition.

Note: To see how to write the server-side adder function, see the section "Write Server-Side Code with SAJAX."

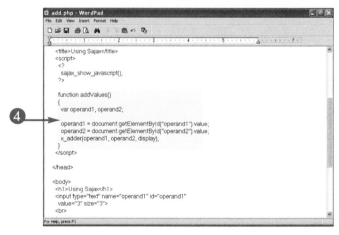

⑤ Add the `display` function, which is passed the result of `add` the two numbers given by the user.

The `display` function displays the sum passed to it in the result text field.

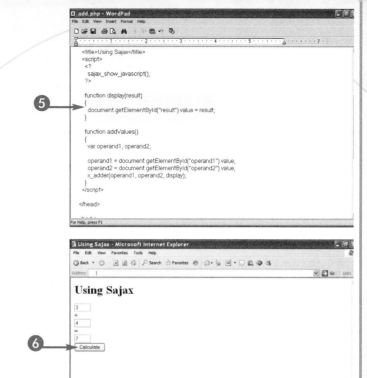

⑥ Open the Web page, type two numbers to add, and click the button.

The sum appears in the result text field.

Extra

Using a server-side framework like SAJAX gives you access to a great deal of power on the server — power you cannot get simply by using JavaScript inside the browser. Server-side languages like PHP and Java offer a great deal more programming power than JavaScript. You can do a great many things in those server-side languages that you can't do with JavaScript, such as work with files. Files on the server can include database files in which you can store all kinds of data, such as what items you have for sale and how many there are in stock, e-mail lists, birthday records, employee data, passwords, spell-checking data, and much more. That kind of data can't easily be downloaded to the browser for use with JavaScript. You can also connect to other servers easily from the server, allowing you to make secure connections to get credit card payments approved, for example.

Although you can only pass a single result to the callback function when working with SAJAX, that single result can hold multiple values if you pass an array to that callback function. Using arrays in that way allows you to pass multiple data items to the callback function.

Install
Xajax

You can use the Xajax Ajax framework to write server-side code that you can access from the browser. Xajax can write JavaScript code for you, allowing you to connect to server-side code using that JavaScript. All you have to do is to write the server-side function you want to call, and let Xajax connect that server-side function to JavaScript you can call in the browser. You can get Xajax free at `http://xajax.sf.net`. Xajax works only with the PHP programming language on the server.

To use Xajax, include the Xajax support file `xajax.inc.php`. This file contains the PHP code that makes Xajax work. Then you define your PHP function or functions that you want to be able to call from the browser. To do that, create a new `XajaxResponse` object, and use that to return your data to the browser. For example, to create an `XajaxResponse` object, you use this code in PHP: `$response = new XajaxResponse()`.

Then to store the result of adding two numbers together in the value property of a text field with the ID result, you execute code like this: `$response->addAssign ("result", "value", $operand1 + $operand2)`.

After creating the function to handle data on the server, you create a new `Xajax` object this way: `$xajax = new Xajax()`. Then you register the function you want to make available to JavaScript in the browser with the `Xajax` object's `registerFunction` method this way: `$xajax->registerFunction("add")`, where `add` is the function you want to make available to the JavaScript in the browser. Finally, you call the Xajax `processRequests` method this way: `$xajax->processRequests()`.

To create the JavaScript in the browser that connects to the `add` function, call `$xajax->printJavascript()`, and then you can reach the `add` function on the server by referring to it as `xajax_add` in JavaScript.

Install Xajax

① Navigate to `http://xajax.sf.net` and click Download Now.

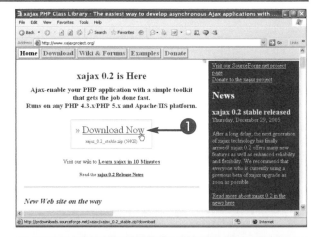

② Click the Download button for the mirror nearest you and download the Xajax ZIP file.

③ Unzip the ZIP file and place the contents in the directory on the server where you want to use Xajax.

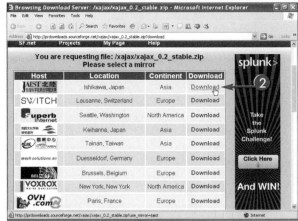

④ Navigate to the Xajax `multiply.add` example, which multiplies two numbers supplied by the user.

Two sample numbers have already been entered for in this example.

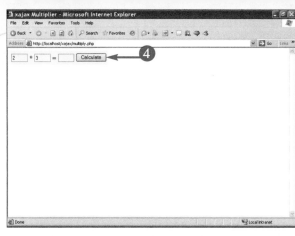

⑤ Click Calculate to see the result of multiplying the two numbers and confirm that Xajax is installed.

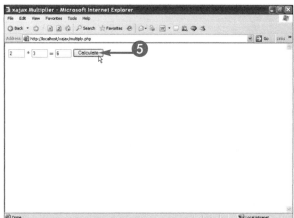

Extra

Xajax has some unique features among server-side Ajax frameworks. One of the most notable is that you can use it to pass multiple results back to the browser. Most server-side Ajax frameworks only allow you to pass back a single result to the browser — a single numeric value, for example. However, Xajax is different, because it allows you to configure an `XajaxResponse` object that permits you to send multiple responses to the browser. For example, if you want to display results in a dozen different controls in a Web page, you can use the `XajaxResponse` object's `addAssign` method to assign results to specific HTML controls. If you use that method a dozen times, you can assign different results to all 12 HTML controls in the Web page.

The Xajax framework also includes a method called getFormValues that is a useful one. This method gathers all the data from an HTML form and stores that data in preparation for sending it to the server all at once, saving you the effort of having to read each data item individually.

Write Server-Side Code with Xajax

You can write code that you want executed on the server and use the Xajax framework to execute that code by calling it from JavaScript inside the browser. To do that, start by writing the server-side code you want to execute.

In order to use Xajax, you must include the PHP support for Xajax in your PHP program, which you do like this: `require("xajax.inc.php")`. That gives you access to the PHP code already written for you in Xajax.

After including `xajax.inc.php` in your PHP program, you write the server-side function you want to execute. For example, to add two numbers, you might write a function named `add`, which you pass two numbers to. In Xajax, you write your server-side code to use an `XajaxResponse` object, which you create this way: `$response = new XajaxResponse()`. To assign data to HTML elements in the Web page, you can use the `XajaxResponse` object's `addAssign` method. For

example, to add two operands together and display the resulting sum in a text field with the ID result, you use this code: `$response->addAssign("result", "value", $operand1 + $operand2)` — the `"value"` part refers to the value property of the result text field. When you are done configuring the `XajaxResponse` object with the data you want to display in the browser, you return that object's internal data using its `getXML` method like this: `return $response->getXML()`.

After you set up the server-side function to handle your code, you create a new `Xajax` object like this: `$xajax = new Xajax()`, and register the function you want to call in the browser this way: `$xajax->registerFunction ("functionName")`. Finally, you call the `$xajax->processRequests()` method to complete the Xajax setup. In the Web page, you must also call the `$xajax->printJavascript()` function to print the JavaScript Xajax creates to that Web page.

Write Server-Side Code with Xajax

① Include `xajax.inc.php` in your PHP program.

② Add a server-side function named `add` that takes two numbers and returns their sum.

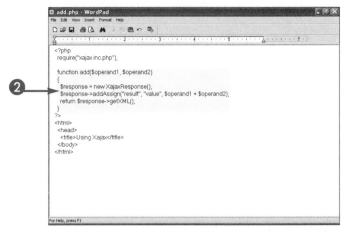

③ Create a new `Xajax` object, call it `registerFunction` to register the `add` function, and call the `Xajax` object's `processRequests` function.

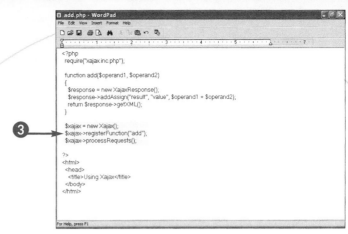

④ Add a call to the Xajax `printJavascript` method to print the JavaScript needed to connect to the `add` function on the server.

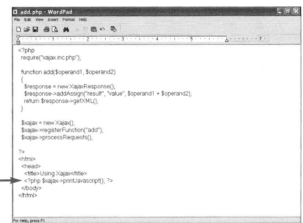

Apply It

The Xajax `XajaxResponse` object lets you bundle multiple results and send them back to the browser. For example, if you want to fill the text fields `result1` to `result4` with the sum, difference, product, and quotient of two numbers, you can use this code:

```
function add($operand1, $operand2)
{
    $response = new XajaxResponse();
    $response->addAssign("result1", "value", $operand1 + $operand2);
    $response->addAssign("result2", "value", $operand1 - $operand2);
    $response->addAssign("result3", "value", $operand1 * $operand2);
    $response->addAssign("result4", "value", $operand1 / $operand2);
    return $response->getXML();
}
```

This code accesses the value property of the text fields `result1` to `result4` and displays the various values in those text fields, saving you the effort of having to use four different functions to do the same thing.

Write Browser-Side Code with Xajax

You can use the Xajax Ajax framework to write browser-side code that connects to server-side code using Ajax techniques and call that server-side code without causing a server refresh.

Xajax lets you connect PHP code to your browser-side JavaScript code. First, set up your server-side PHP function in a Web page. You use an `XajaxResponse` object to store and return the data in the function you create. For example, if you add two numbers in a PHP function named `add`, you can set up that function in PHP like this: `function add($operand1, $operand2) { $response = new XajaxResponse(); $response->addAssign("result", "value", $operand1 + $operand2); return $response->getXML(); }`. In this function, you store your result in an `XajaxResponse` object and return that object's XML data using the `XajaxResponse` object's `getXML` method.

After creating a PHP function on the server like `add`, you create a new `Xajax` object, register the function you want to make available to your JavaScript, and call the `Xajax` object's `processRequests` method to start handling user data: `$xajax = new Xajax(); $xajax->register Function("add"); $xajax->processRequests();`.

To connect your browser's code to the server-side code, execute the PHP `<?php $xajax->printJavascript(); ?>` in your browser, which makes Xajax add the JavaScript needed to connect to the server in code. In the browser, you can access the `add` function on the server by calling that function as `xajax_add` instead of simply `add`. For example, to add the values in two variables, `operand1` and `operand2`, you could use this call in JavaScript: `xajax_add(operand1, operand2);`.

Because you have used this line in the PHP `add` function: `$response->addAssign("result", "value", $operand1 + $operand2)`, the sum of the two operands is assigned to the value property of the text field named result.

Write Browser-Side Code With Xajax

① Add two text fields so that the user can enter two numbers to add.

② Add a third text field in which to display the result of the addition.

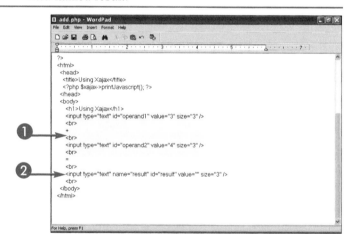

③ Add a button that calls a function named `calculate` that the user can call to add the two numbers entered.

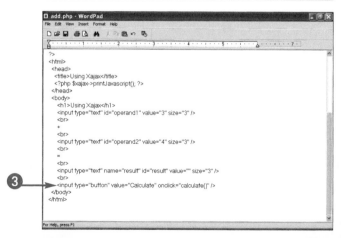

④ Add the `calculate` function to pass the two numbers the user has entered to the PHP version of the `add` function on the server.

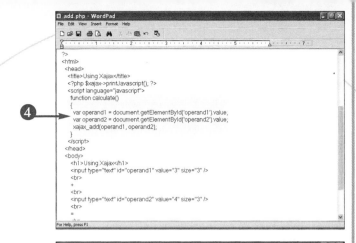

⑤ Open the page in a browser, enter two numbers to add, and click the button.

Your numbers are passed to the server-side `add` function, and the sum of those numbers appears in the Web page.

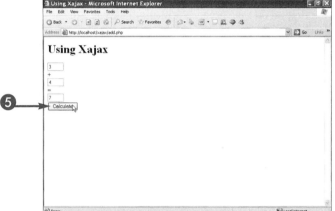

Apply It

If you have more than one PHP function you want to make available to your JavaScript, register each function separately:

```php
function add($operand1, $operand2)
{
  $response = new XajaxResponse();
  $response->addAssign("result", "value", $operand1 + $operand2);
  return $response->getXML();
}
function subtract($operand1, $operand2)
{
  $response = new XajaxResponse();
  $response->addAssign("result", "value", $operand1 - $operand2);
  return $response->getXML();
}
$xajax = new Xajax();
$xajax->registerFunction("add");
$xajax->registerFunction("subtract");
$xajax->processRequests();
```

Install LibAjax

You can use the LibAjax Ajax framework to connect to server-side code using Ajax techniques. Once you install LibAjax, you can write functions in PHP on the server and connect to and execute those functions from JavaScript. Being able to execute functions on the server and get access to the results without a page refresh in the browser is a very important capability in Ajax. Now you can contact the server-side code with your data, have that code execute on the server, and have the results returned to you.

Some code must be on the server, not in the browser. For example, code that checks a huge database may work fine on the server, where the database is, but does not work at all in JavaScript in the browser. Or you may want to check a password, but not download the whole password file to the browser, where it is accessible from your JavaScript. Here is how LibAjax works. Start with the server-side, PHP code. In that code, you include the

file `libajax.php` this way: `require("libajax.php")`, which makes the code in `libajax.php` accessible to you. Then you define the function you want to run on the server; for example, you may want to create a function named `add` to add two numbers, which looks like this in PHP: `function add($operand1, $operand2) { print $operand1 + $operand2; }`.

To make the `add` function available to your JavaScript code, you create a new `Ajax` object, set the `HTTP` method it should use to connect to the server, export the `add` function, and then call the `Ajax` objects' `client_request` method to initialize the `Ajax` object. Here is what that entire process looks like in PHP: `$ajax = new ajax(); $ajax->mode = "POST"; $ajax->export = array("add"); $ajax->client_request();`. Now you can pass data to the `add` function on the server like this: `ajax_add(operand1, operand2, display)`. In this case, the sum of the two operands is passed to the display function in your JavaScript.

Install LibAjax

Note: LibAjax does not work on IIS servers.

① Navigate to `http://sourceforge.net/projects/libajax` and click the Download button.

② Click the `libajax100.zip` link.

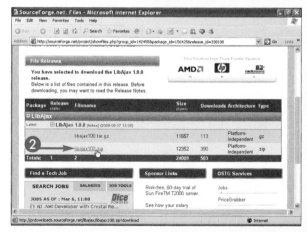

③ Select a download mirror close to you, and download `libajax100.zip`.

Unzip `libajax100.zip` and place `libajax.php` in the same directory as the Web page you plan to use it in.

④ Include `libajax.php` in your Web page.

LibAjax is now installed.

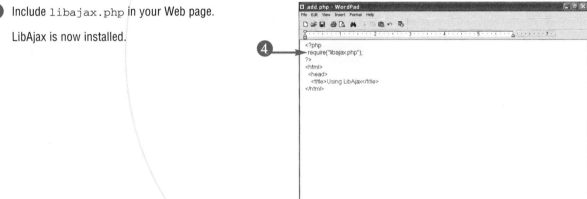

```php
<?php
require("libajax.php");
?>
<html>
 <head>
  <title>Using LibAjax</title>
</html>
```

Extra

LibAjax is an interesting framework. Unlike some other Ajax frameworks, you do not have to configure and work with specialized objects in your PHP code to return values. On the other hand, the LibAjax framework is a relatively simple one and comes without adequate documentation or sample programs. The number of options you have at your disposal to configure your code is very limited compared to other Ajax frameworks. On the other hand, when you get a LibAjax-based program working, it is easy to adapt and extend into other programs.

You can use either the HTTP GET or POST method with the LibAjax framework, but not other methods like HEAD. To set the HTTP method you want to use, you set the Ajax object's mode property. For example, you can create a new Ajax object in PHP like this: `$ajax = new ajax()`, and then you can set the HTTP method using the mode property of this object. To set the HTTP method to GET, use this code: `$ajax->mode = "GET"`. To set the method to POST<, use this code: `$ajax->mode = "POST"`.

Write Server-Side Code with LibAjax

You can write code you want executed on the server with the LibAjax framework. You place that code in the PHP file that creates the Web page that appears in the user's browser. Like other server-side Ajax frameworks, LibAjax lets you create the server-side code you want to execute in the same page as the rest of the Web page that the user sees. LibAjax adds the JavaScript to let you connect to the server-side code from JavaScript to the Web page.

To write the server-side code for your LibAjax-enabled Web application, you include the file libajax.php, which holds the PHP support for LibAjax, this way require("libajax.php"). Then you create a new Ajax object with this code: $ajax = new ajax(), and you are ready to use the LibAjax framework.

You create the PHP function you want to call from the browser. For example, if you want to add two numbers together, you might call the PHP function add like this: function add($operand1, $operand2) { print $operand1 + $operand2; }.

After you set up the PHP function you want to call from JavaScript, you configure the Ajax object, setting the HTTP method to use when you contact the server with the Ajax object's mode property, and the URL of the PHP page with the url property. You set the name of the PHP functions you want to make accessible in JavaScript with the export property like this: $ajax->export = array("add");. After configuring the Ajax object, you call this object's client_request method, which prepares the object for use.

Finally, you place this PHP in the Web page's <script> element, which makes LibAjax print the JavaScript it generates so that you can connect to your server-side function: <?php $ajax->output(); ?>.

Write Server-Side Code with LibAjax

1 Include libajax.php in your Web page to make the LibAjax code available.

2 Create a new Ajax object.

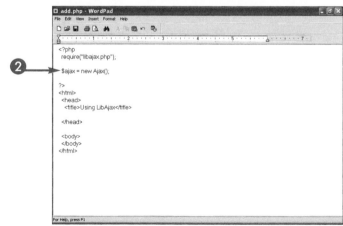

③ Add the PHP function you want to call from JavaScript.

④ Configure the `Ajax` object.

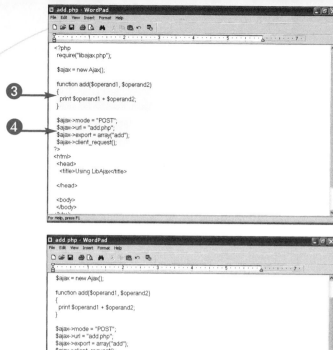

⑤ Make LibAjax create the JavaScript that allows you to call the PHP function on the server by including this line of PHP inside a `<script>` element: `<?php $ajax->output(); ?>`.

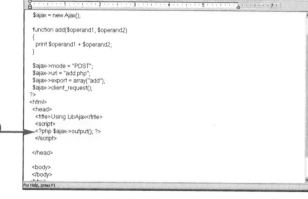

Apply It

You can export more than one function using LibAjax: Simply list all the exported functions in the export array. Here is example code showing how to do that:

```php
require("libajax.php");
$ajax = new Ajax();
function add($operand1, $operand2)
{
   print $operand1 + $operand2;
}

function subtract($operand1, $operand2)
{
   print $operand1 - $operand2;
}

$ajax->mode = "POST";
$ajax->url = "add.php";
$ajax->export = array("add", "subtract");
$ajax->client_request();
```

Write Browser-Side Code with LibAjax

You can write browser-side code that will connect to server-side code using the LibAjax framework. After writing your server-side code, you can make LibAjax write the JavaScript that will connect to your server-side code.

At this point, the LibAjax framework only supports PHP on the server. You can write your server-side function in PHP and let the LibAjax framework write the JavaScript that lets you call the server-side function in your Web page, using Ajax techniques. To write your server-side code, include `libajax.php` in your PHP, create a new `Ajax` object, and write the function you want to be able to call from the browser. For example, to add two numbers together, you could create a function named `add` this way in PHP: `function add($operand1, $operand2) { print $operand1 + $operand2; }`.

After creating the server-side function to call, you configure the `Ajax` object, assigning the `mode` property

the `HTTP` method to use with Ajax — `"GET"` or `"POST"`; the `url` property, the URL of the PHP page itself; and the `export` property, an array containing the name(s) of the function(s) to make available to your JavaScript. Finally, you call the `Ajax` object's `client_request` method and use the `Ajax` object's output method to write the JavaScript that lets you connect to the server-side code.

Now you can connect to your server-side PHP function, named `add`. To call that server-side function from your browser-side JavaScript code, you can call the `ajax_add` function. That is how LibAjax gives you access to your server-side functions — you prefix their names with `"ajax_"`. Here is the call: `ajax_add(operand1, operand2, display)`, which passes `operand1` and `operand2` to the PHP `add` function and passes the result to a JavaScript function named `display`. In the `display` function, you can display the sum of the two numbers in the Web page.

Write Browser-Side Code with LibAjax

① Add two text fields that let the user enter two numbers to add.

② Add a text field to display the results of adding the two numbers together.

③ Add a button that calls a function named `add` when the user wants to add the two numbers that are entered.

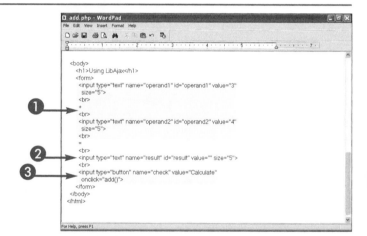

④ Create the `add` function, and pass the two numbers to add to the `add` function on the server, accessing that server-side function as `ajax_add`. Also pass the name of a callback function, `display`.

5 Create the `display` function, which is passed the results of adding the two operands, and display that result in the Web page.

6 Open the Web page, enter two numbers, and click the button.

LibAjax passes the two numbers to the server-side `add` function using Ajax and displays the result.

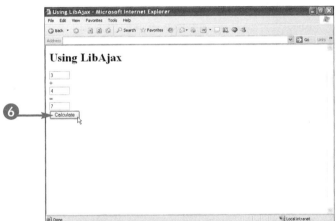

Apply It

This task only passes two parameters to the `add` function, but you can pass as many as you like. To do that, just declare the server-side function with all the parameters you need:

```php
<?php
    require("libajax.php");
    $ajax = new Ajax();
    function add($operand1, $operand2, operand3, operand4)
    {
        print $operand1 + $operand2 + $operand3 + $operand4;
    }
    $ajax->mode = "POST";
    $ajax->url = "add.php";
    $ajax->export = array("add");
    $ajax->client_request();
?>
```

Then call the `ajax_add` function, passing all the required parameters:

```
ajax_add(operand1, operand2, operand3, operand4, display);
```

Chat with Direct Web Remoting

Y ou can use Direct Web Remoting (DWR) with Java on the server instead of using PHP. DWR works much like a standard PHP-based Ajax framework, except that you connect to Java on the server, not PHP. You can get DWR free at `www.getahead.ltd.uk/dwr`. There is an introduction to DWR at `http://getahead.ltd.uk/dwr/`, and the DWR documentation appears at `http://getahead.ltd.uk/dwr/documentation`.

When you use DWR, you have access to the full power of Java. That kind of programming power is not available to you in the browser, which only supports JavaScript. With Java, you can handle thousands of tasks, such as using integrated database support, connecting to other servers, creating files on the fly, and much more.

To work with DWR, you need a Java-enabled Web server. Web-based applications on Java-enabled Web servers have a specific directory layout, and the installation of DWR follows that layout. To install DWR, you start by

downloading the dwr.jar file — a JAR file stands for Java Archive file — from `http://getahead.ltd.uk/dwr/download`. The `dwr.jar` file goes into the `WEB-INF/lib` directory of your Java Web application, which is the directory that commonly stores JAR files.

DWR is based on a Java servlet whose class is `uk.ltd.getahead.dwr.DWRServlet`, and that class is in `dwr.jar`. To install that servlet so that your Web server knows about it, you must edit `web.xml`, the standard configuration file for Java-enabled Web applications, as shown in the DWR documentation. You must also create a `dwr.xml` configuration file that goes into the Web application's `WEB-INF` directory where `web.xml` resides. After you install DWR, you can call its Java methods to create Ajax applications. To see what DWR has to offer, look online at `http://getahead.ltd.uk/dwr/examples/chat`.

Chat with Direct Web Remoting

① Navigate to `http://getahead.ltd.uk/dwr/examples/chat`.

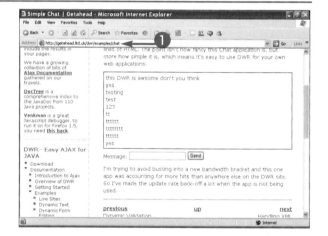

② Type **Hello world.** in the chat application's Message field.

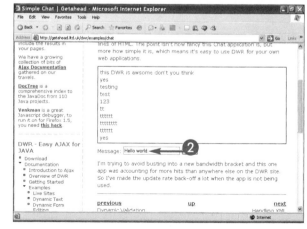

3 Click Send.

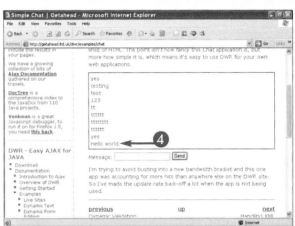

4 The text appears in the chat box, using Ajax techniques, which means the Web page is not refreshed.

Extra

One of the most popular of the Java-based servers is Apache Tomcat, which you can get free at http://jakarta.apache.org/tomcat. You can install Tomcat on your own computer and test your Ajax Web applications instantly. Installation is easy on Windows machines: Just download Tomcat and double-click it to start the installation. Many Web servers already have Tomcat installed, and they are ready to use. All you have to do is to upload the DWR files, such as dwr.jar, to the correct directory in your Web application. Tomcat is a particularly good choice, because it is the standard Web server for online Java applications. Sun Microsystems, the creator of Java, often uses Tomcat to test its Java servlet and JavaServer Pages (JSP) frameworks.

DWR also comes in a WAR, or Web archives file, version. Instead of having to copy dwr.jar to WEB-INF/lib, modify web.xml, and create dwr.xml, you can simply place dwr.war in your Java-based Web server's webapps directory, restart the server, and dwr.war expands into a full, working DWR installation.

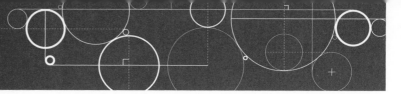

Edit an Interactive Table with DWR

ou can use the Direct Web Remoting (DWR) Ajax framework for creating instant-update HTML tables. DWR comes with many utility functions built in, and that includes support for updating HTML tables interactively. The data the user enters is sent to the server and back to the Web page, all behind the scenes. In fact, you can even save that data using cookies.

One of the DWR example programs displays a Web page with an HTML table that the user can edit interactively, using Ajax. Much of the support for this application comes from the DWR Java library of methods, such as the `Util.setValues` and `Util.getValues` methods, which let you read values from HTML controls, and set those values as well.

Here is how this example works in code. This example displays a table and a set of text fields that the user can

use to edit data. When the user clicks Edit next to a row in the table, the code uses DWR to copy the data in the table row and display that data in the editing text fields. Behind the scenes, each text field has the same ID as a corresponding property name in a JavaBean, and that JavaBean is populated with the data from the text fields in the Web page. The bean can be used to pass data around the Web application online, much as beans are used in the popular Java Struts framework. You can access data from the Web page simply by reading the corresponding property values in the bean on the server.

To populate the server-side bean with data, just use the DWR `Util.getValues` method; to store data in the text fields in the Web page, use the DWR `Util.setValues` method. In that way, you can pass data around the application, and handle any changes made by the user.

Edit an Interactive Table with DWR

① Navigate to `http://getahead.ltd.uk/dwr/examples/table`.

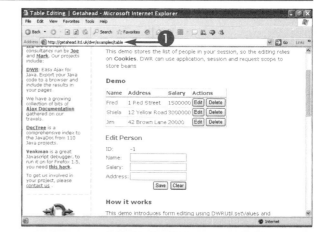

② Click the Edit button next to the top row in the table.

③ Change the person's salary.

④ Click Save.

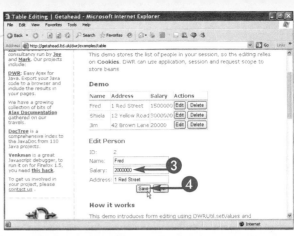

⑤ The new salary appears in the table.

Extra

DWR is a useful Ajax framework that is worth checking out if you use Java online. The DWR framework is especially useful if your Java applications are built using servlets and JSP pages, as the standard Model/View/Controller online Java applications are. DWR is also useful when developing Apache Struts applications — because DWR passes data around using JavaBeans, DWR fits right in with Struts, which does the same thing. It takes some work to install DWR, but it has proven itself a reliable framework and is in fairly widespread use now. Besides simply letting you connect to your server-side Java code, DWR also supplies a large library of Ajax-enabled methods.

DWR also comes with a JavaScript library of functions that let you display data and write interactive Web pages using dynamic HTML. That can be particularly useful when you want to perform manipulations in your Web page, as when you want to update controls or text in those Web pages.

Handling E-Mail with Echo2

You can use the Echo2 framework to create Ajax applications. Echo2 is an online Java framework with a great deal of support for Web application creation built in. And it has recently been upgraded to provide Ajax support.

Echo2 is a professional-level application framework that lets you develop in Java online. Because Echo2 has long been designed to create applications that look and feel as though they are working on the user's desktop computer, it is natural that Ajax support appears in Echo2. Version 2 has made large-scale improvements in performance and in the capabilities of Echo.

In fact, when you use Echo2, you do not need to know anything about HTML, HTTP, or even JavaScript. Echo2 handles the details behind the scenes for you. You can host Echo2 applications on any server that supports Java servlets.

There is an online demo program that shows some of what Echo2 is capable of in Ajax terms at `http://demo.nextapp.com/Email/app`. That demo is an online e-mail program that lets you browse through fictitious e-mail messages online. When you click an e-mail message's header, that e-mail appears in another part of the window, using Ajax techniques. Because the application uses Ajax, the e-mail's body appears without a page refresh, just as it would in a standard e-mail program. But this e-mail program works in your browser.

Other browser e-mail applications can also display e-mail in a browser, but when you want to display the text of individual messages, the browser refreshes the entire page. That does not happen in the Echo2 Ajax-enabled e-mail application. And the good part is that using Echo2, you do not have to write the code that creates the application in the browser — Echo2 can handle the details for you.

Handling E-mail with Echo2

 ① Navigate to `http://demo.nextapp.com/Email/app`.

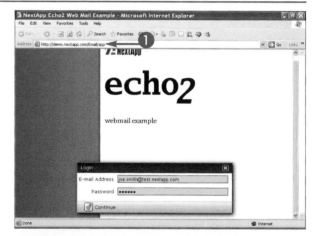

② Click Continue.

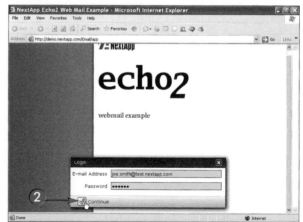

③ Click an e-mail message.

The message's text appears at the bottom of the window without a browser refresh.

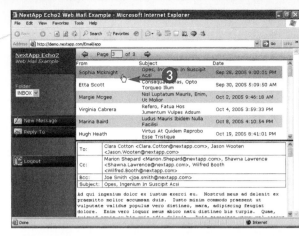

④ Click another e-mail message.

That new message's text appears at the bottom of the window, also without a browser refresh.

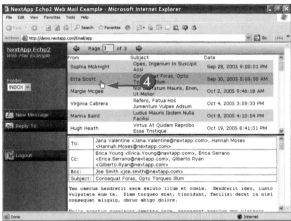

Extra

You can download the Echo2 framework at
www.nextapp.com/platform/echo2/echo/
download/. Echo2 is distributed using the
Mozilla public license, which you can find at www.
nextapp.com/products/mpl_license.html,
and which gives you largely free use of this
framework. Echo2 is not a typical Ajax framework
of a few files — it is an extensive package, including
969 files inside the ZIP file currently. You do not
need to invest a lot of time creating individual
Web pages with Echo2 — Echo2 does all that for
you automatically. You can learn how to write
Echo2 applications by studying the three example
applications that come with this framework,
including the source code for all example
applications. The example applications include a
simple "Hello world" application, the e-mail
application, and a chat application.

The Echo2 distribution also comes with a number
of WAR — Web archive — files that you can use
for easy installation of this framework. All you have
to do is place the WAR files in your Java server's
webapps directory, and they are expanded and
installed automatically.

Support Auto-complete with the Ajax Tag Library

You can use the Ajax tag library to create Ajax applications on a Java-enabled Web server. The Ajax tag library uses JavaServer Page (JSP) tags in your application to understand what you want to do. The JSP tags insert the code needed to make what you want to have happen actually happen in your Web page. You can get the Ajax Tag Library at `http://ajaxtags.sourceforge.net` free. There are a number of built-in JSP tags in the Ajax tag library that support many of the standard tasks that Ajax applications perform.

For example, there is an autocomplete JSP tag that lets you support auto-completion of text in a text field — you just provide a list of possible completion items, and the Ajax tag library takes it from there, showing auto-completion candidate terms when the user enters a partial term in a text field.

There is a callout tag that lets you display a pop-up, tooltip-like balloon for a particular item in a Web page. For example, when the user moves the mouse over that element, you can display help information for that item.

There is a Select Ajax library tag that lets you create an HTML `<select>` control. This tag sets the contents of the `<select>` control based on the user's selection in another `<select>` control.

The Ajax tag library supports a Toggle JSP tag that lets you switch images between two different image sources without a browser refresh. Switching images without a browser refresh is a common Ajax technique.

The Ajax tag library Update lets you update the text in a specific text field, depending on what data the user enters in another text field.

Support Autocomplete With the Ajax Tag Library

① Navigate to `http://ajaxtags.no-ip.info/` and click the Run link for the Auto-Complete example.

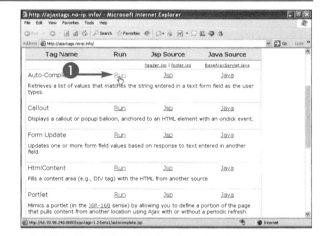

② Type the letter **A** in the Name text field.

The application suggests a car name using Ajax.

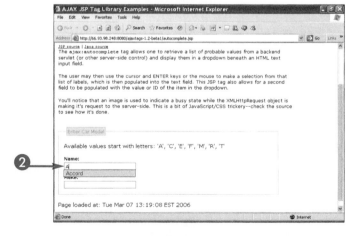

3 Select the Accord entry.

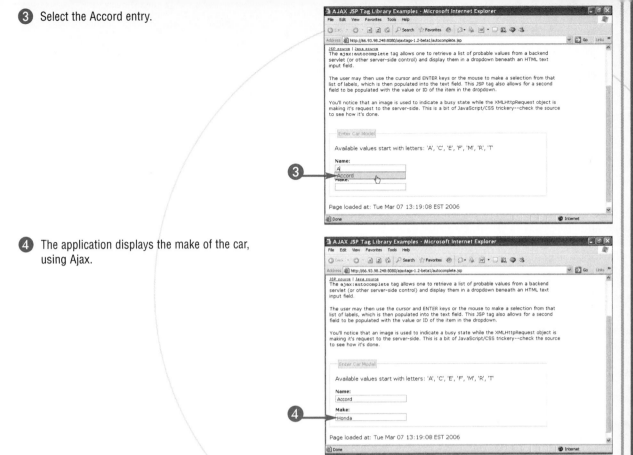

4 The application displays the make of the car, using Ajax.

Extra

Another good example showing what the Ajax tag library can do is the Callout example at http://66.93.98.248:8080/ajaxtags-1.2-beta1/callout.jsp. In this example, the user can move the mouse over several hyperlinks. When the mouse is over a hyperlink, a titled window appears at the location of the mouse containing a black title bar with a close link, header text, and some explanatory text for the hyperlink. Using pop-up windows like this can be a great help in a Web application because it can give your users more information about the elements in your Web page easily, without having to cause a screen refresh. The text and data in the pop-ups are fetched from the server using Ajax techniques.

There is another good Ajax tag library demonstration at http://66.93.98.248:8080/ajaxtags-1.2-beta1/formupdate.jsp, which shows how to update data in a text field, depending on the data in another text field. In this case, you enter a speed in miles per hour in one text field, click Calculate, and the same speed is displayed in kilometers per hour in another text field.

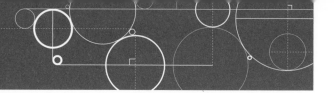

Update HTML Elements with Ajax Tag Library

You can use the Ajax tag library to use Ajax to update HTML controls in a Web page. This is a normal task to perform using Ajax, but using the Ajax tag library makes writing the code easier by using a number of JavaServer Page (JSP) tags to write your code with and then handle any additional programming on the server in Java.

You can use the Ajax JSP tag `<ajax:htmlContent>` to download and store data in HTML elements like `<div>` elements, using Ajax. For example, you have a `<div>` element with the ID `targtDiv` like this: `<div id="targetDiv"> </div>`. You can connect that `<div>` element to your Ajax code using the `<ajax: htmlContent>` tag.

For example, you have an HTML `<select>` control that displays a number of options in a drop-down list, using this HTML: `<select id="select1" name="select1"> <option value="">Select a fruit</option> <option value="apples">Apples</option> <option value="oranges">Oranges</option> <option value="bananas">Bananas</option></select>`.

This `<select>` control displays the choices Apples, Oranges, and Bananas. When the user selects an item, you can display information about that type of fruit in the `targetDiv` `<div>` element.

When the user chooses a fruit in the `<select>` element, a change event occurs in that element, and you can handle that event with an Ajax tag library `<ajax:htmlContent>` tag. You start by giving this tag an `eventType` attribute, which indicates what kind of HTML event you want to handle — that is a change event in this case, so you set `eventType="change"`. You use the source attribute to indicate the HTML control that causes the event you are interested in, like this: `source="select1"`. The target attribute specifies the HTML element that will display the results, so you set `target="targetDiv"`. The parameters attribute specifies the data to send to the server, which might look like this: `parameters="fruit={select1}"`. Finally, you specify the code you want the data from the `<select>` control sent to on the server, which might look something like this: `baseUrl="${contextPath}/htmlcontent.view"`.

Update HTML Elements with Ajax Tag Library

① Navigate to `http://66.93.98.248:8080/ ajaxtags-1.2-beta1/htmlcontent.jsp`.

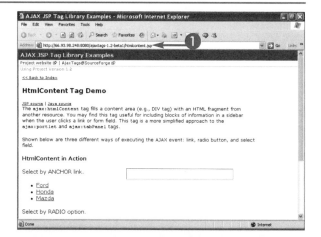

② Click the Ford link.

Using Ajax, the application updates the `<div>` element with information.

3 Select the Honda radio button.

The application updates the `<div>` element using Ajax.

4 Select the Mazda list item.

The application updates the `<div>` element using Ajax.

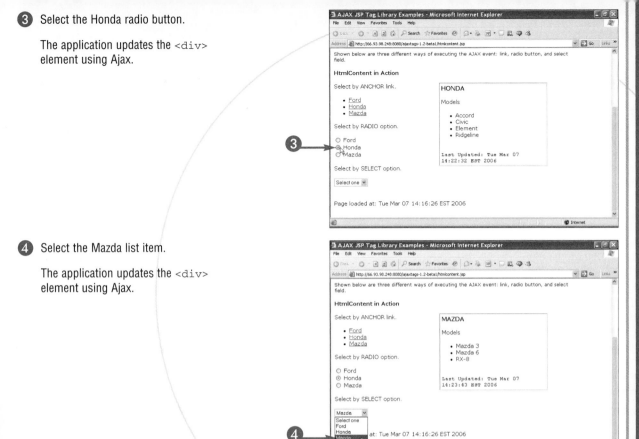

Apply It

The Java code on the server extends the `BaseAjaxServlet` class. All you have to do is to return the HTML you want displayed in the target `<div>` element. Here is what some sample Java looks like to return data from the server:

```java
public class FruitHandler extends BaseAjaxServlet {
  public String getXmlContent(HttpServletRequest request,
    HttpServletResponse response)
      throws Exception {
    String fruit = request.getParameter("fruit");

    StringBuffer html = new StringBuffer();
    html.append("You selected ");

    html.append(fruit);
    return html.toString();
  }
}
```

Create an XML Document

You can create XML documents if you know the rules. You can create your own tags in XML documents, because you do not have to use a predefined set of tags, as in HTML. There is a set of rules for creating XML documents, however, and you can find the full set of rules in the XML specification at www.w3.org/TR/REC-xml/.

To create an XML document, you must begin with the XML declaration, which must specify the version of XML you are using — currently, only versions 1.0 and 1.1 are allowed. Here is an XML declaration: `<?xml version="1.0"?>`. Note that the XML declaration is not an XML element.

XML documents must also contain a document element, which is an element that contains all other elements in the document. For example, if your document element is `<products>`, that might look like this in an XML document: `<?xml version="1.0"?> <products>...</products>`.

Each XML element has an opening tag, like `<products>`, and a closing tag, like `</products>`, unless the element is an empty XML element, which means there is only one tag. You end an empty XML element with the markup `/>` like this: `<actor />`. Note also that there are some rules on what tag names are legal: You cannot start a tag name with a number, and they cannot contain spaces and cannot contain a few other characters such as quotation marks.

As in HTML, you can also use attributes in opening tags or empty element tags like this: `<products date="Tuesday">`. All values you assign to attributes must be quoted. As in HTML, XML elements may also contain text, such as `<?xml version="1.0"?> <products>printer</products>`. And XML elements may be nested, one inside the other, like this: `<?xml version="1.0"?> <products><product>printer</product></products>`.

Create an XML Document

① Create a document named employees.xml, add the XML declaration and a document element named `<corporation>` to your XML document.

② Nest a `<human_resources>` element inside the document element, and an `<employees>` element inside the `<human_resources>` element.

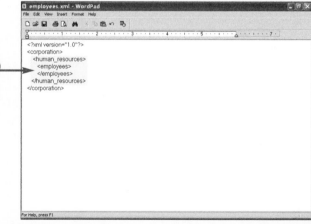

3 Add three `<employee>` elements, each of which contains a `<first_name>` and `<last_name>` element.

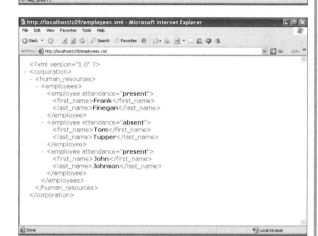

4 Open the XML document in Internet Explorer.

The XML document appears in the browser.

Extra

Note the minus (–) icons at left in Internet Explorer. You can click those icons in the browser to collapse XML elements, hiding all the elements nested inside them. That makes it much easier to deal with larger XML documents — just collapse the elements you do not need to see. When an element is collapsed, you see a plus (+) icon next to it, and if you click that icon, the element expands. A minus icon means that an element is already expanded, and a plus icon indicates that an element can be expanded. Knowing how to use those icons gives you a fruitful way of dealing with XML inside Internet Explorer.

Internet Explorer also gives you a simple way to test your XML documents — if Internet Explorer cannot read an XML document, it tells you what is wrong with it. In technical terms, if Internet Explorer cannot read your XML document, that document is not considered well formed. See the section "Write Well-Formed XML" for more details.

Write Well-Formed XML

You can create *well-formed* XML documents if you follow a few rules. Being well formed means that your XML document can be read by an XML parser. The XML data you pass to Ajax applications must be well formed, and it is worth learning the basic rules for well formedness in XML.

Besides being well formed, XML documents can also be *valid*, which means that they specify the syntax rules that their contents must obey — for example, that a <human_resources> element must be nested inside a <corporation> element, or that an <employee> element must have an attendance attribute, and so on. You can see more about creating valid XML documents in the section "Create a Valid XML Document."

There are many rules for creating well-formed XML documents in detail, and you can see them all at www.w3.org/TR/REC-xml/. However, the main rules are easily explained. To be well formed, an XML document must start

with an XML declaration, such as <?xml version="1.0" ?>. Such a declaration is required for all XML documents.

A well-formed XML document must also have a document element that contains all the other elements in the document. The document element is the first element in an XML document. Its opening tag is the first element tag in the document, and its closing tag is the last element tag in the document. For example, if your document element is <corporation>, that might look like this in an XML document: <?xml version="1.0"?> <corporation>...</corporation>.

All elements in a well-formed XML document must be properly nested. For example, this XML is not nested correctly: <corporation> <human_resources> </corporation> </human_resources>, because the closing </corporation> tag appears before the closing </human_resources> tag. Here is the correctly nested version: <corporation> <human_resources> </human_resources> </corporation>. In fact, the term "well formed" originally meant "properly nested."

Write Well-Formed XML

① Create an XML document that has a nesting error by closing an enclosing XML element too soon.

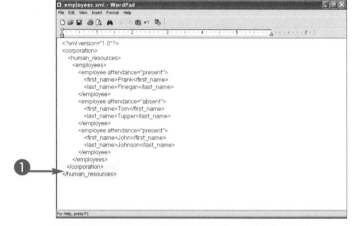

② Try to open the XML document in Internet Explorer. Internet Explorer indicates it cannot read the document because of a problem.

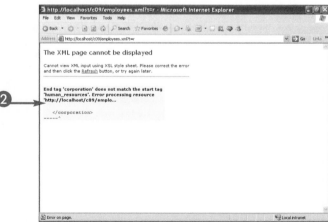

3 Fix the nesting error.

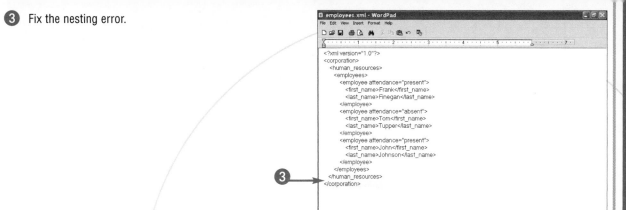

4 Open the document in Internet Explorer.

Internet Explorer opens the document successfully.

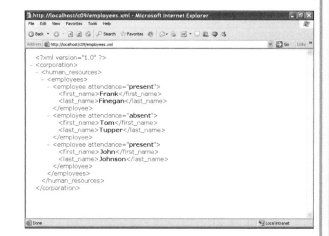

Extra

Internet Explorer is surprisingly helpful in telling you what the problem is if an XML document is not well formed. Internet Explorer error messages for JavaScript are nearly always useless, such as simply "Object expected", which tells you that Internet Explorer could not run the code — that is why it is good to have Firefox when you are debugging your Ajax applications, because the JavaScript error message in the JavaScript console is very helpful. However, Internet Explorer does give good error descriptions when XML is not well formed, as seen in this task: "End tag 'corporation' does not match the start tag 'human_resources'. Error processing resource 'http://localhost/c09/emplo...'". In this error message, Internet Explorer says that it found a `</corporation>` tag when it was expecting a `</human_resources>` tag, which is a classic well-formedness error. When you fix a well-formedness error and want to view an XML document again in Internet Explorer, just click the Refresh button.

Handle XML in JavaScript

You can use JavaScript to work with XML in Ajax applications. In JavaScript, XML is treated as a collection of nodes, and JavaScript can handle XML as nodes using special built-in properties and methods.

Being able to handle XML in JavaScript is crucial to Ajax applications. Ajax applications download XML from the server and process it in the browser. You then use JavaScript to process the XML.

JavaScript is an excellent tool for this purpose, because it enables you to handle your XML using programming. When it is downloaded, your XML may have elements nested among other elements, text mixed in with those elements, and information stored in attributes as well — all of which must be extracted if you are going to use the data in your XML. In addition, learning how to handle XML in your Ajax-enabled Web pages with JavaScript enables you to extract that data.

JavaScript handles XML as a collection of nodes. You can operate on each node independently, extracting the data it contains, as well as navigating to the next node in the sequence.

For example, look at this simple XML document: `<?xml version="1.0" ?> <document> <greeting>No worries.</greeting> </document>`. The document element is `<document>`, and it has one subnode, the `<greeting>` element. The `<greeting>` element, in turn, has a subnode — the text node containing the text `"No worries."`.

Handling Child Nodes

The `childNodes` property holds an array of the child nodes of the current node. You usually use this property with element nodes. For example, if you had an element named `<a>` that contained other elements as children, such as `<a><b></b><c></c></a>`, then the `childNodes` property of the `<a>` element would contain an array with the `<b>` and `<c>` elements in it.

The `firstChild` property gives you the first child node of the current node. This property is often used to extract the text node inside an element node. For example, if you store an element node in a variable named `elementNode`, and want to extract the text in that element, you can use the expression `elementNode.firstChild.nodeValue`. Here, you are extracting the text node inside the element node, and then getting the text itself.

The `lastChild` property gives you the last child node of the current node. For example, if you had an element named `<a>` that contained other elements as children, such as `<a><b></b><c></c></a>`, then the `lastChild` property of the `<a>` element node gives you the `<c>` element node.

Handling Sibling Nodes

The `nextSibling` property of a node gives you a node corresponding to the next sibling of the current node. For example, if you have three elements in a row, `<a></a><b></b><c></c>`, and you have a node object corresponding to the `<a>` element, then the `nextSibling` property of that object would contain the `<b>` element node.

The `previousSibling` property contains the previous sibling node. If you have three elements in a row, `<a></a><b></b><c></c>`, then the previous sibling of the `<c>` element is the `<b>` element, and the previous sibling of the `<b>` element is the `<a>` element.

Note that siblings are on the same level in the document. For example, in the XML `<a><b></b><c></c></a><d></d>`, the `<b>` and `<c>` elements are child elements of the `<a>` element, not sibling elements of the `<a>` element. So the next sibling of the `<a>` element here is the `<d>` element. Also, the `<b>` and `<c>` elements are siblings here, because they are on the same level.

XML as a Tree of Nodes

You can think of an XML document like this one as a tree of nodes. The top node is the document node, which is the very beginning of the document, even before the document element. After the document node can come processing instruction nodes, which are not covered in this book, and then the document element node, which contains the document element.

After the document element node comes the element nodes in the document. Element nodes themselves may be nested as well, one within another — a parent node can contain child nodes in this way. In programming terms, therefore, you can think of XML documents as trees of nodes, and for each type of node, you have a node object in JavaScript.

Types of Nodes

There are various types of nodes, such as element nodes, text nodes, attribute nodes, and so on, and JavaScript can handle them all. JavaScript has built-in properties you can use to work with the nodes in XML document objects, such as the objects that are contained in the `XMLHttpRequest` object's `responseXML` property.

For example, the `documentElement` property of the XML document object you get in the `XMLHttpRequest` object's `responseXML` property gives you the element node corresponding to the XML data's document element. This is where you typically start when working with an XML document object: with the documentElement property, which gives you the document element — as an element node object — for the XML data that is retrieved from the server.

Using the nodeType and nodeValue Properties

The `nodeType` property of any node object in JavaScript gives you the type of the node. The values in the `nodeType` property are numbers, and they correspond to the different types of nodes. Here are the possible values — note that some only make sense if you have used XML in depth before: 1 stands for an element node; 2 stands for an attribute node; 3 stands for a text node, which contains simple text, such as the text you would find inside an element; 4 stands for an XML CDATA section, which contains text data that is not supposed to be treated as XML; 5 stands for an XML entity reference; 6 stands for an XML entity node; 7 stands for an XML processing instruction; 8 stands for an XML comment, which is just like an XML comment, starting with `<!--` and ending with `-->`; 9 stands for an XML document node, corresponding to the very beginning of the document; 10 stands for an XML Document Type Definition, a DTD; 11 stands for an XML document fragment; and 12 stands for an XML Notation.

The `nodeValue` property of a node in JavaScript holds the value of the node. For example, the value of a text node is the text in the node, so if the variable `textNode` contains a text node, then `textNode.nodeValue` contains the text inside that text node. That is the usual way that you retrieve the text from a text node — using the `nodeValue` property.

The name property contains the name of the node. For example, if you have an element node in a variable named `elementNode`, and that element node corresponds to an element named `<corporation>`, then the expression `elementNode.name` gives you the name of the element, `"corporation"`. Using the name property gives you a way of navigating through an XML document and determining which element you are currently dealing with.

Getting XML Attributes

You use the attributes property in JavaScript to get an array of the attributes contained in a particular node. Because only elements can contain attributes, only element nodes support the attributes property.

Get the XML Document Element from Downloaded XML

You can extract an object corresponding to the document element of XML data that you download from the server using Ajax techniques. It is important to know how to handle the XML you download from the server using Ajax. Because that XML data is in XML document object form, you can handle that XML simply by using the JavaScript `documentElement` property.

Ajax relies on downloading XML from the server, and you have to work with that XML in JavaScript. Programmers often expect the downloaded XML from the server will be available in text form. However, when you want to download text, use the `XMLHttpRequest` object's `responseText` property. When the data you download is in XML form, you use the `XMLHttpRequest` object's `responseXml` property instead.

The data in the `XMLHttpRequest` object's `responseXml` property is stored in a JavaScript XML document object. This object represents an XML document, and you use

JavaScript properties and methods to work with it. In particular, you usually start by using the JavaScript `documentElement` property of this object to get an object that contains the XML data's document element. And the document element contains all the other XML elements in the downloaded data.

Once you have the document object, you can use the other JavaScript properties of the document element to navigate through your XML data. For example, if the XML document you downloaded is `<>xml version = "1.0"><data>No worries.</data>`, then you can extract the text from the text node in this document this way in JavaScript: `XML HttpRequestObject.responseXml.documentElement. firstChild.nodeValue`. In other words, you get a JavaScript object corresponding to the document element, then get the text node inside that element with the `firstChild` property, then extract the text from the text node with the `nodeValue` property.

Get the XML Document Element from Downloaded XML

① Store the XML data downloaded from the server in a variable named `xmlDocument`.

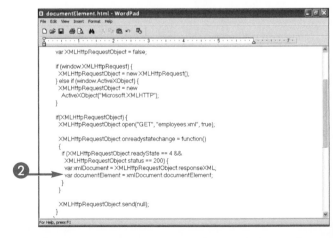

② Get the document element of the downloaded XML data with the `documentElement` property, and store the document element in a variable named `document Element`.

The document element contains all the other elements in the XML data.

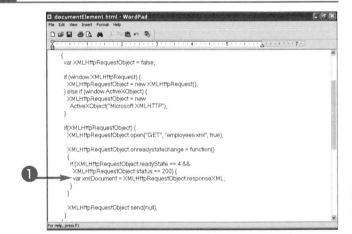

③ Notify the user that you got the document element.

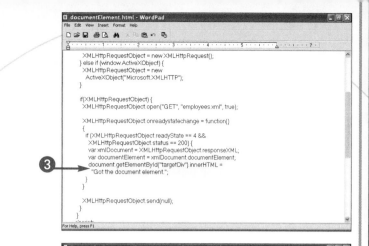

④ Open the Web page in a browser and click the button to download the XML data.

The message "Got the document element" appears.

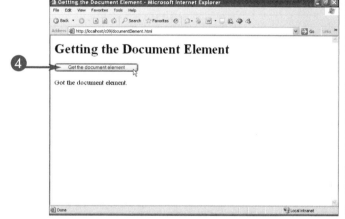

Extra

If you want to take a good look at the XML data that is stored in the XMLHttpRequest object's responseXML property, you actually can convert that XML into simple text to display it. To see the downloaded XML as text, you simply use the xml property. For example, to display the XML in an XMLHttpRequest object in an alert box, use this JavaScript code: alert(XMLHttpRequest Object.responseXML.xml). If you have trouble navigating around inside your XML data using JavaScript properties and methods, it can be a good idea to look at the XML data in readable form, not as an object. And using the XML document object's xml property, you can see the XML data you downloaded in simple text form. When you are debugging an Ajax application, being able to see the XML you are working with directly can be invaluable.

You do not need to use the document element to work with a JavaScript document object. You can use other methods on that object, such as the JavaScript getElementsByTagName method, to fetch the XML elements you want from the XML data, bypassing the document element.

Navigate XML Using firstChild and lastChild

You can use JavaScript properties like `firstChild` and `lastChild` to navigate through an XML document's data. After you download your XML data, you can read that data from the `XMLHttpRequest` object's `responseXML` property. That property holds a JavaScript XML document object, and you can navigate through the items in that object using JavaScript methods and properties.

You usually start by getting the document element for the XML data you have downloaded. When you have the document element, you have access to all the elements in the XML document, because the document element contains all the other elements. Once you have the document element, you can navigate through the document easily, using the available JavaScript properties.

The `firstChild` property lets you recover the first child of the current node. For example, if you had the XML `<a><b></b><c></c></a>`, the first child of the `<a>`

element is the `<b>` element, so if you store the `<a>` element as a node object in a JavaScript variable named element, then the JavaScript expression element.firstChild gives you a node object containing the `<b>` element.

The `lastChild` property gives you access to the last child of the current node. For example, if you use the same XML, `<a><b></b><c></c></a>`, the last child of the `<a>` element is the `<c>` element. So, for example, if you store a node object corresponding to the `<a>` element in a variable named element, then the expression `element.lastChild` gives a node object corresponding to the element `<c>`. As you can see, the `firstChild` and `lastChild` properties are very useful for navigating around inside your downloaded XML data in JavaScript.

To get the document element for XML data downloaded from the server, see the section "Get the XML Document Element from Downloaded XML."

Navigate XML Using firstChild and lastChild

① Examine the XML document you want to extract data from.

In this case, you can extract the first name of the third employee using JavaScript after downloading this XML data using Ajax.

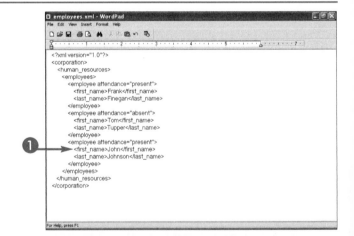

② Get the document element of the downloaded data.

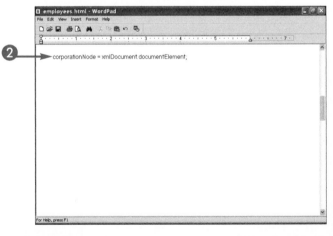

③ Navigate to the `<employee>` node containing the third employee's data.

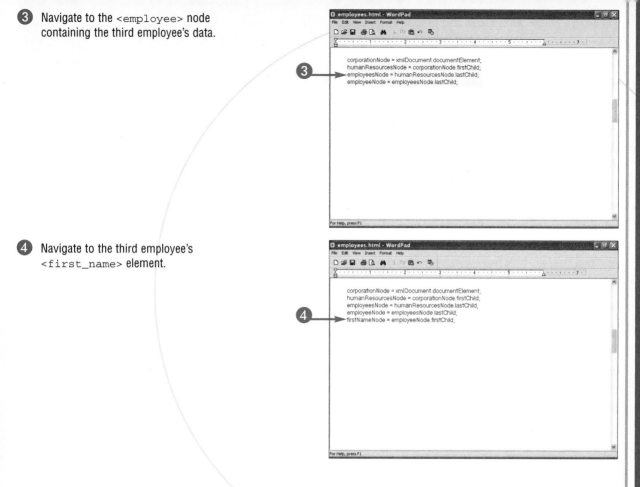

```
corporationNode = xmlDocument.documentElement;
humanResourcesNode = corporationNode.firstChild;
employeesNode = humanResourcesNode.lastChild;
employeeNode = employeesNode.lastChild;
```

④ Navigate to the third employee's `<first_name>` element.

```
corporationNode = xmlDocument.documentElement;
humanResourcesNode = corporationNode.firstChild;
employeesNode = humanResourcesNode.lastChild;
employeeNode = employeesNode.lastChild;
firstNameNode = employeeNode.firstChild;
```

Extra

After reaching the third employee's `<first_name>` element, you can extract the name from that element, which is `<first_name>John</first_name>`. Remember that the text in an XML element is stored in a text node as far as JavaScript is concerned. If you have stored the `<first_name>` element in a JavaScript object named firstNameNode, you can extract the text node that contains the employee's name this way: firstNameNode.firstChild. In other words, the text node contained inside the `<first_name>` element is the first child of that element. When JavaScript programmers work with XML data, it is a common mistake to forget that the text inside XML elements is actually stored in text nodes.

After you recover the text node holding the text inside the third employee's `<employee>` element, you can read the actual text in the text node with the nodeValue property. In JavaScript, you use this expression to do that: firstNameNode.first Child.nodeValue, assuming that you have stored the `<employee>` element in the variable named firstNameNode.

Navigate XML Using nextSibling and previousSibling

You can navigate through XML document objects using JavaScript properties like nextSibling and previousSibling. After you download XML data using Ajax techniques, you get an XML document object in the XMLHttpRequest object's responseXML property, and you can use JavaScript to work with that XML data. The usual first step is to extract the XML data's document element, which contains all the other elements in the XML data. When you have the document element, you can move throughout the XML data easily using the JavaScript properties of the nodes in the data.

You can use the firstChild property to move to the first child node of the current node. That is useful when you want to move from the document element, which contains all other elements, to the children of that element. It is also useful when you want to extract the text in an element, because that text is stored in a text node, which is the first child contained in the element.

You can also use the lastChild property to move to the last child of the current node.

Properties like firstChild and lastChild let you navigate through your XML data by moving down successive levels as you target the data you want. For example, if you have the XML <a> <b></b> <c></c> <d></d> </a>, and you start with a node corresponding to the <a> element, that node's firstChild property contains a node object corresponding to the <c> element, and the lastChild property contains a node object corresponding to the <d> element.

However, if you want to access the <c> element, you have to navigate among the <b>, <c>, and <d> elements, all of which are siblings. For example, if you start at the <a> element and want to get the <c> element, you could use firstChild.nextSibling or lastChild.previousSibling.

Navigate XML Using nextSibling and previousSibling

① Select the XML element you want to navigate to using JavaScript.

In this case, target the <last_name> element of the third employee.

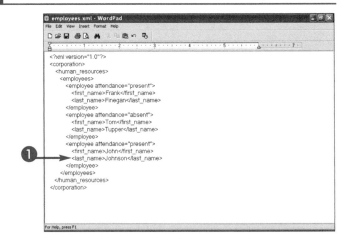

② To reach the <first_name> element of the third employee, you can use the firstChild and lastChild properties.

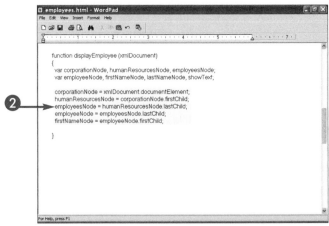

③ Navigate to the `<last_name>` element using the `nextSibling` property, and inform the user that you reached that element.

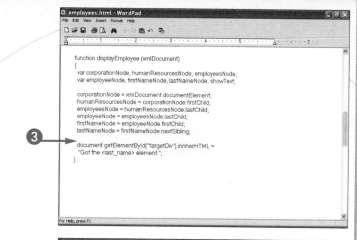

```
function displayEmployee (xmlDocument)
{
  var corporationNode, humanResourcesNode, employeesNode;
  var employeeNode, firstNameNode, lastNameNode, showText;

  corporationNode = xmlDocument.documentElement;
  humanResourcesNode = corporationNode.firstChild;
  employeesNode = humanResourcesNode.lastChild;
  employeeNode = employeesNode.lastChild;
  firstNameNode = employeeNode.firstChild;
  lastNameNode = firstNameNode.nextSibling;

  document.getElementById("targetDiv").innherHTML =
  "Got the <last_name> element.";
}
```

④ Open the Web page in a browser, and click the button.

The message "Got the <last_name> element" appears.

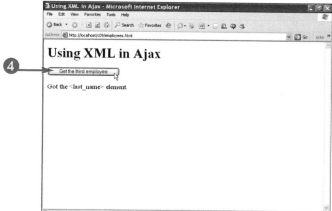

Using XML in Ajax

Get the third employee

Got the <last_name> element.

Apply It

This example uses the `nextSibling` property to navigate, but say that you had been at the `<last_name>` element and wanted to get back to the `<first_name>` element instead:

```
<employee attendance="present">
    <first_name>John</first_name>
    <last_name>Johnson</last_name>
</employee>
```

In that case, you can use the `previousSibling` property instead, this way:

```
corporationNode = xmlDocument.documentElement;
humanResourcesNode = corporationNode.firstChild;
employeesNode = humanResourcesNode.lastChild;
employeeNode = employeesNode.lastChild;
lastNameNode = employeeNode.firstChild;
firstNameNode = lastNameNode.previousSibling;
```

Extract Text Data from an XML Element

You can extract text data from XML elements using JavaScript. When you locate the XML element you want to get text from, all you have to do is to extract the text node inside that element and use the text node's `nodeValue` property to get the text.

Many JavaScript programmers have difficulty extracting text data from XML elements. If the element you want to extract text data from is `<first_name>John</first_name>`, it looks like extracting the text data here is a simple task. Say that this element is stored as a node object in the JavaScript variable `firstNameNode`. It seems that you could access the text in the `<first_name>` element simply using the `nodeValue` property this way: `firstNameNode.nodeValue`.

However, that does not work. The reason is that the text in the `<first_name>` element is stored in a text node. So the `<first_name>` element node itself has a child node,

the text node that contains the text "John". Enclosing text inside text nodes may seem like a needless additional level of complexity, but there are occasions in which you can have text in XML documents next to other text, and to keep those text items separate, you need to place them in separate nodes. To access the text contained in the `<first_name>` element, you must first access the text node that contains the text.

Because the text node inside the `<first_name>` element is the first child of that element, you can access that text node as `firstNameNode.firstChild`. You can reach the text inside the text node with the text node's `nodeValue` property, so finally, you can access the text in the `<first_name>` element as `firstNameNode.firstChild.nodeValue`. That is the way to access the text in an element — first access the text node, then extract the text in that node.

Extract Text Data from an XML Element

1 Locate the XML elements you want to extract from text.

In this example, that is the first and last names of the third employee in the `employees.xml` document.

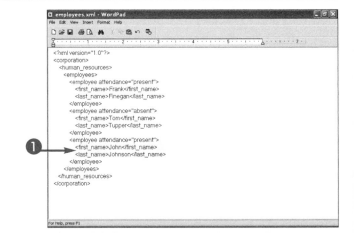

2 Get node objects corresponding to the elements whose text you want to extract.

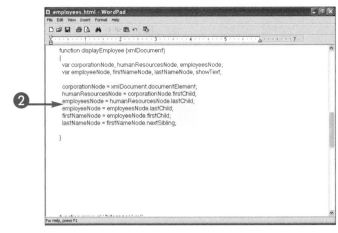

③ Extract the text from the text nodes inside the elements, and display that text.

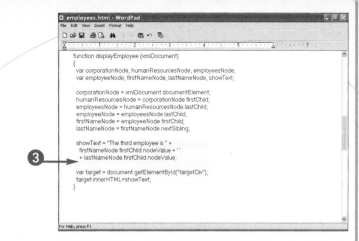

④ Open the Web page in a browser, and click the button.

The application displays the message "The third employee is John Johnson."

Apply It

The example in this task extracts the text node in the target XML elements using the firstChild property. However, it is also worth noting that if an XML element has a text node, that is usually the only child node in the element — you can technically place both text and child elements as siblings inside an element, but that is rarely done. When the text node is the only node inside an element, you can use the lastChild property instead of the firstChild property to access the text node.

Example:

```
corporationNode = xmlDocument.documentElement;
humanResourcesNode = corporationNode.firstChild;
employeesNode = humanResourcesNode.lastChild;
employeeNode = employeesNode.lastChild;
firstNameNode = employeeNode.firstChild;
lastNameNode = firstNameNode.nextSibling;

showText = "The third employee is " +
  firstNameNode.lastChild.nodeValue + ' '
  + lastNameNode.lastChild.nodeValue;
```

Handle White Space in Mozilla and Firefox

You can navigate through XML data using JavaScript, but how you navigate differs in Internet Explorer, Mozilla, and Firefox. In Mozilla and Firefox, text nodes that are pure white space — spaces, tabs, carriage returns, and so on — are considered real text nodes in JavaScript terms, although they are not in Internet Explorer. That is when you navigate around in XML data in Mozilla and Firefox, you have to take white space text nodes into account, but you do not in Internet Explorer.

For example, you have XML data starting a document element named `<corporation>`. The opening tag of that element is followed by some spaces used for indentation before the next opening tag, `<human_resources>`, like this: `<corporation>      <human_resources>`. Also, there were additional spaces before the next child element, `<employees>`, like this: `<corporation>` `<human_resources>      <employees>`. That white space is treated as text nodes in Mozilla and Firefox, but not in Internet Explorer.

If you want to use JavaScript to navigate XML data in Ajax applications in Mozilla and Firefox, you must navigate over those white space nodes. For example, in Internet Explorer, if you store a node corresponding to the `<corporation>` element in the variable `corporationNode`, you can navigate to the `<employees>` element this way: `corporationNode = xmlDocument.documentElement; humanResourcesNode = corporationNode.firstChild; employeesNode = humanResourcesNode.firstChild;`. But in Mozilla and Firefox, the `<corporation>` element's first child is a white space text node, so you would have to do this: `corporationNode = xmldoc.documentElement; humanResourcesNode = corporationNode.firstChild.nextSibling; employeesNode = humanResourcesNode.lastChild.previousSibling;`.

That is how it works — you navigate past the text nodes with the `nextSibling` and `previousSibling` properties. See the section "Create the removeWhitespace Function in Mozilla and Firefox" to remove white space nodes from XML data so that you can treat XML data the same in Mozilla, Firefox, and Internet Explorer.

Handle White Space in Mozilla and Firefox

1 Examine the XML data you have to navigate through.

In this example, assume you want to extract the first and last names of the third employee.

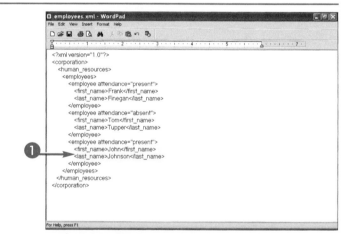

2 Navigate to the two elements you want to extract, taking care to navigate over white space text nodes.

3 Extract the text data from the elements and display that data.

```
function displayGuest(xmldoc)
{
  var corporationNode, humanResourcesNode, employeesNode;
  var employeeNode, firstNameNode, lastNameNode, showText;

  corporationNode = xmldoc.documentElement;
  humanResourcesNode = corporationNode.firstChild.nextSibling;
  employeesNode = humanResourcesNode.lastChild.previousSibling;
  employeeNode = employeesNode.firstChild.nextSibling
    .nextSibling.nextSibling.nextSibling.nextSibling;
  firstNameNode = employeeNode.firstChild.nextSibling;
  lastNameNode = firstNameNode.nextSibling.nextSibling;

  showText = "The third employee is: " +
    firstNameNode.firstChild.nodeValue + ' '
    + lastNameNode.firstChild.nodeValue;

  var target = document.getElementById("targetDiv");
  target.innerHTML=showText;
}

</script>
```

4 Open the page in the Mozilla or Firefox browser, and click the button.

The message "The third employee is John Johnson" appears.

Extra

You may think that you can avoid having to deal with white space nodes by removing all indentation white space this way:

```
<?xml version="1.0"?>
<corporation>
<human_resources>
<employees>
<employee attendance="present">
<first_name>Frank</first_name>
<last_name>Finegan</last_name>
</employee>
<employee attendance="absent">
<first_name>Tom</first_name>
<last_name>Tupper</last_name>
</employee>
</employees>
</human_resources>
</corporation>
```

However, even carriage returns count as white space, so you actually must put all your XML on one line:

```
<?xml version="1.0"?><corporation><human_resources><employees>....
```

Create the removeWhitespace Function in Mozilla and Firefox

You can handle the whitespace nodes used in XML documents for indentation in the Mozilla and Firefox browsers by explicitly navigating over those white space nodes. That is one way of handling such white space nodes. On the other hand, that means you must write very different code for Mozilla and Firefox in your JavaScript, compared to your code for Internet Explorer. It is far easier to simply strip out the white space nodes in the XML you download in Ajax applications, which will let you handle that downloaded XML using the same JavaScript navigation code in all these browsers.

The difference in handling XML data in Mozilla and Firefox compared to Internet Explorer is how you handle white space nodes. The problem is that in JavaScript in Mozilla and Firefox, white space text nodes are considered true text nodes, while they are ignored by Internet Explorer by default. So if you have this XML: `<corporation>` `<human_resources>` `<employees>`, you must navigate over the white space nodes like this in Mozilla and Firefox:

```
corporationNode = xmldoc.documentElement;
humanResourcesNode = corporationNode.
firstChild.nextSibling; employeesNode =
humanResourcesNode.lastChild.previous
Sibling;
```

In Internet Explorer, you can ignore the pure white space nodes, so the JavaScript is

```
corporationNode = xmlDocument.
documentElement; humanResourcesNode =
corporationNode.firstChild; employeesNode =
humanResourcesNode.firstChild;
```

One solution is to remove all the white space nodes from the XML data in a function named `removeWhitespace`, which allows you to handle the XML data as you would in Internet Explorer. To find pure white space nodes, you can use a regular expression in JavaScript this way: `/^\s+$/.test(currentNode.nodeValue)`. If the current node is indeed a white space node, you can remove it with the JavaScript `removeChild` method. For more on how to create and use regular expressions, see `http://perldoc.perl.org/perlre.html`.

Create the removeWhitespace Function in Mozilla and Firefox

1 In the `removeWhitespace` function, loop over all the child nodes in the XML object passed to the function.

2 If the current node is an element, pass it to the `removeWhiteSpace` function again to handle all children of that element.

③ Check to see if the current node is a text node, which is `nodeType 3`, and if it contains only white space.

④ If the current node is a pure white space node, remove it from your XML data.

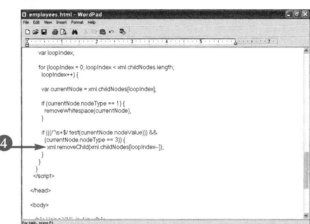

Apply It

You can adapt the removeWhitespace function to remove any kinds of text nodes you want. For example, here is how you can remove any text nodes with the word "comment" in them:

Example:
```
function removeCommentTextNodes(xml)
{
  var loopIndex;
  for (loopIndex = 0; loopIndex < xml.childNodes.length;
    loopIndex++) {
    var currentNode = xml.childNodes[loopIndex];
    if (currentNode.nodeType == 1) {
      removeWhitespace(currentNode);
    }
    if ((((/comment/.test(currentNode.nodeValue))) &&
      (currentNode.nodeType == 3)) {
        xml.removeChild(xml.childNodes[loopIndex--]);
    }
  }
}
```

Use the removeWhitespace Function in Mozilla and Firefox

Y ou can use the `removeWhitespace` function to remove white space from XML data downloaded using Ajax techniques. When you do so, you strip out the white space text nodes from that XML data. Using the `removeWhitespace` function is very useful, because after you have removed that white space, you can use JavaScript to navigate around inside your XML data in the same way in the Mozilla, Firefox, and Internet Explorer browsers.

The main issue is simply to know when your code is executing in the Mozilla or Firefox browsers. When you determine that, you can call the `removeWhitespace` function if your code is operating in one of those browsers.

One easy way to determine if your Web page is in the Mozilla or Firefox browser is to see how your code creates the `XMLHttpRequest` object. The standard `XMLHttpRequest` object creation code has two different

parts — one for the Mozilla and Firefox browsers, and one for Internet Explorer. In the Mozilla and Firefox browsers, `window.XMLHttpRequest` exists, and you create a new `XMLHttpRequest` object this way: `XMLHttpRequestObject = new XMLHttpRequest()`. If `window.XMLHttpRequest` exists, you can set a variable, which you might call `mozilla`, to true. Checking that variable tells you if you should pass the downloaded XML data to the `removeWhitespace` function.

If you do pass your XML data to the `removeWhitespace` function, all white space text nodes are removed, and you can then work with the downloaded XML data just as you would in Internet Explorer, where you do not have to worry about white space nodes in the first place. In that way, you can use the same JavaScript navigation code across all three browsers. To see how to create the `removeWhitespace` function, see the section "Create the removeWhitespace Function in Mozilla and Firefox."

Use the removeWhitespace Function in Mozilla and Firefox

① Create a new variable named `mozilla`, and initialize it to false.

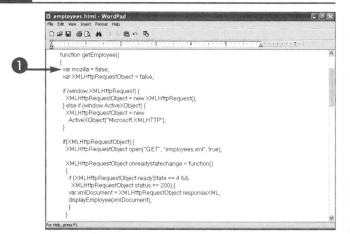

② Set the mozilla variable to true if your code is executing in the Mozilla or Firefox browsers.

③ If the `mozilla` variable is true, remove the white space nodes from the XML data with the `removeWhitespace` function.

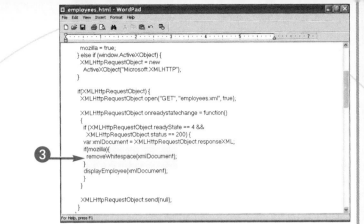

④ Open the Web page in Firefox and click the button.

The Web page now works in Firefox, using the same XML navigation code as in Internet Explorer.

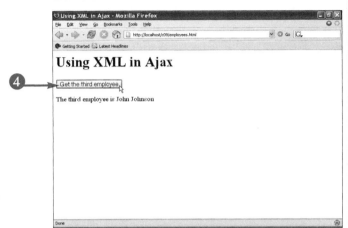

Apply It

Another way of checking if your code is being executed in the Mozilla or Firefox browsers is to check the navigator object's `appName` property. If that property contains the word "Firefox", for example, your code is executing in the Firefox browser:

```
var XMLHttpRequestObject = false;

if (window.XMLHttpRequest) {
  XMLHttpRequestObject = new XMLHttpRequest();
} else if (window.ActiveXObject) {
  XMLHttpRequestObject = new
    ActiveXObject("Microsoft.XMLHTTP");
}
if(navigator.appName == "Netscape") {
  if(navigator.userAgent.indexOf("Firefox") > 0) {
      removeWhitespace(xmlDocument);
  }
}
```

259

Find XML Elements by Name

Y ou can find XML elements in an XML document by name. You can navigate through an XML document using the JavaScript node properties like nextSibling, firstChild, and so on. However, navigating from node to node means that you must know the exact structure of the XML data you are dealing with, and that structure cannot change. And it is more difficult to navigate from node to node throughout an entire document than simply to pluck out the elements you want by name.

To fetch the elements you want from an XML document, you can use the JavaScript XML document object's getElementsByTagName method. Note that this method is called getElementsByTagName — plural — not just getElementByTagName. The reason is that your XML data may contain a number of elements with the same name.

For example, say that you have this XML data and that you want to extract the name of the third employee:

```
<employee attendance="present">
```

```
<first_name>Frank</first_name> <last_name>
Finegan</last_name> </employee>
<employee attendance="absent"> <first_name>
Tom</first_name> <last_name>Tupper</
last_name> </employee> <employee attendance
="present">   <first_name>John</first_name>
<last_name>Johnson</last_name> </employee>
```

If you call getElementsByTagName("first_name") on the document object that contains this XML data, you get a JavaScript array that holds three <first_name> elements. In order to extract the element you want from that array of elements, you can simply use a numeric index. For example, if you have placed the array in a variable named firstnamenodes, you can access the first name of the third employee like this: firstnamenodes[2]. firstChild.nodeValue. Remember that arrays start with index 0, so the third element has index 2. Using the getElementsByTagName method is often easier than navigating through your data node by node because you can simply specify the elements you want.

Find XML Elements by Name

1 Identify the data you want to extract from your downloaded XML, such as the first and last names of the third employee here.

2 Use the getElementsByTagName method on the XML document object from the XMLHttpRequest object's responseXML property to get the elements you want.

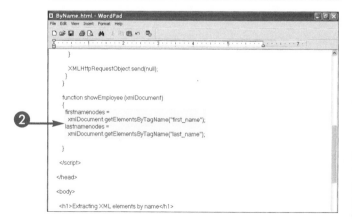

③ Get the text data you want from the element arrays and display that text.

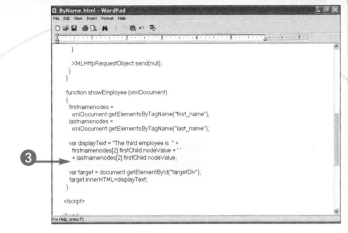

④ Open the Web page in a browser and click the button.

The name of the third employee is downloaded and displayed.

Apply It

JavaScript lets you condense the process of getting the arrays holding the elements you want and referencing those elements in your code. Putting everything together into single statements can make your code much more compact. Here is what the code that takes advantage of that JavaScript capability looks like:

```
function showEmployee (xmlDocument)
{
  var displayText = "The third employee is: " +
    xmlDocument.getElementsByTagName("first_name")[2]
    .firstChild.nodeValue + ' '
    + xmlDocument.getElementsByTagName[2]
    .firstChild.nodeValue;

  var target = document.getElementById("targetDiv");
  target.innerHTML=displayText;
}
```

Extract XML Attributes

Y ou can extract attribute values from XML data. XML elements can have text content, but they can also have attributes. For example, say you have an XML element named `<employee>` like this: `<employee attendance="present"> <first_name>John</first_name> <last_name>Johnson</last_name> </employee>`. Note that the opening tag has an attribute, `attendance`. You can extract the value assigned to that attribute, which is `"present"` in this example, using JavaScript.

For example, you want to extract the value of the attendance attribute for the third employee in an XML document named `employees.xml`. First navigate to that `<employee>` element using the navigational technique you prefer — you can use node properties like `nextSibling` and `firstChild` to get the `<employee>` element you are interested in, or you can use the JavaScript XML document object `getElementsByTagName` method instead.

After you have a JavaScript object corresponding to the element you want to extract an attribute or attributes

from, you can use the element's attributes property, which contains a JavaScript named node map of attributes. A *named node map* is a JavaScript object that lets you access items by name, not just numeric index. For example, you store the `<employee>` element as a node object in a variable named `employeeNode`. You can get a named node map of the element's attributes this way: `var attributes = employeeNode.attributes`.

Now you have a named node map, named attributes, that holds the attributes of the `<employee>` element. You can get the value of the attribute you are interested in, the attendance attribute, using the named node map's `getNamedItem` method this way: `var attendance Employee = attributes.getNamedItem ("attendance")`.

At this point, you have an attendance node stored in the variable named `attendanceEmployee`. To extract the text assigned to the `attendance` attribute, you can use the node's `nodeValue` property this way: `attendance Employee.nodeValue`.

Extract XML Attributes

① Select the `<employee>` element whose attendance attribute you want to access.

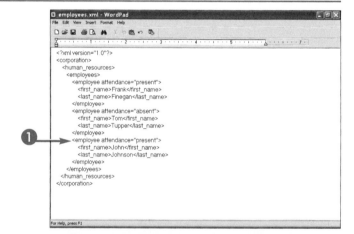

② Navigate to the `<employee>` element and get a named node map of its attributes.

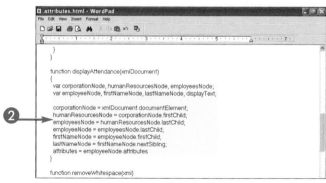

3 Get a node corresponding to the attribute you are interested in and display that attribute's value.

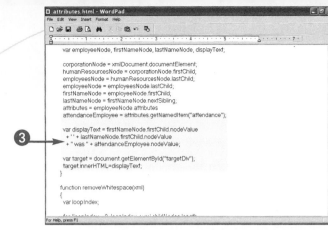

4 Open the Web page and click the button.

The attendance attribute is read, and the message "John Johnson was present" appears.

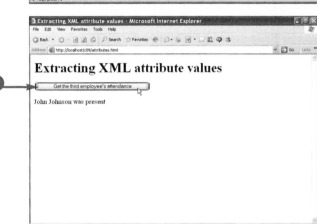

Apply It

In much Ajax code, you do not display the values of attributes, but you use those values to filter the data you want. For example, if you only want to display data in English, you might look for elements whose language attribute is set to "English". If you only want to display employees who are present, you might use code like this:

```
firstNameNode = employeeNode.firstChild;
lastNameNode = firstNameNode.nextSibling;
attributes = employeeNode.attributes
attendanceEmployee = attributes.getNamedItem("attendance");
if(attendanceEmployee.nodeValue == "present"){
  var displayText = firstNameNode.firstChild.nodeValue
    + ' ' + lastNameNode.firstChild.nodeValue;
}
var target = document.getElementById("targetDiv");
target.innerHTML=displayText;
```

Create a Valid XML Document

You can create XML documents that are *valid* as well as well formed. A valid XML document meets a set of requirements you specify for its syntax. There are two ways of specifying the syntax of an XML document by using a Document Type Definition (DTD), or with an XML schema. For official details on DTDs, see www.w3.org/TR/REC-xml/; for XML schema, see www.w3.org/XML/Schema.

DTDs are the easiest to create. The DTD for a document may be placed at the beginning of the document using a `<!DOCTYPE>` element. For example, if the document element is `<corporation>`, then you start an XML DTD listing that document element this way: `"<!DOCTYPE corporation ["`. The rest of the DTD follows the square brace, `[`, and you end the DTD with the markup `]>`.

Say that the `<corporation>` element contains a `<human_resources>` element. You can indicate that in the DTD this way: `<!ELEMENT corporation (human_resources)>`. In turn, say that the `<human_resources>`

element contains an `<employees>` element. You can indicate that in the DTD this way: `<!ELEMENT human_resources (employees)>` .

Now say that the `<employees>` element can contain zero or more `<employee>` elements. You can indicate that in the DTD this way: `<!ELEMENT employees (employee*)>`. Note the asterisk, *, which means that you can have zero or more `<employee>` elements.

In addition, say that an `<employee>` element contains both a `<first_name>` and a `<last_name>` element, in that order. You specify that in the DTD this way: `<!ELEMENT employee (first_name,last_name)>`.

You can specify that the contents of the `<first_name>` and `<last_name>` elements are just text with the PCDATA keyword: `<!ELEMENT first_name (#PCDATA)>`. And finally, you can indicate that the `<employee>` element should have an attribute named attendance, which may be assigned simple text, this way: `<!ATTLIST employee attendance CDATA #IMPLIED>`.

Create a Valid XML Document

1 Create a DTD, giving the name of the document element.

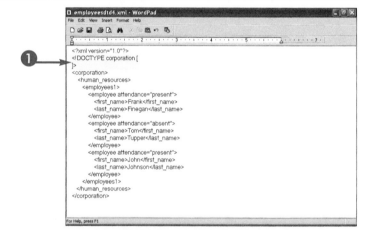

2 Declare the XML elements that contain other elements in your document in the DTD.

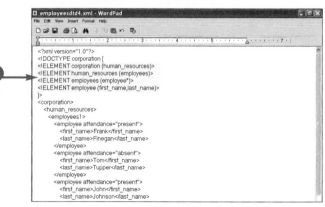

③ Declare the elements that contain plain text, called parsed character data, or PCDATA, in XML.

④ Declare the attendance attribute of the `<employee>` element.

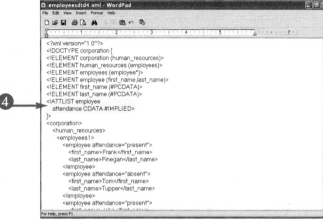

Extra

You can specify any number of attributes for an element in the `<!ATTLIST>` declaration — "ATTLIST" stands for attribute list. To add a date, time, location, and attendance attribute to the `<employee>` element, you can use this `<!ATTLIST>` declaration:

```
<!ATTLIST employee
    date CDATA #IMPLIED
    time CDATA #IMPLIED
    location CDATA #IMPLIED
    attendance CDATA #IMPLIED>
]
```

You can also indicate that an element must contain one or more of another element. For example, to specify that the `<employees>` element must contain one or more `<employee>` elements, you can use this like in a DTD:

```
<!ELEMENT employees (employee+)>
```

You can use the + and * symbols when declaring sequences of elements as well:

```
<!ELEMENT employees (employee+, consultant*)>
```

You can use XML parsers to validate XML documents. Doing so in Ajax applications can be especially useful to make sure that the XML data you download downloads intact — if it cannot be validated, there is a problem with the XML data. Internet Explorer has an XML parser built in to it that you can use to validate XML documents.

When you use an XML schema or an XML DTD, you specify the syntax of an XML document. When you download XML using Ajax, you can test the validity of the data you download in Internet Explorer. You can download XML data using an `XMLHttpRequest` object's `responseXML` property. That property holds a JavaScript XML document object that you can parse directly using Internet Explorer's XML parser.

You start by storing the XML document object in a variable: `var xmlDocument = XMLHttpRequest`

`Object.responseXML`. To work with and parse that object for validity errors, you can pass it to the load method of the Internet Explorer parser.

To create a parser object, you use this JavaScript in Internet Explorer: `var parser = new ActiveXObject ("MSXML2.DOMDocument")`. That gives you the object you need to parse XML and to determine if there are any validity errors. By default, this parser only reads in XML data and makes it available as a document object, but you can turn on validity checking by setting the `validateOnParse` property of the parser to true: `parser.validateOnParse = true`.

To validate the XML document object, just pass it to the parser's load method this way: `parser.load(XMLHttp RequestObject.responseXML)`. If there is an error, the `parser.parseError.errorCode` property holds a nonzero value. To create a sample DTD, see the section "Create a Valid XML Document."

Validate an XML Document

① Create a validity error in `employees.xml` by changing `<employee>` to `<employees1>`.

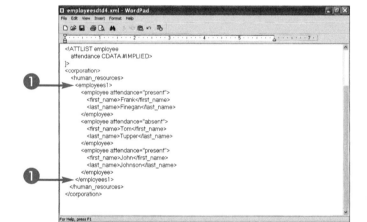

② Parse the downloaded XML.

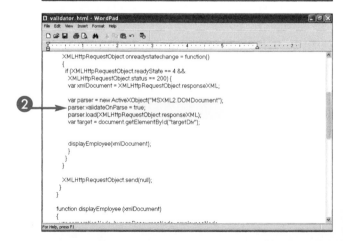

③ Display an error message if there is
a validity error.

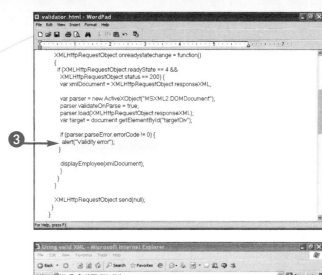

④ Open the Web page and click the
button.

The validity error is caught and an
error dialog box appears.

Apply It

You can also use the MSXML2.DOMDocument object to download XML documents from the server in Internet
Explorer. As the example is written, it parses an XML document downloaded from the server using Ajax
techniques — you pass it that document from the XMLHttpRequest object's responseXML property:

```
var parser = new ActiveXObject("MSXML2.DOMDocument");
parser.validateOnParse = true;
parser.load(XMLHttpRequestObject.responseXML);
var target = document.getElementById("targetDiv");
```

However, you can also download XML documents by giving their URL:

```
var parser = new ActiveXObject("MSXML2.DOMDocument");
parser.validateOnParse = true;
parser.load("http://www.noisp.com/user/employee.xml");
var target = document.getElementById("targetDiv");
```

Although this works, this code downloads XML data synchronously, waiting for that data to appear, as
opposed to the asynchronous Ajax method.

Report XML Validation Errors

You can use Internet Explorer's built-in parser to report exactly what validity errors there are in the XML data you download from the server, if any. When there is a validation error, you can get an error object in the Internet Explorer XML parser's `parseError` property. That error object contains a number of properties that you can use to determine more about the error.

To validate the XML data you download using Ajax in Internet Explorer, you can create an XML parser this way: `var parser = new ActiveXObject("MSXML2. DOMDocument")`. Then you set the parser's `validate OnParse` property to true, and pass that parser the XML data you download this way: `parser.load (XMLHttpRequestObject.responseXML)`.

If there is a validity error, then the `parser.parseError. errorCode` is nonzero — if this property is zero, there is no error. When there is a validity error, you can use the properties of the `parser.parseError` object to get more information about the error.

The `parser.parseError.url` holds the URL of the XML document that caused the problem. If there is no URL, as when you pass an object to the load method — as in this example, where you pass the downloaded XML text to the parser this way: `parser.load(XMLHttpRequest Object.responseXML)` — then this property does not hold any text.

The `parser.parseError.line` holds the line in the XML document that caused the error. That kind of information is very useful, letting the user locate the problem immediately.

The `parser.parseError.linepos` property holds the position in the line where the error happened. Using the `parser.parseError.line` property, you can locate the line where the error occurs, and the `parser. parseError.linepos` tells the user what character position in the line the error starts at.

The `parser.parseError.srcText` holds the XML text that causes the error; and the `parser.parseError. reason` contains a message holding the reason for the error.

Report XML Validation Errors

① Check if there is a validation error.

② Report the file name, line, and position of the error.

③ Report the source, reason for the error, and the error code.

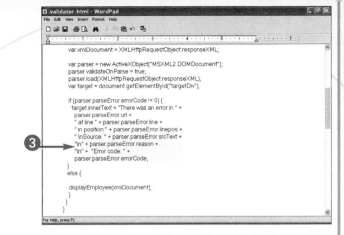

③

④ Open the Web page in Internet Explorer and click the button.

If there is a validation error, a complete error report appears.

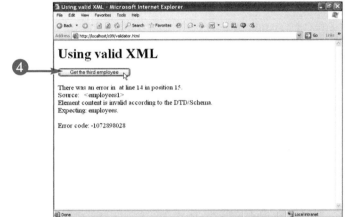

④

Apply It

You can display your own error messages instead of relying on the error messages that the Internet Explorer parser creates. To do that, simply determine which error occurred by checking the `parser.parseError.errorCode` property, and display an error message to match:

```
if (XMLHttpRequestObject.readyState == 4 &&
  XMLHttpRequestObject.status == 200) {
  var xmlDocument = XMLHttpRequestObject.responseXML;

  var parser = new ActiveXObject("MSXML2.DOMDocument");
  parser.validateOnParse = true;
  parser.load(XMLHttpRequestObject.responseXML);
  var target = document.getElementById("targetDiv");

  if (parser.parseError.errorCode == -1072898028) {
    alert("The parser found an unexpected element.");
  }
```

Set Up CSS Styles

Y ou can use Cascading Style Sheets (CSS) with Ajax to display Ajax results in a Web page. When you download data using Ajax, CSS lets you display those results in a Web page without needing to refresh the Web page. You can display pop-ups, replace text, change colors, and move elements in the page, all using CSS and Ajax.

To work with CSS, you create style *rules*. A rule specifies how you want to set a particular style property, such as the color used for hyperlinks. You assign a value to a style property, such as text-decoration: underline, which underlines text by setting that text's text-decoration style property to underline. To find the complete list of style properties, look at www.w3.org/TR/REC-CSS1/ for CSS1 and www.w3.org/TR/REC-CSS2/ for CSS2. For a more user-friendly site, you may go to www.w3schools.com/css/default.asp.

The style rule text-decoration: underline underlines text, but you have to know how to connect that style rule to the text you want to underline. One way of connecting style rules to HTML elements is to use a <style> element. For example, <style type="text/css"> body {background: white; color: black;} </style> assigns two style rules to the <body> element in a Web page, setting the background color to white and the color of text to black.

You can also set the style of elements with a particular ID. For example, if you have a <div> element with the ID targetDiv, you can set that element's styles this way: <style type="text/css"> #targetDiv {background: #FF0000; color:#0000FF;}</style>.

You can also set styles using an inline style attribute instead of a <style> element. Every HTML element that can appear in a Web page has a style attribute. For example, if you want to underline text, you can use a <span> element's style attribute this way: <span style="text-decoration: underline">.

Set Up CSS Styles

① Create an HTML document and use a <style> element to style HTML elements.

This example sets the colors of hyperlinks and removes any underlining under them.

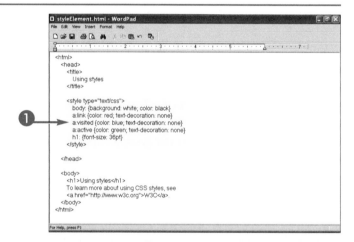

② Open the Web page in a browser.

The hyperlink to W3C is not underlined.

3 Create a new HTML document that uses inline styles to set the spacing between letters to 15 pixels, underlines and overlines text, and indents text to 20 percent of the browser's window's width.

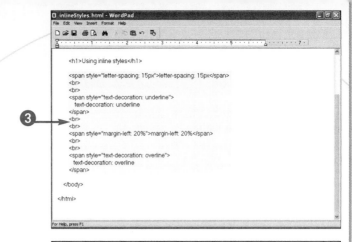

4 Open the HTML document in a browser and observe the applied inline styles.

Apply It

You can also specify the particular HTML element you want to set styles for in a `<style>` element. You can specify the element using that element's ID. For example, if a `<div>` element's ID is "display", you can set the styles for that element referring to it as `#display` this way:

Example:
```html
<html>
  <head>
    <style type="text/css">
      #display {
        background: #FF0000;
        color:#0000FF;
      }
    </style>
  </head>

  <body>
   <div id="display"></div>
  </body>
</html>
```

Set Font Family and Size

You can set the typeface and font style used in your Ajax applications using CSS styles. In particular, you use the `font-family` style property to set the typeface to use, and the `font-size` property to set the size of the font to display.

You might think you use a style property named `font-face` to set the typeface, such as Courier or Arial, but in fact, you use the `font-family` style property. For example if you want to set the font used in a `<span>` element to Arial, you can do this using inline styles: `<span style="font-family: Arial">This text is in Arial font.</span>`. If you want to use a `<style>` element instead of using the inline style HTML attribute, you can do that also — say, you want to style the text in a `<div>` element with the ID `targetDiv`: `<div id="targetDiv"></div>`. You can then use a `<style>` element like this to style the text in the `targetDiv` element to use Arial font: `<style type="text/css"> #targetDiv: {font-family: arial}</style>`. You

can also set up the style for an entire HTML element, such as the `<body>` element, like this: `<style type="text/css"> body: {font-family: arial}</style>`.

Note that the computer your Web page executes in might not have the font you want to use, such as the Arial font, available. To address that, you can specify a list of possible font families to use, not just a single family. For example, if Arial is not available, you might want to use Courier instead. You can tell the browser to use a comma-separated list of font family names, like this: `<span style="font-family: Arial, Courier"> This text is in Arial font, or Courier font if Arial is not available.</span>`.

You can also set the size of the font to use with the `font-size` property. For example, you can specify a font size by appending "pt", such as 36pt, which means 36-point font: `<span style="font-size: 36pt"> This text is in 36 point font.</span>`.

Set Font Family and Size

1 Display a line of text using the Arial font.

If Arial is not available, use the browser's default font.

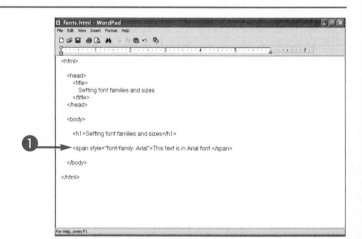

2 Display another line of text in Arial font.

If Arial is not available, use Courier.

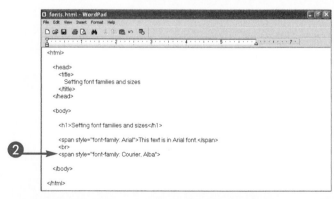

③ Display a line of text using 36-point font.

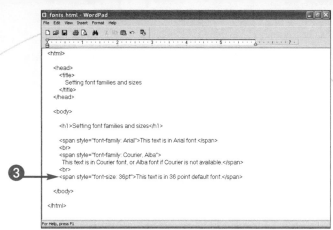

④ Open the document in your browser and observe the styles that the browser has applied.

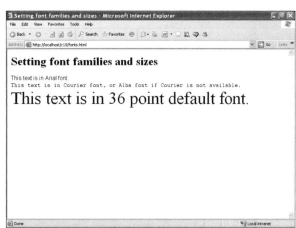

Extra

There is no limit to the number of font families you can specify when using the `font-family` style property. For example, you can specify that you want the first of the available Courier, Alba, Times, Tunga, or Verdana font families used this way:

```
<body>

  <h1>Setting font families and sizes</h1>

  <span style="font-family: Arial">This text is in Arial font.</span>
  <br>
  <span style="font-family: Courier, Alba, Times, Tunga, Verdana">
    This text is in Courier, Alba, Times, Tunga, or Verdana
      font.</span>
  <br>
  <span style="font-size: 36pt">
    This text is in 36 point default font.</span>

</body>
```

Underline or Italicize Text

Y ou can underline text or italicize it using the text-decoration and font-style properties. The text-decoration property lets you specify how to underline text by specifying no underline, a single underline, or even an overline. The font-style property lets you specify how you want text to be displayed; for example, you can set this property to "italic" to make the text you are styling appear in italic.

Do not use a style property like font-style to underline text, use the text-decoration property. You can set this property to "none" to remove any underlining or overlining, "underline" to underline the text, "overline" to display text with a line over it, "line-through" to display text with a line through it, or "blink" to make it blink. Note that blinking works in Mozilla and Firefox, it does not work in Internet Explorer.

For example, the text in this <span> element appears underlined: <span style="text-decoration: underline">This text is underlined.</span>. The text in this <span> element will appear with an overline: <span style="text-decoration: overline">This text is overlined.</span>.

The font-style property is the one that lets you specify whether or not text should appear in italics. You can set the font-style property to "normal" to make the text appear normally, without italics, or you can set this property to "italics" to make the text appear in italics. You can also set the font-style property to "oblique", which is a browser-dependent setting. In Mozilla, Firefox, and Internet Explorer, setting font-style to "oblique" simply displays the styled text in italics.

In Ajax applications, these style properties are useful to draw the user's attention. When you display new text for example, you can display it in italics or underlined, which makes it stand out.

Underline or Italicize Text

1 Display text in italics, styling it with the font-style property.

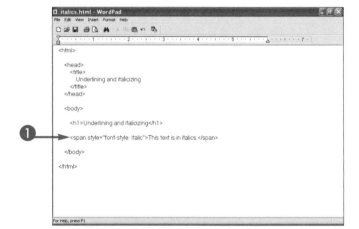

2 Display text that is underlined, using the text-decoration property.

③ Use the `text-decoration` property to display text that is overlined.

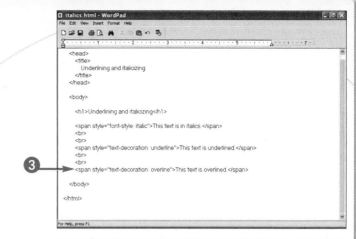

④ Open the Web page in a browser and observe the properly styled text.

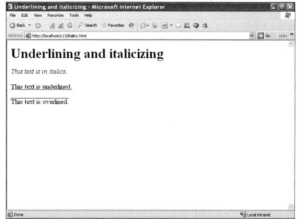

Apply It

You can set styles like underlining and italics in JavaScript. In JavaScript, you use style properties with JavaScript names — `text-decoration` becomes `textDecoration`, `font-style` becomes `fontStyle`, and so on. Here is some HTML that underlines a header when you click the button:

Example:
```
<head>
  <script>
    function italicize()
    {
      document.getElementById("header").style.fontStyle = "italic";
    }
  </script>
</head>
<body>
  <h1 id="header">Underlining and italicizing</h1>
  <form>
    <input type="button" onclick="italicize()" value="Click me">
  </form>
</body>
```

Make Text Bold

You can use CSS styles to display text as bold. To do that, use the `font-weight` property. You can make text appear simply bold or use a variety of numeric settings to indicate just how bold you want the text.

Set the `font-weight` property to `"bold"` to make the text you are styling bold. That is the default action for the `font-weight` property and makes the text you are styling stand out from the rest of the text on the page. To make text appear not bold, or normal, set the `font-weight` property to `"normal"`.

You can also make text appear bolder than its surrounding text by setting the `font-weight` property to `"bolder"`. That makes the text you are styling stand out from the surrounding text, even if that surrounding text has been made more bold than normal for text in the

Web page. You can also assign the `font-weight` property the value `"lighter"` to lighten the text you are styling compared to the rest of the text in the page.

Besides `"normal"`, `"bold"`, `"bolder"`, and `"lighter"`, you can also set the `font-weight` property to a numeric value, as long as you enclose that number in quotation marks. The allowed values are `"100"`, `"200"`, `"300"`, `"400"`, `"500"`, `"600"`, `"700"`, `"800"`, or `"900"`, in increasing boldness increments.

The `font-weight` property is a good one to use in Ajax applications because you can use it to make new text stand out. For example, you may have just downloaded text from the server and want to display that text in a Web page, where it replaces old text — to make the new text stand out, consider making it bold.

Make Text Bold

1 Display a line of text in bold.

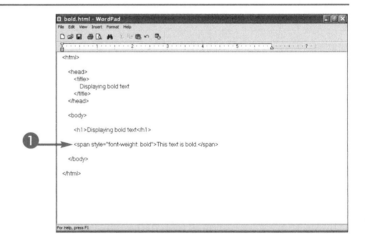

2 Display text in 100 bold.

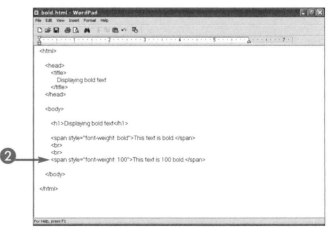

3 Display text in 600 bold.

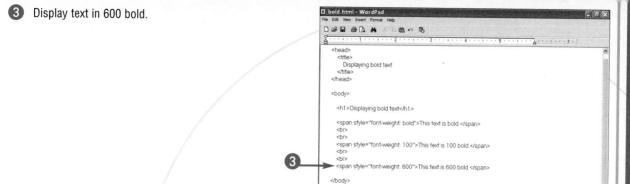

```
    <head>
        <title>
            Displaying bold text
        </title>
    </head>

    <body>

        <h1>Displaying bold text</h1>

        <span style="font-weight: bold">This text is bold.</span>
        <br>
        <br>
        <span style="font-weight: 100">This text is 100 bold.</span>
        <br>
        <br>
        <span style="font-weight: 600">This text is 600 bold.</span>

    </body>

</html>
```

4 Open the Web page in a browser and observe the styling.

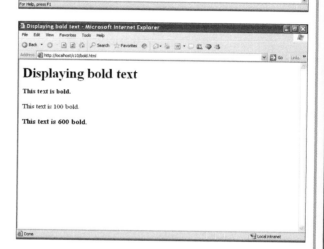

Apply It

You can make new text in a Web page bold using JavaScript. In JavaScript, the `font-weight` property becomes `fontWeight`. Here is some HTML that bolds text in a header when you click the button:

Example:
```
<head>
  <script>
    function bold()
    {
       document.getElementById("header").style.fontWeight = "bold";
    }
  </script>
</head>
<body>
  <h1 id="header">Bolding text</h1>
  <form>
    <input type="button" onclick="bold()" value="Click me">
  </form>
</body>
```

Align Text

You can align text in a Web page using the CSS `text-align` property. Formerly, you could use HTML elements to align text in Web pages, such as the `<center>` element this way: `<center> This text is centered. </center>`. However, the `<center>` element was made obsolete in HTML version 4.0, and you are instead supposed to use CSS styles to align text now although you can still use HTML elements like `<center>`, and modern browsers will still use them.

You can use the `text-align` property only with HTML *block* elements. A block element is one that takes up its own line in a Web page, such as an `<h1>` header element. The HTML `<div>` element also counts as a block element. However, inline elements like `<span>` do not count as block elements — they are simply HTML inline elements and are not given their own line in the browser's display.

You can set the `text-align` property to `"left"` to left-align block elements in a Web browser. This displays any elements starting with their left edges at the left edge of the browser's client area, which is the display area of the browser that excludes borders, menus and toolbars, the status bar, and so on. Left-aligning text in the browser is the default, so when you assign `text-align` the value `"left"`, there may not be much difference in the way your page displays.

You can also set the `text-align` property to `"center"`, which centers text in the browser's client area. This is the way you are supposed to center text now instead of using the `<center>` element.

Finally, you can set the `text-align` property to `"right"`, which aligns the right side of the styled text with the right edge of the client area.

Align Text

① Use the `text-align` property to align text left in the Web page.

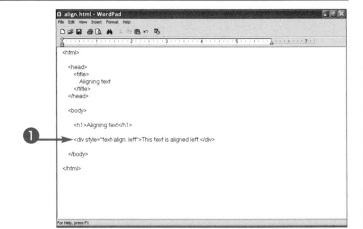

② Use the `text-align` property to center text in the Web page.

③ Use the `text-align` property to align text right in the Web page.

④ Open the Web page in a browser and observe the alignment of the text.

Apply It

You can align new text in a Web page using JavaScript. In JavaScript, the `text-align` property becomes `textAlign`. Here is some HTML that aligns text in a header when you click the button:

```
<head>
  <script>
    function center()
    {
      document.getElementById("header").style.textAlign = "center";
    }
  </script>
</head>
<body>
  <h1 id="header">Centering text</h1>
  <form>
    <input type="button" onclick="center()" value="Click me">
  </form>
</body>
```

Set Foreground Colors

You can set foreground colors — that is, the color used for text in a Web page — using the `color` CSS style property. This property is a very useful one in Ajax, because you can use it to make new text stand out in a Web page. When you download new text and display it, you can make it bright red to help it get noticed. Unless you make some effort to make new text stand out, the user may not notice that anything has changed in the Web page.

To set the color of text, you only need to assign a value to the `color` style property. For example, to display text in red, you could use this HTML: `<span style="color: red">This text is red.</span>`.

You can specify the colors you assign to the `color` property using color names, such as red, green, yellow, blue, purple, orange, and so on. You can find a list of predefined colors supported in Internet Explorer at `http://msdn.microsoft.com/library/default.asp ?url=/workshop/author/dhtml/reference/colors/ colors.asp`. There are many interesting colors in the list, such as aliceblue, antiquewhite, aqua, honeydew,

aquamarine, bisque, ivory, lavender, lemonchiffon, ghostwhite, and others.

You can find a list of the predefined colors in Mozilla and Firefox at `http://wp.netscape.com/eng/mozilla/ 3.0/handbook/javascript/colors.htm`. The list includes many that are the same in Internet Explorer, and many interesting colors such as aliceblue, blanchedalmond, crimson, darkmagenta, deepskyblue, lightseagreen, papayawhip, and others.

You can also define your own colors using color triplets that specify the red, green, and blue components you want to use in a color, as in HTML. Each component is given as a two-digit hexadecimal number in the triplet like this: rrggbb, where rr is the red value, gg the green value, and bb the blue value. Each component can vary from 00 to FF in hexadecimal, just as in HTML. There's a good list of color triplets and what they look like at `www.w3schools.com/tags/ref_color_tryit.asp`. You can also use decimal color values, 0 – 255, with the rgb function like this: rgb(255, 255, 255).

Set Foreground Colors

1. Give the `<body>` element the foreground color blue, making the default color of text in the document blue.

2. Style individual elements in the page with color, such as making text in a header red.

3 Use color triplets.

This example uses FF00FF for purple.

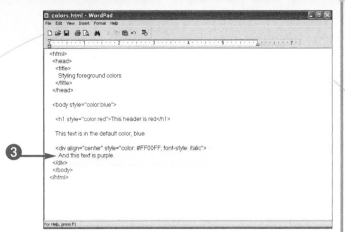

4 Open the Web page in a browser.

The text should appear in various colors.

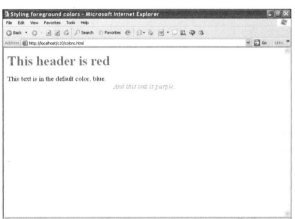

Apply It

The color property is available to you in JavaScript. To access the color property of an element, and to change it at runtime, you only need to create a JavaScript object corresponding to that element and use that object's style.color property:

```
<head>
  <script>
    function colorText()
    {
      document.getElementById("header").style.color = "indigo";
    }
  </script>
</head>
<body>
  <h1 id="header">Coloring text</h1>
  <form>
    <input type="button" onclick="colorText()" value="Click me">
  </form>
</body>
```

Make New Text More Noticeable

Y ou can use JavaScript to change the color of newly downloaded text as the user watches, emphasizing what text is new in the Web page. This is a good technique. Ajax critics often complain that one of the problems with Ajax is that newly displayed text that is downloaded using Ajax does not get noticed.

For example, you can use JavaScript to display the new text in color, and then go back to black text after a short interval. Doing so makes it evident what text has just been added to your Web page. To set the color of text in a `<div>` element to red, for example, you can do this: `var targetDiv = document.getElementById ("targetDiv"); targetDiv.style.color = "#FF0000";`.

Any text displayed in the `<div>` element is now red — and you can change it back to black after a moment

using JavaScript. To do that, use the JavaScript `setTimeout` function to call the `backToBlack` function this way: `setTimeout(backToBlack, 400);`. The `setTimeout` function lets your script wait the specified number of milliseconds before calling a JavaScript function that you have written.

In the `backToBlack` function, you can change the color of the text in the `<div>` element to black, like the text in the rest of the page, this way: `targetDiv = document.getElementById("targetDiv"); targetDiv.style.color = "black";`.

Originally, then, the newly downloaded text in the `<div>` element appears red. After the user notices it, the text reverts to the default text color for the page, which is black. The impression the user gets is that new text flashes in red for a moment, drawing the user's attention to it.

Make New Text More Noticeable

① Style the color for downloaded text as red.

② Make the JavaScript function `setTimeout` call the `backToBlack` function in 400 milliseconds.

3 In the `backToBlack` function, set the color of the downloaded text to black.

4 Open the Web page in a browser and click the button.

The newly downloaded text appears in red, then turns to black after a moment.

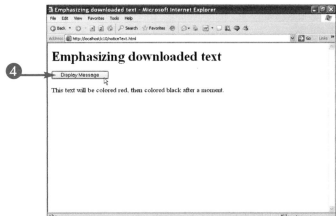

Apply It

You can use the JavaScript `setTimer` function for many purposes, including displaying scrolling text in the status bar of the browser. Here is a script that scrolls the text "Sorry, a server error occurred!!!" in the status bar:

```
<script language="JavaScript">

  var text = "Sorry, a server error occurred!!! ";

  function displayer()
  {
    window.status = text
    text = text.substring(1, text.length) + text.substring(0, 1)
    setTimeout("displayer()", 120)
  }

</script>
```

Set Background Colors

You can set the background color of HTML elements using CSS styles and the `background-color` property. This property can be useful in Ajax applications to make the cells in a table flash as the data they contain updates with new data downloaded from the server.

You can set the background color of an HTML element like a table cell like this: `<td style="background-color: black">Hello</td>`, which sets the background color to black. Modern browsers come with many built-in predefined colors. There is a list of predefined colors in Internet Explorer at `http://msdn.microsoft.com/library/default.asp?url=/workshop/author/dhtml/reference/colors/colors.asp`, and a list of the predefined colors in Mozilla and Firefox at `http://wp.netscape.com/eng/mozilla/3.0/handbook/javascript/colors.htm`. You can find many predefined colors for these browsers at those sites, but if you want

to handle all three browsers, make sure that the color names you select are supported in all three browsers.

You can also use the same color triplets in style properties like `background-color` that you can assign to HTML color properties. To create a color triplet, you can use three two-digit hexadecimal values ranging from 00 to FF like this: rrggbb, where rr is the red value, gg the green value, and bb the blue value. For example, pure red is FF0000, pure green is 00FF00, and pure blue is 0000FF. You can see a list of color triplets and the colors they correspond to at `www.w3schools.com/tags/ref_color_tryit.asp`.

You can also use decimal color values, 0 – 255, with the rgb function like this: rgb(255, 255, 255). For example, this sets the background color of a table cell to green: `<td style="background-color: rgb(0, 255, 0)">Hello</td>`.

Set Background Colors

① Set the background color of a Web page using the `<body>` element's style attribute.

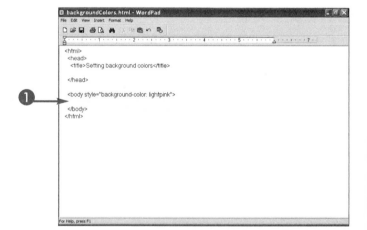

② Create an HTML table.

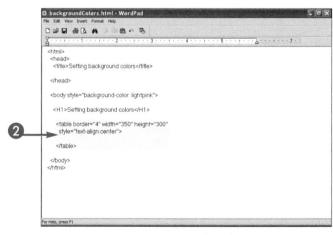

③ Set the background colors of the
table cells to various colors.

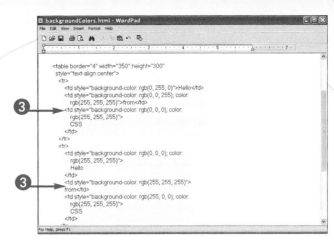

④ Open the Web page in a browser.

The table cells should appear in
various colors.

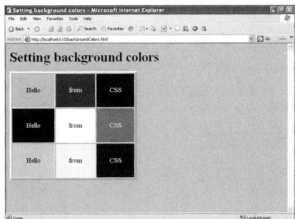

Apply It

The `backgound-color` property is available to you in JavaScript as `backgroundColor`. To access the
`backgroundColor` property of an element and to change it at runtime, you only need to create a JavaScript
object corresponding to that element and use that object's `style.backgroundColor` property:

```
<head>
  <script>
    function setBackgroundColor()
    {
      document.getElementById("targetDiv")
        .style.backgroundColor = "pink";
    }
  </script>
</head>
<body>
  <div id="targetDiv">Coloring text</div>
  <form>
    <input type="button" onclick="setBackgroundColor()"
      value="Click me">
  </form>
</body>
```

Set Background Images

You can use CSS to display background images in a Web page. You use the `background-image` style property to set the URL of the image to use. You can also use other CSS style properties to specify if the image should repeat in the background or not, whether the image should scroll with the rest of the document, and more.

You must assign a URL to the CSS style property `background-image`, and you can create a URL in CSS style rules using the `url` function. For example, if you want to use `image.jpg` as the background image in a Web page, and `image.jpg` is in the same directory on the server as that Web page, you can assign the `background-image` property the value `url(image.jpg)`. You can also use URLs to point to images at other locations on the Internet, such as `url(www.noisp.com/user/image.jpg)`.

The `background-repeat` property specifies if the background image should be tiled in the browser. Set this property to "repeat", `"repeat-x"` to repeat in the x direction, `"repeat-y"` to repeat in the y direction, or `"no-repeat"`.

You can use the `background-attachment` property to specify if the background image or images should scroll with the rest of the document as the user uses the scroll bars. You can set this property to either `"scroll"` to let the background image scroll with the rest of the document, or `"fixed"` to make the background image not scroll. Letting the content of the Web page scroll while the background image remains fixed can provide a striking effect.

You can also use the `background-position` property to set the starting position of the background. You set this property to `"top"`, `"center"`, `"bottom"`, `"left"`, or `"right"`.

Set Background Images

① Give the `<body>` element a background image.

② Set the background image to repeat.

3 Set the starting position of the repeated images at the top of the page.

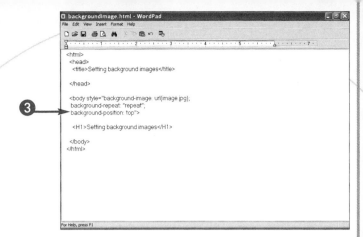

4 Open the Web page in a browser.

The Web page displays the background image.

Apply It

You can use the `backgound-image` property in JavaScript, where it is named `backgroundImage`. To set the background image of a Web page, you only need to use that the document body's `style.backgroundImage` property:

```
<head>
  <script>
    function setBackgroundImage()
    {
      document.getElementById("body")
        .style.backgroundImage = "url(image.jpg)";
    }
  </script>
</head>
<body id="body">
  <h1>Setting background images</h1>
  <form>
    <input type="button" onclick="setBackgroundImage()"
      value="Click me">
  </form>
</body>
```

Position Elements Using Absolute Positioning

You can position elements using CSS styles. There are two ways to position elements — absolute positioning and relative positioning. If you use absolute positioning, you can specify where in a Web page a particular HTML element should appear. That is useful in Ajax applications to support pop-up menus or windows like tool tips and other messages to the user.

To work with absolute positioning, you set the `position` style property to `"absolute"`. When you use absolute positioning, you can specify the location for the top and left locations of the HTML element you want to position in the Web page. The x origin is at the left of the client area in the browser, and positive x extends to the right. The y origin is at the top of the client area, and positive y extends downward. By default, all screen measurements are in pixels.

You set the `top` style property to the location you want to set for the top of the element you are positioning. The `bottom` style property specifies the location of the bottom of the element in the browser's client area. The `left` property specifies the location of the left edge of the element you are positioning, and the `right` property specifies the location of the right edge of the property you are positioning.

For example, to position a `<div>` element at x location 350 and y location 100, you can use this style attribute: `<div style="position:absolute; left:350; top:100; background: orange">`. To move elements in a Web page, you can change an element's position properties like `top` and `left` interactively in JavaScript. Doing so allows you to move elements in a Web page, as when you allow the user to drag and drop those elements.

Position Elements Using Absolute Positioning

① Create a `<div>` element that uses absolute positioning.

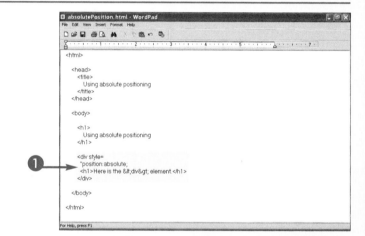

② Set the x location of the `<div>` element with the `left` style property.

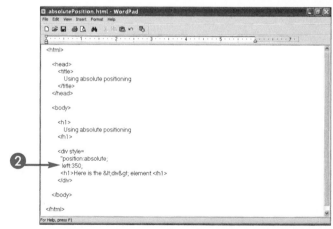

③ Set the y location of the `<div>`
element with the `top` style property.

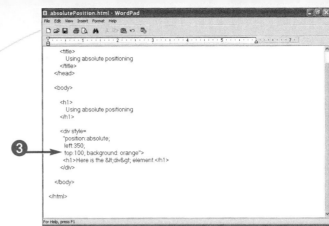

④ Open the Web page in a browser.

The `<div>` element appears as you
have positioned it in the Web page.

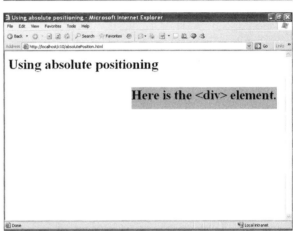

Extra

Although the default measurement is in pixels, you
can use inches if you append `"in"` to
measurements, such as `"3in"`; centimeters if you
append `"cm"`; or millimeters if you append `"mm"`.
To make sure that the browser uses pixel
measurements, you can append `"px"`, as in the
measurement `"350px"`. Note that although you can
use physical measurements like inches or
millimeters, all nonpixel measurements should be
treated as approximate. Although there are other
measurement systems available, pixel measurements
are the most commonly used screen measurements
in browser-hosted applications.

Do not forget that the positive y direction is
downward on the screen. Some people get confused
because it can seem that positive y should extend
upward from the bottom of the client area, but
screen measurements were designed to work like a
page of text, which is read from left to right, and
top to bottom. For that reason, y measurements
start at the top of the client area and extend
downward, not upward.

Position Elements Using Relative Positioning

You can position elements in a Web page using relative positioning and CSS styles. When you position something using relative positioning, you specify its location with respect to its default position in the Web page. For example, if you specify the relative position of a word in a sentence, you give its location with respect to where the browser normally places it. Using relative positioning, you can specify how far away, and in what direction, you want an element placed with respect to where it is normally displayed. In other words, relative positioning moves HTML elements out of the normal flow of where they would usually go in the browser's client area.

In order to use relative positioning, you assign the CSS style property position a value of "relative" this way:

"position: relative". Doing so makes the browser realize that you want to specify the location of the associated HTML element relative to where it would otherwise be displayed. As with other kinds of positioning, all measurements are in pixels by default.

As with absolute positioning, you can specify the relative location of an HTML element using style properties. You use the top style property to indicate how far the top of the element you are positioning should be offset from its default position. You use the bottom style property to specify where the bottom of the HTML element should go relative to its default position. Using these two properties lets you displace an HTML element up and down in a Web page. You can also use the left and right style properties to move elements to the left and right of their normal position in the browser's display.

Position Elements Using Relative Positioning

① Place text in a Web page to establish the normal flow of that text.

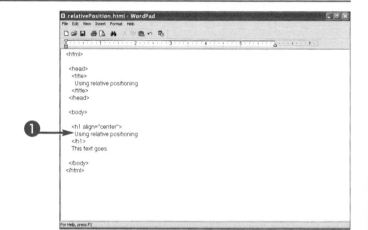

② Displace additional text upward from its default placement by 5 pixels.

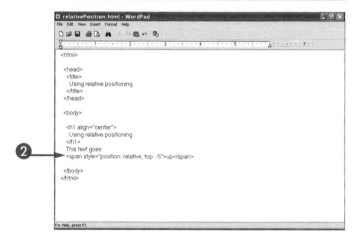

290

3 Displace additional text downward by 5 pixels.

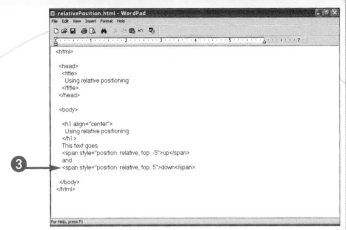

4 Open the Web page in a browser.

The text appears positioned as you specified.

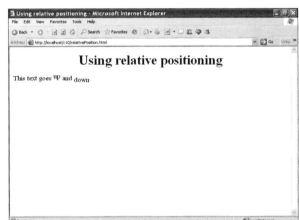

As with other types of measurements in browser-hosted applications, the default measurement is in pixels, but you can use other physical measurements if you prefer. If you want to use millimeters instead of pixel measurements, you can append `"mm"` to the end of measurements. For example, if you want to specify a measurement of 10 millimeters, express that measurement as `"10mm"`. To move an HTML element up by 10mm, you can use this CSS: `"position: relative; top: -10mm"`. If you want to use inches, use `"in"`, as in `"3in"`. If you want to use centimeters, use `"cm"`, as in this example: `"10cm"`. Although you can give physical measurements like inches and centimeters, you should treat all such measurements on the screen as approximate. To make sure the browser uses pixel measurements, you can append `"px"` to the end of measurements like `"350px"`.

Keep in mind that the positive y direction is downward on the screen. That means that if you want to move an item upward, you use a negative value for the top property, such as

```
<span style="position: relative;
top: -5">up</span>
```

Set HTML Element Visibility

You can make HTML elements visible or invisible using CSS styles. In particular, you use the CSS visibility style to control an element's appearance on the screen. Making elements visible and invisible in Web pages is valuable in Ajax applications because you can display pop-ups, or display elements with new data when that data is downloaded.

To set an element's visibility, you use the CSS style property named `visibility`. You can set this property to `"visible"` to display the associated HTML element, or `"hidden"` to hide it. Making items appear and disappear can be useful to Ajax applications that are not supposed to rely on page refreshes to display data.

One thing you should know here is that some browsers do not seem to handle the visibility style property well as an inline style. For example, if you create a `<div>` element like this: `<div style="visibility:hidden">`, some browsers ignore the visibility property. To make that property effective, you should use it in a `<style>` element instead.

Here is how that works: You give the `<div>` element an ID like this: `<div id="targetDiv">`. Then you can refer to that element as `#targetDiv` in a `<style>` element this way: `<style> #targetDiv </style>`. To set the `<div>` element's visibility property to hidden, you can use this HTML: `<style> #targetDiv {visibility : hidden}</style>`.

That sets the `<div>` element's visibility to hidden when the page first loads. The next step is to make the element visible, which you can do with JavaScript. To do that, create an object corresponding to the `<div>` element and set its visibility style to `"visible"` this way: `document.getElementById("targetDiv").style.visibility = "visible";`. When you execute that code, the `<div>` element appears on the screen.

Set HTML Element Visibility

① Create a `<style>` element, setting the visibility of a `<div>` element to `hidden`.

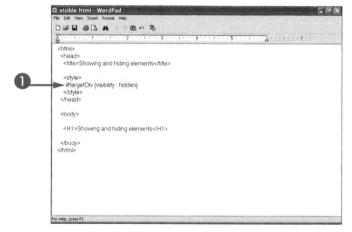

② Create the `<div>` element.

③ Add a button connected to a function named `showData`.

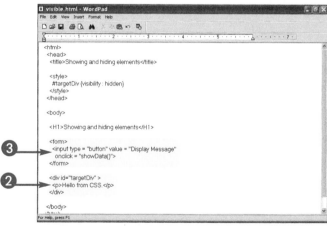

④ In the `showData` function, set the
`<div>` element's `visibility`
property to `visible`.

⑤ Open the Web page in a browser,
and click the button.

The message "Hello from CSS"
appears in the `<div>` element.

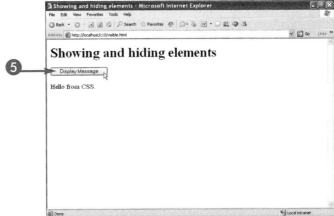

Apply It

You can also reverse the process, and hide an HTML element that was previously visible. Here is the CSS and
JavaScript for doing that:

```
<head>
  <title>Showing and hiding elements</title>

  <style>
    #targetDiv {visibility : visible}
  </style>
  <script language = "javascript">
    function showData()
    {
      document.getElementById("targetDiv").style.visibility =
        "hidden";
    }
  </script>
</head>
```

Create Web Page Pop-Ups

You can use CSS to create pop-up windows in Web browsers. That is useful in Ajax applications to display newly downloaded data. When important new data is read from the server, you can bring it to the user's attention immediately by displaying that data in a pop-up window.

To create a pop-up, you can use a `<div>` element to hold text. For example, a `<div>` element with the ID `"popup"` looks like this: `<div id = "popup" style="left:300; top:200; width:100; height: 70;">Hello from CSS.</div>`. You can make this pop-up appear and disappear in a Web page using JavaScript and CSS. To make the pop-up invisible when the Web page first appears, you can set its visibility property to hidden in a `<style>` element: `<style> #popup {background-color: #EE3333; font-weight: bold; font-family: arial; position: absolute; visibility: hidden; }`.

You can also set the position of the pop-up as needed in your JavaScript code. You already set the position of the pop-up when you created the `<div>` element this way: `<div id = "popup" style="left:300; top:200; width:100; height: 70;">Hello from CSS.</div>`. However, if you want to make the pop-up appear in various places in the Web page connected with the text in a number of different text fields; for example, you can change the location of the pop-up like this: `document.getElementById("popup").style.top = "300px"` and `document.getElementById ("popup").style.left = "600px"`.

To make the pop-up actually appear, all you have to do is set its visibility property to visible: `document .getElementById("popup").style.visibility = "visible"`. And to make the pop-up disappear, just set its visibility property to hidden.

Create Web Page Pop-ups

① Style a `<div>` element as a pop-up.

② Create the pop-up `<div>` element.

③ Add two buttons, one to show the pop-up and one to hide the pop-up.

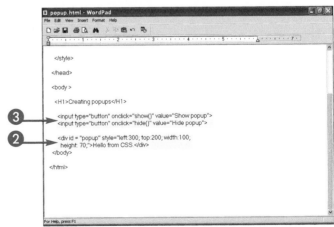

④ Add the JavaScript to show and hide the pop-up.

⑤ Open the Web page, and click each button.

The pop-up appears and disappears as you click each button.

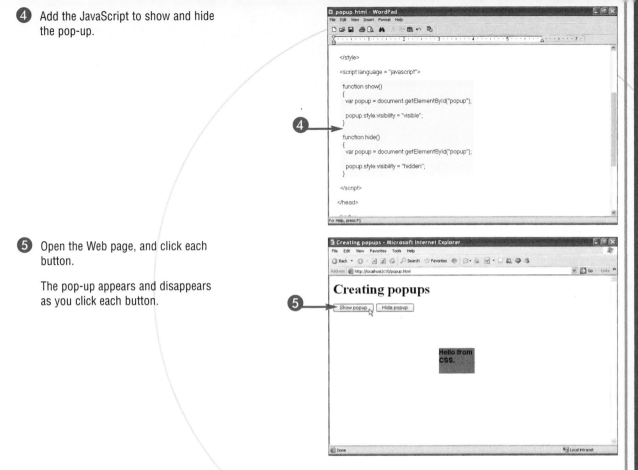

Apply It

You can alter the text in the pop-up using the innerHTML property of the pop-up, document.getElementById("popup").innerHTML, as you download new data from the server:

```
if(XMLHttpRequestObject) {

    XMLHttpRequestObject.open("GET", dataSource);

    XMLHttpRequestObject.onreadystatechange = function()
    {

        if (XMLHttpRequestObject.readyState == 4 &&
            XMLHttpRequestObject.status == 200) {
                document.getElementById("popup").innerHTML =
                    XMLHttpRequestObject.responseText;
        }

    }
```

Move Elements
in a Web Page

You can move HTML elements in a Web page using CSS styles. This is a useful technique when creating drag-and-drop applications, such as Ajax-based shopping-cart applications that let the user drag items to a shopping cart. When the item is dropped in the cart, your application can use Ajax to let the server know about the purchase.

To move an element in a Web page, you can use CSS and JavaScript. An element that can be moved in a Web page using CSS must be placed using absolute positioning, so you must specify that you are using absolute positioning for the element you want to move.

For example, if you want to move a pop-up around a Web page, you might set up its styles in a `<style>` element, making sure to give it absolute positioning: `<style> #popup { background-color: #EE3333;`

`font-weight: bold; font-family: arial; position: absolute; }`.

When you want to move an HTML element using CSS styles in JavaScript, you can use the positioning properties. For example, you can use the top style property to change the location of the top of the HTML element you want to move. If you originally set the top of a `<div>` element to a y value of 200 pixels like this: `<div id = "popup" style="left:300; top:200; width:100; height: 70;">Hello from CSS.</div>`, then you can move the `<div>` element downward in the Web page by 100 pixels if you execute this JavaScript: `document.get ElementById("popup").style.top = "400"`. As soon as you execute that line of code, the `<div>` element moves to its new position in the Web page. Besides the top style property, you can also use the right, left, and bottom properties to move HTML items in Web pages.

Move Elements in a Web Page

① Give the element you want to move absolute positioning.

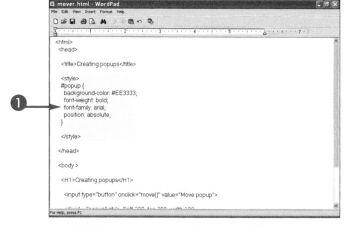

② Create the HTML element to move.

   In this example, it is a `<div>` element.

③ Add a button, and connect it to a function named `move`.

④ In the `move` function, move the
`<div>` element to the right.

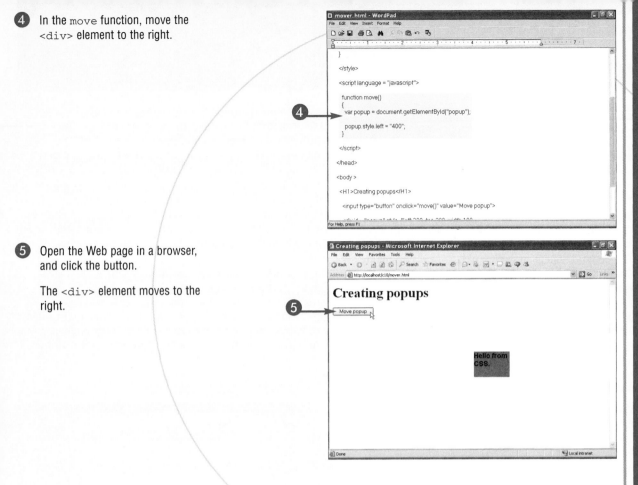

④

⑤ Open the Web page in a browser,
and click the button.

The `<div>` element moves to the
right.

⑤

Apply It

Although the example in this task simply moves the pop-up to the right, you are not restricted to motion in
any one dimension. If you want to move the pop-up in both the x and y directions, simply do so in successive
operations, like this:

```
<script language = "javascript">

  function move()
  {
    var popup = document.getElementById("popup");

    popup.style.left = "400";

    popup.style.top  = "500";
  }

</script>
```

Overlap HTML Elements

ou can use CSS to position elements in a Web page, and some of those elements may overlap each other. When you place elements in a Web page using absolute positioning, the one you place in a particular location may be covered by ones you place overlapping that position later. To handle overlap the way you want it, you use the CSS style z-index.

When you use absolute positioning with CSS styles in a Web page, you set an HTML element's position style attribute to "absolute", which allows you to specify the location of that element in a Web page. Once you make the positioning of HTML elements absolute, you can use the location CSS style properties to actually set the position of element — the top, left, right, and bottom style properties. All of these properties may be set to a measurement, which is usually in pixels.

By default, screen measurements are made in pixels in browser-based applications. You can specify other

measurement systems by appending "in" to measurements for inches, as in "4in"; or "cm" for centimeters; or "mm" for millimeters.

When you position more than one HTML element in a Web page, you run the risk that such elements may overlap. If you do not mind that, but want to be sure that you control which element appears on top of which other elements, use the z-index CSS style property. When you use this property, elements with a high z-index appear on top of elements with a lower z-index or no z-index setting.

Using z-index, you have control over which elements appear on top of which other elements, which is very valuable when you are writing drag-and-drop Ajax applications — if you do not control which element rides over which other elements as the user drags elements, your application may give some strange visual results.

Overlap HTML Elements

① Style three <div> elements to use absolute positioning.

② Create the three <div> elements.

298

③ Give the middle `<div>` element a high `z-index` value, 200, so it appears on top of the other two `<div>` elements.

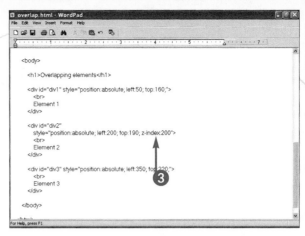

④ Open the Web page in a browser.

The middle `<div>` element appears on top of the other two `<div>` elements.

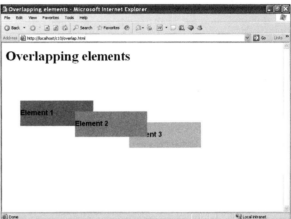

Apply It

You can access the `z-index` property in JavaScript as the `zIndex` property of JavaScript objects. Using that property means that you can change the z-index of an HTML element at runtime, using JavaScript like this:

```javascript
<script language = "javascript">

  function overlap()
  {
    var popup = document.getElementById("popup");

    popup.style.zIndex = "400";

  }

</script>
```

Being able to change HTML elements's `z-index` property like this in JavaScript means you can change which elements appear on top of which other elements.

Create a PHP Page

You can create PHP pages on the server that react to data sent from the browser, handle that data, and send data back to the browser. PHP is commonly used with Ajax, and most of the Ajax examples you see on the Web use PHP as their server-side language. Creating PHP-enabled pages is not difficult — you simply need to enclose your PHP code inside the markup `<?` and `?>`.

When you write a PHP page, you use standard HTML, as usual for a Web page. A PHP-enabled server sends that HTML back to the browser without changing it. To work with PHP in the page, you insert PHP code where you want the results of that code to appear in the page and surround that code with the markup `<?` and `?>`. You save your work in a file with the extension .php so a PHP-enabled server knows that your page uses PHP.

For example, you might have a standard Web page that has a header section like this: `<html>` `<head>` `<title>`

A first PHP page `</title>` `</head>`. And the body might look like this: `<body>` `<h1>` A first PHP page `</h1>` `</body>` `</html>`.

So far, there's nothing in this Web page's body besides an `<h1>` element with the text "A first PHP page" in it. You can add PHP code to this page if you insert PHP code where you want it in the page. You can insert as many PHP code sections as you want — all you have to do is surround each such section with `<?` and `?>`.

For example, the PHP function `phphinfo` returns an HTML table giving the details of your PHP installation, and you can insert that table in your Web page's body like this: `<body>` `<h1>` A first PHP page `</h1>` `<? phpinfo();  ?>` `</body>` `</html>`. Note that, like JavaScript, each line of PHP ends with a semicolon. You can also comment out lines with `//` in PHP.

Create a PHP Page

① Create an HTML document and give it a `<body>` element.

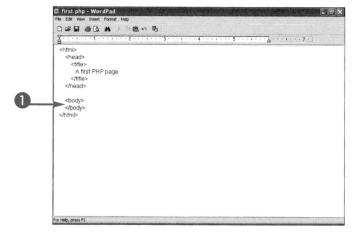

② Add an `<h1>` header to the body of the page.

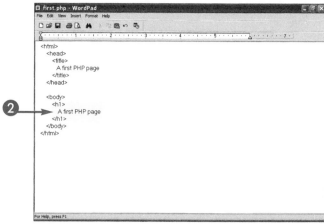

③ Add the PHP code `<? phpinfo(); ?>`, and save the document with the extension .php.

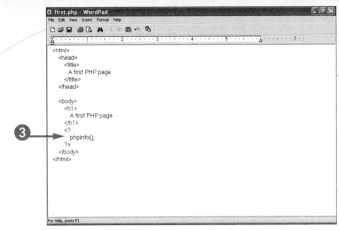

④ Open the document in a browser to see the details of your PHP installation.

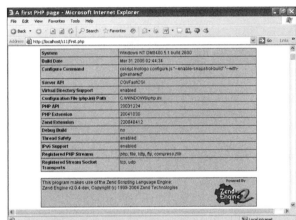

Apply It

If your Web server supports other scripting languages, such as JavaSever Pages (JSP), you might want to specifically indicate that your scripts are written in PHP, which you can do by using the markup `<?php` and `?>` instead of just `<?` and `?>`.

Example:

```
<body>

  <h1>
    A first PHP page
  </h1>

  <?php
    phpinfo();
  ?>

</body>
```

Create HTML to Send to the Browser

You can create your own HTML text using PHP to send to the browser. To send text to the browser from your PHP code, you can use the PHP echo statement. The echo statement is very popular in PHP because you can use it to send the results of your calculations back to the browser. Rather than relying on sending static text to the browser, you can perform your calculations in PHP and then use the echo statement to send the results to the browser.

As an example, you might start a PHP page in the standard way with an HTML head section: `<html> <head> <title> Using echo in PHP </title> </head>`. Then you can add a body section: `<body> <h1> Using echo in PHP </h1> </body> </html>`.

You might want to display some text from your PHP code in this Web page, such as "Greetings from PHP."; you can do that like this: `<body> <h1> Using echo in PHP </h1> <? echo "Greetings from PHP."; ?> </body> </html>`. Note that the text you pass to the echo statement is enclosed in quotation marks, just as you would handle text strings in JavaScript.

When someone views your Web page by navigating to it on the server, the server reads your PHP and sees that you are using the echo statement to echo text to the browser. It reads the text you want to echo and sends it to the browser. That text is displayed at the location of the PHP script that uses the echo statement, so this is the HTML sent to the browser: `<html> <head> <title> Using echo in PHP </title> </head> <body> <h1> Using echo in PHP </h1> Greetings from PHP. </body> </html>`.

Create HTML to Send to the Browser

① Create a new Web page and give it a `<body>` section.

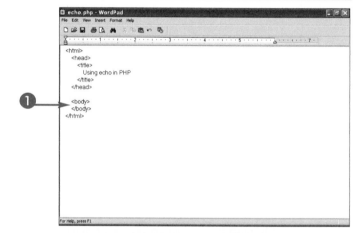

② Add an `<h1>` header to the page to explain what the page does.

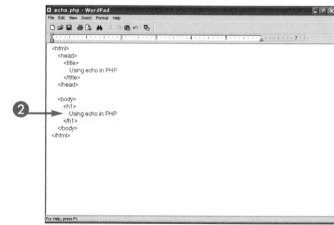

3 Use the PHP echo statement to send the text "Greetings from PHP." to the browser.

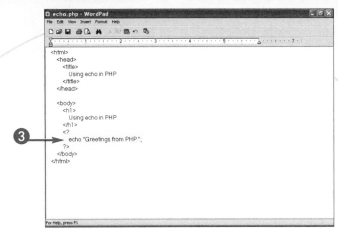

4 Open the document in your browser.

The message "Greetings from PHP." appears.

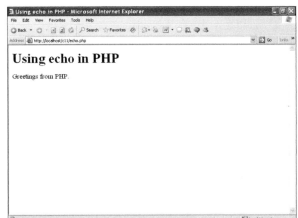

Apply It

This example only sends plain text back to the browser, but you can use the echo statement to send back HTML markup as well, like this:

```
<html>
    <head>
        <title>
            Using echo in PHP
        </title>
    </head>
    <body>
        <h1>
            Using echo in PHP
        </h1>
        <?
            echo "<h1>Greetings from <i>PHP</i></h1>.";
        ?>
    </body>
</html>
```

Work with Variables

You can handle variables in PHP just as you can in JavaScript. Variable names in PHP start with a dollar sign ($) like this: $temperature. You can assign values to variables in PHP just as you can in JavaScript, and you can use operators on the values stored in variables just as you can in JavaScript.

You do not have to declare variables in PHP before you use them. For example, you might have a collection of cars and keep track of the number of cars you own in a variable named $cars. To start, you might buy five cars: <body> <h1> Using variables in PHP </h1> <? echo "Buying five cars...
"; $cars = 5;.

That stores a value of 5 in the variable $cars. As with JavaScript, you can store numbers, text, or objects in variables in PHP. Now that you have stored a value in the $cars variable, you can display that value using the

echo statement like this: <? echo "Buying five cars...
"; $cars = 5; echo "Current number of cars: ", $cars, "<br>";.

Note the use of the echo statement here. You can list the items you want to echo back to the browser by separating them with a comma, as you see: echo "Current number of cars: ", $cars, "<br>";. This statement sends the text "Current number of cars: ", followed by the value in the variable $cars, followed by the HTML "<br>" to the browser.

You can use operators with variables as well. Say that you buy seven more cars; you could add 7 to the current value in the $cars variable this way: $cars = $cars + 7;. Then you can display the new number of cars in your collection this way: echo "New number of cars: ", $cars, "<br>";.

Work with Variables

① Create a PHP page and store a value of 5 in a variable named $cars.

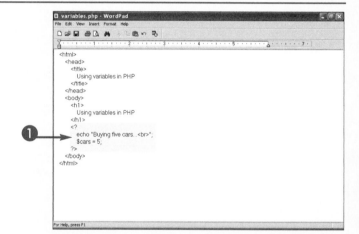

② Display the value in the $cars variable in the browser.

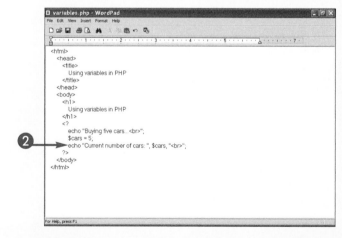

③ Buy seven more cars and display the new total of cars.

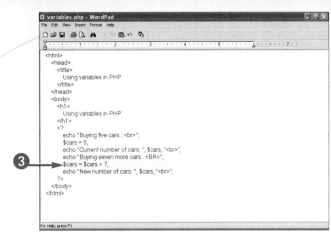

③ → `$cars = $cars + 7;`

④ Open the Web page in a browser to track the number of cars in your collection.

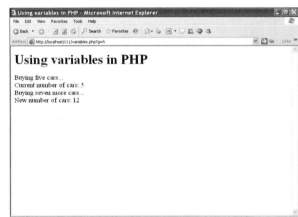

Apply It

This example separates the items to send to the browser with commas in the echo statement. But you can also use the PHP concatenation operator, which is a dot (.) to combine items into a single text string.

Example:

```php
<?
  echo "Buying five cars...<br>";
  $cars = 5;

  echo "Current number of cars: " . $cars . "<br>";
  echo "Buying seven more cars...<BR>";

  $cars = $cars + 7;

  echo "New number of cars: " . $cars . "<br>";
?>
```

Create Arrays

You can create arrays in PHP and work with them as you can in JavaScript. To create an array in PHP, you can use the PHP array statement. After you have created an array, you can access the values in the array using an index, and read and set the values in that array in the same way as you can using JavaScript. As in JavaScript, arrays start with the index 0, not 1.

To create an array, you can use the PHP array statement. For example, say that you want to keep track of the scores of students in a class you are teaching on PHP and that you want to use an array named `$scores` for that purpose — (note that array names, like variable names, start with $ in PHP).

To create the new array named `$scores`, you use a statement like this in PHP: `$scores = array();`, which creates an empty array. To initialize the array with the

students' scores 56, 29, and 98, you can use this statement in PHP: `$scores = array(56, 29, 98);`. That creates a one-dimensional array named `$scores`, whose contents are the scores given. You can access the values in the array as you would in JavaScript — just use a numeric index inside square brackets like this: `$scores[index]`. In particular, `$scores[0]` holds the value 56, `$scores[1]` holds the value 29, and `$scores[2]` holds the value 98.

As with other programming languages, you can also assign values to the elements in an array much as you would with simple variables. For example, to assign the value 78 to `$scores[1]`, you simply use the PHP assignment operator, =, like this: `$scores[1] = 78;`. All of which is to say, if you know how to use arrays in JavaScript, you have a good head start on using arrays in PHP.

Create Arrays

① Create a new PHP page with a `<body>` element.

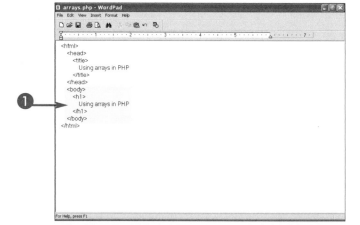

② Create an array named `$scores` with the values 56, 29, 98.

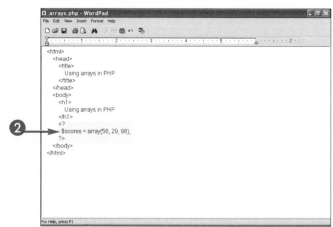

③ Display the values stored in the
`$scores` array.

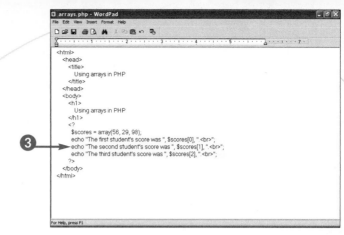

④ Open the Web page in a browser.

The array values appear.

Apply It

You can also use text indexes in PHP arrays, not just numeric indexes. Here is an example:

```
<?
  $scores = array();

  $scores["Allen"] = 56;
  $scores["Tina"] = 29;
  $scores["Mike"] = 98;

  echo "The first student's score was ", $scores["Allen"],
    ".<br>";
  echo "The second student's score was ", $scores["Tina"],
    ".<br>";
  echo "The third student's score was ", $scores["Mike"],
    ".<br>";
?>
```

Operators

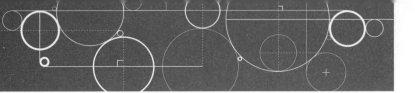

You can use operators in PHP just as you can in JavaScript. All the operators you know from JavaScript, except the === object comparison operator, are available in PHP. And you use them just as you do in JavaScript.

The most basic PHP operator is the = assignment operator. For example, if you want to store the value 219 in a variable named $apples, you can assign that value this way: $apples = 219;.

The basic PHP math operators are the + operator for addition, the - operator for subtraction, the * operator for multiplication, and the / operator for division. There is also a modulus operator, %, as in JavaScript. For example, if $apples holds 219, then you can multiply the value in $apples by 2 this way: $apples = 2 * $apples;.

In fact, just as in JavaScript, you can shorten the operator/assignment process by combining an operator

with an equals (=) sign. For example, to multiply the value in $apples by 2, you can do this: $apples *= 2;, using the compound *= operator. To add 400 apples to the value in $apples, you can do this: $apples += 400. Here are the possible compound operators in PHP: = += -= *= /= .= %= &= |= ^= <<= >>=.

PHP also supports operators of the kind you use in if statements, such as the == and != comparison operators. For example, if you want to test if the number in $apples is the same as the number in $oranges, you can compare them with this expression: $apples == $oranges. This expression is true if the value in $apples is the same as the value in $oranges. In addition to the comparison operators, you can also use the && and || logical operators to combine expressions like this: $apples == $oranges && $bananas == $lemons.

Use PHP Operators

① Create a new PHP page with a `<body>` section.

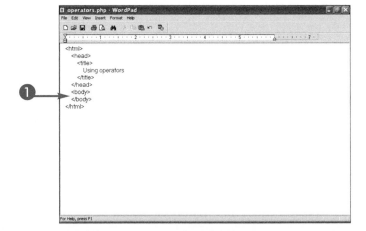

② Test the addition and subtraction operators by adding and subtracting values.

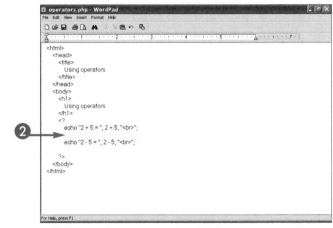

3 Test the multiplication and division operators by multiplying and dividing values.

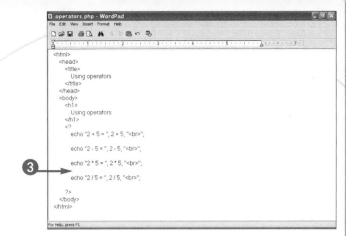

4 Open the Web page in a browser.

The results of your calculations appear in the Web page.

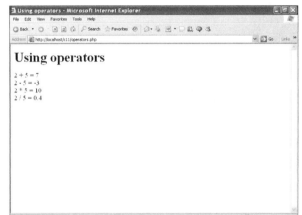

Apply It

Besides the standard +, -, *, and / operators, PHP also supports the ++ increment and -- decrement operators. For example, this PHP code places a value of 1 in $data, increments it, and decrements it, giving you 1, 2, 1:

```
<?

  $data = 1;
  echo $data, "<br>";

  $data++;
  echo $data, "<br>";

  $data--;
  echo $data, "<br>";

?>
```

Handle Text String Data

You can work with text in PHP because PHP supports string functions, just as JavaScript does. Being able to work with string data can be very important in Ajax applications. For example, when you send text data to the server, you may want to extract commands from that text, and you can use string functions to do that.

There are plenty of string functions to work with in PHP; in fact, that is one of PHP's strengths. For example, the `strtoupper` function converts text to uppercase: You simply pass the text you want to convert to uppercase, and this function returns that text in uppercase. For example, `strtoupper("No worries.")` returns the text "NO WORRIES." Similarly, the `ucfirst` function converts just the first character of the text you pass to it to uppercase.

The trim function is a useful one, because you can use it to trim leading and trailing spaces from text. That is

handy to work with user input because there are frequently some extra spaces at the beginning or end of such text. If you had the text " No worries.", for example, and passed that text to the trim function, that function returns "No worries."

The `strlen` function returns the length of a string, measured in characters. Knowing the length of a string can be useful when you want to extract substrings from that string because you have to supply numbers of characters to extract.

You can also search through strings to see if they contain specific text using the `strpos` function. For example, if you want to determine where the word "worries" starts in the text "No worries", you can use this expression: `strpos("No worries.", "worries")`. In this case, the word "worries" starts at position 3 in the text "No worries" — that is, you count character positions starting from 1, not 0 as you do elements in a PHP array.

Handle Text String Data

① Display the text you are working with, and then capitalize that text with the `strtoupper` function.

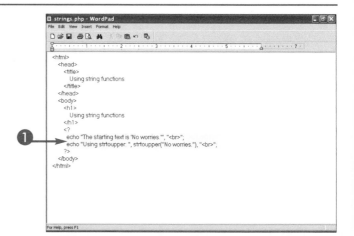

② Use the `trim` function to remove leading and trailing spaces, and the `strlen` function to determine the length of the text.

③ Use `ucfirst` to capitalize the first letter in some text, and use the `strpos` function to determine the location of a substring.

```
<html>
  <head>
    <title>
      Using string functions
    </title>
  </head>
  <body>
    <h1>
      Using string functions
    </h1>
    <?
      echo "The starting text is 'No worries.'", "<br>";
      echo "Using strtoupper: ", strtoupper("No worries."), "<br>";
      echo "Using trim: ", trim("    No worries."), "<br>";
      echo "Using strlen: ", "The text is ", strlen("No worries."),
        " characters in length.<br>";
      echo "Using ucfirst: ", "No ", ucfirst("worries."), "<br>";
      echo "Using strpos: ", "'worries' is at position ",
        strpos("No worries.", "worries"), "<br>";
    ?>
  </body>
</html>
```

④ Open the Web page in a browser.

The PHP string functions display data about the string "No worries."

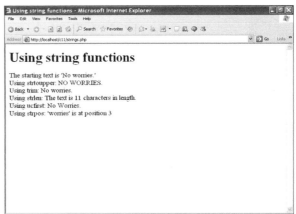

Using string functions

The starting text is 'No worries.'
Using strtoupper: NO WORRIES.
Using trim: No worries.
Using strlen: The text is 11 characters in length.
Using ucfirst: No Worries.
Using strpos: 'worries' is at position 3

Apply It

You can use the `substr` function to extract a substring from a string of text. You supply the string to extract from, the starting position of the string to extract, and the number of characters to extract. For example, `substr("No worries.", 3, 7)` gives you "worries". You can also use the `substr_replace` function to replace a substring with other text. For example, `substr_replace("No worries.", "troubles.", 3, 8)` gives you "No troubles." Here is what sample code using these two functions looks like:

```
<body>
  <h1>Using additional string functions</h1>
  <?
    echo "Using substr: ", substr("No worries.", 3, 7), "<br>";
    echo "Using substr_replace: ",
      substr_replace("No worries.", "troubles.", 3, 8), "<br>";
  ?>
</body>
```

Make Choices with the if Statement

You ou can use the `if` statement in PHP to make choices in your code, just as you can with the `if` statement in JavaScript. If you know how the `if` statement works in JavaScript, you already know how the `if` statement works in PHP. The syntax is the same.

For example, say that you want to use PHP to see if you are a millionaire by checking the amount of dollars you have in your bank account, as stored in a variable named `$bankAccount`. Say that you start with `$bankAccount` set to 750000. You can check with an `if` statement to see if you are a millionaire this way: `if ($bankAccount < 1000000)`.

You can execute code if the test condition of the `if` statement is true, just as you can with JavaScript. For example, if you want to display the message "Sorry, you are not a millionaire." if you do not have enough money,

you can use an `if` statement like this: `if ($bankAccount < 1000000) { echo "Sorry, you are not a millionaire."; }`. As in JavaScript, you can enclose multiple statements to execute in curly braces (`{`, `}`) if the `if` statement's test condition is true.

You can also use additional operators in the `if` statement's test condition to test several conditions at once. For example, you might have a variable named `$lottery`, which can hold the text "wins" or "loses". If it holds "wins", you are a millionaire; if "loses", you are not — at least, not from winning the lottery. You can test the values in the `$bankAccount` and `$lottery` in the same `if` statement this way: `if ($bankAccount < 1000000 && $lottery == "loses") { echo "Sorry, you are not a millionaire."; }`.

Make Choices with the if Statement

① Set up two variables in PHP.

This example uses `$bankAccount`, which holds 750000, and `$lottery`, which holds the text `"loses"`.

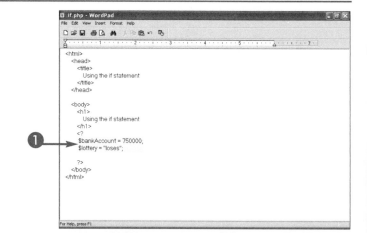

② Create an `if` statement to check if `$bankAccount` holds a value less than 1000000 and `$lottery` holds the value `"loses"`.

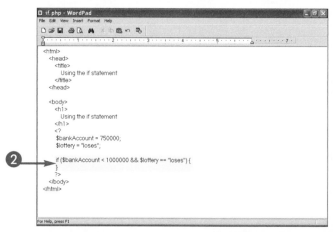

③ Display the bad news that you are not a millionaire if the `if` statement's test condition is true.

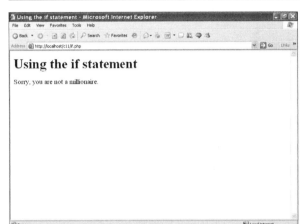

④ Open the Web page in a browser.

The Web page displays the text "Sorry, you are not a millionaire."

Apply It

The PHP `if` statement also supports an `else` clause, just as the JavaScript `if` statement does. The code you place inside the curly braces of the `else` clause is executed if the `if` statement's test condition turns out to be false, not true. Here is an example showing how to use the `else` clause in an `if` statement:

```php
<?
   $bankAccount = 750000;
   $lottery = "loses";

   if ($bankAccount < 1000000 && $lottery == "loses") {
      echo "Sorry, you are not a millionaire.";
   }
   else {
      echo "Congratulations, you are a millionaire.";
   }
?>
```

Read Data from Text Fields

Y ou can use PHP to extract the data from the HTML controls in Web pages sent to the server. In particular, if you give a name to an HTML control such as a text field, you can access the data in that control in PHP by passing the control's name to the built-in PHP $_REQUEST array.

To set up a Web page to send data to the server you need to use an HTML <form> element with a Submit button with two attributes: action and method. The action attribute holds the URL to which you want to send data, and if you are using PHP, that is the URL of the PHP script that handles your data. That URL can be a relative URL, containing simply the name of the PHP script if that script is in the same server directory as the Web page whose data the script is supposed to process. In addition, the method attribute holds the HTTP method you want to use to send data to the server — usually "GET" or "POST".

For example, say that you want to ask users their names, and that you want to send that data to a PHP script named textfield.php. You can use this HTML form to collect the data in a Web page: <form method="post" action="textfield.php"> Enter your name: <input name="name" type="text"> <input type="submit" value="Submit"> </form>. When the user clicks Submit, the text in the text field is sent to textfield.php.

In the textfield.php script, you can recover the text in the text field using the text field's name, which is just "name" like this: $name = $_REQUEST["name"]. That is all it takes.

Note that the data you send to PHP scripts does not have to come from HTML controls — if you URL-encode that data, you can send it using the GET or POST methods yourself to PHP on the server, which can use the $_REQUEST array to read that data.

Read Data from Text Fields

① Add a form to a Web page, and set the action attribute to textfield.php.

② Add a text field with the name "name" and a Submit button.

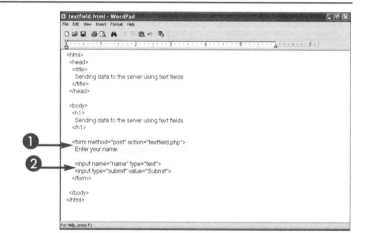

③ Use the expression $_REQUEST["name"] in textfield.php to read the name the user enters.

④ Open the Web page that contains the text field, type a name, and click Submit.

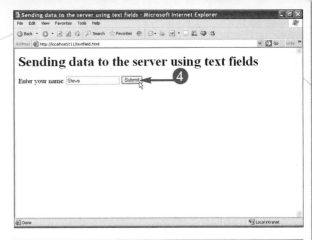

The Web page created by `textfield.php` appears, displaying the name you typed.

Apply It

This example uses the POST method to send data to the server, but you can also use the GET method:

```
<form method="get" action="textfield.php">
  Enter your name:

  <input name="name" type="text">

  <input type="submit" value="Submit">
</form>
```

In your PHP, you still use the $_REQUEST array to read data, whether you send data using GET or POST:

```
<body>
  <h1>
    Reading data from text fields on the server
  </h1>
  Your name is
  <?
    echo $_REQUEST["name"];
  ?>
</body>
```

Read Data from Check Boxes

You can use PHP to read data from check boxes — in particular, which check boxes have been checked in a Web page. You can work with check boxes by giving them a value when you create them in a Web page and reading that value in your PHP script.

To create a check box, you use the `<input>` HTML element and set the `type` attribute to `"checkbox"`. You also need to assign a value to the `name` attribute if you want to be able to access the check box's setting in PHP. And you can assign a value to the check box using the `value` attribute. The `value` property holds the text that is sent to the server. For example, if you ask users what items they want to buy along with a computer, such as a screen, your check box might look like this in HTML: `<input name="screen" type="checkbox" value="screen">`. If the user selects this check box, the value `"screen"` is sent to the server-side PHP script, and

you can access that value using the `$_REQUEST` array.

In PHP, you can access the setting of this check box this way: `$_REQUEST["screen"]`. This expression gives you the value set for the check box, but there is a possible problem here: If the check box is not selected, trying to find an element in the `$_REQUEST` array for the element named `"screen"` gives you an error, because there is no such element.

Instead, check to see if the `$_REQUEST["screen"]` exists before trying to work with it. You can do that with the PHP `isset` function, which checks to see if an array element exists, and if it does, returns true. So you can safely echo the value of the check box named `"screen"` to the browser if you use this PHP: `if (isset($_REQUEST["screen"])){ echo $_REQUEST["screen"]; }.`

Read Data from Check Boxes

① Create two check boxes, and give them the names `"screen"` and `"mouse"`.

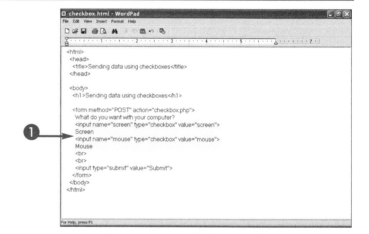

② In the PHP script, check if values have been assigned to the check boxes, and if so, display those values.

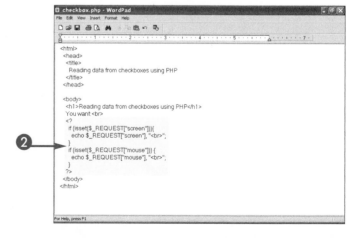

③ Open the Web page, click an item or items, and click Submit.

The PHP script indicates the item or items you selected.

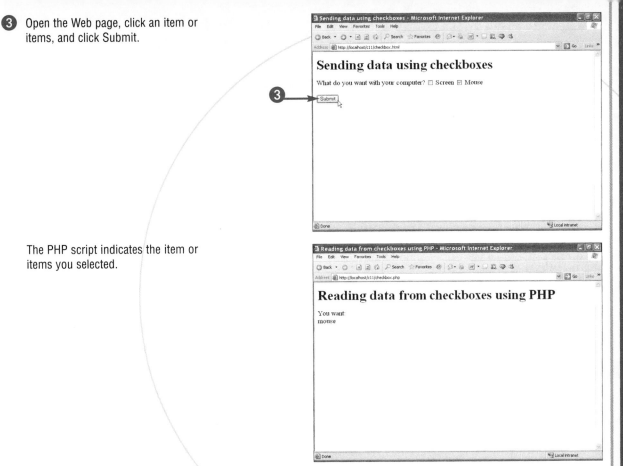

Apply It

If you simply want to determine if a check box is checked or not, use the `isset` function. You do not need to check the value of the selected check boxes.

```
<body>
  <h1>Reading data from checkboxes using PHP</h1>
  You want:<br>
  <?
    if (isset($_REQUEST["screen"])){
      echo "You selected the screen.<br>";
    }

    if (isset($_REQUEST["mouse"])) {
      echo "You selected the mouse.<br>";
    }
  ?>
</body>
```

Read Data from Radio Buttons

You can read data from radio buttons in Web pages using PHP on the server. To create radio buttons in a Web page, you use a number of radio button controls, giving them all the same value in their `name` property. That groups the radio buttons together as far as the browser is concerned, which means that when the user selects one of the group of radio buttons, that radio button is selected, and all the other radio buttons in the group are deselected. When the data in the radio button group is sent to the server, you can access it using the `$_REQUEST` array, using the name of the radio button group as an index in that array.

You create a radio button using the `<input>` element, setting the type attribute to `"radio"` this way: `<input name="radios" type="radio">`. To be able to pass a value to the server-side script, you assign a value to the `value` attribute. For example, you might ask the user a question in a Web page, such as "Do you want a raise?", and then offer two radio buttons in the same radio button group — one with the value `"Yes"`, and one with the answer `"No"` like this: `<input name="radios" type="radio" value="Yes">Yes<input name="radios" type="radio" value="No"> No`.

If the user selects a radio button and clicks Submit, the server-side PHP script can determine which radio button is clicked by examining the expression `$_REQUEST["radios"]`. This expression returns the value of the radio button that is selected when the Submit button is clicked in the Web page. Because only one radio button in a group can be selected at once, only one value needs to be read for the radio group.

Read Data from Radio Buttons

① Create two radio buttons with the values Yes and No.

② In the PHP script, determine which radio button the user selected, and display that selection.

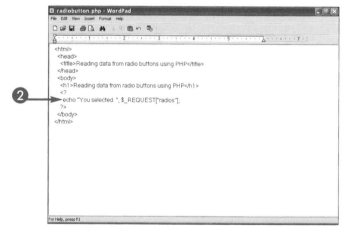

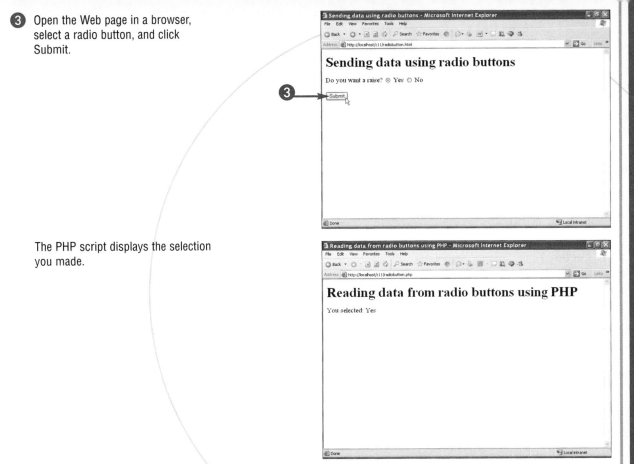

3 Open the Web page in a browser, select a radio button, and click Submit.

The PHP script displays the selection you made.

Apply It

When a Web page with radio buttons is first displayed in the browser, no radio button is selected unless you specify that one should be, using the HTML checked attribute. To handle the case where the user does not select a radio button, you can use the isset function to test if a radio button has been selected before trying to work with it in code.

Example:
```
   <html>
 <head>
   <title>Reading data from radio buttons using PHP</title>
 </head>
 <body>
   <h1>Reading data from radio buttons using PHP</h1>
   <?
     if (isset($_REQUEST["radios"])) {
       echo "You selected: ", $_REQUEST["radios"];
     }
   ?>
 </body>
</html>
```

Send XML to the Browser

You can send XML back to the browser using PHP if you set the correct HTTP header. When you send data back to the browser, the HTTP header named Content-Type sets the type of the data you are sending to the browser, so the browser can interpret that data properly.

By default, the data you send to the browser using PHP is HTML text, and you can read it using the XMLHttpRequest object's responseText property. To change that so that you send XML to the browser, which you can read in the XMLHttpRequest object's responseXml property, you must change the setting of the Content-Type HTTP header of your data.

You set HTTP headers with the built-in header function in PHP. To specify that the HTTP Content-Type header should indicate that the data you send back to the browser is XML, you call the header function this way:

header('Content-Type: text/xml'). To indicate that the data you send back to the browser is HTML, you call the header function this way: header('Content-Type: text/html'). When you set the Content-Type header, make sure you do so before sending any data back to the browser.

When you set the Content-Type header, you are setting the MIME type of your data. MIME means Multipurpose Internet Mail Extensions, and every common data type, from plain text to JavaScript, has an assigned MIME type. You can find the complete list of MIME types at www.iana.org/assignments/media-types/. For example, the MIME type for JPG images is image/jpeg; the MIME type for plain text is text/plain.

After setting the Content-Type header to indicate that you are sending XML data back to the browser, do not forget to send an XML declaration to start the actual data.

Send XML to the Browser

① Set the Content-Type header to "text/xml" in a PHP file.

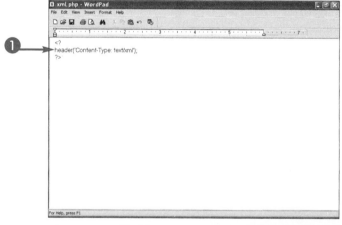

② Send an XML declaration to the browser.

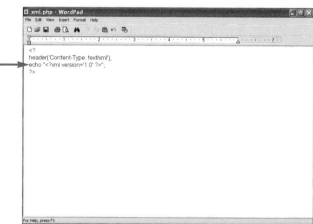

③ Send your XML data to the browser.

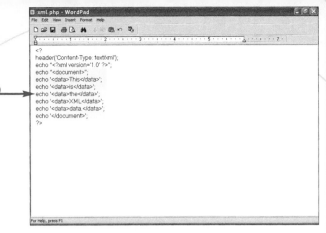

④ Open the PHP file in a browser.

The XML data you want to send back to the browser appears.

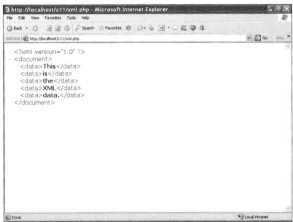

Apply It

You can also generate XML under program control. Here is some PHP code that sends the same XML, as in this task's example, using PHP code:

```
<?
header('Content-Type: text/xml');

$data = array('This', 'is', 'the', 'XML', 'data.');

echo '<?xml version="1.0" ?>';
echo '<document>';
foreach ($data as $value)
{
  echo '<data>';
  echo $value;
  echo '</data>';
}
echo '</document>';
?>
```

Work with the for Loop

You can use loop statements in PHP, just as you can in JavaScript. The most basic loop in PHP is the for loop, and that loop works just as it does in JavaScript. In PHP, you supply a loop index, initialize it, and test that loop index as you iterate through the loop.

You construct a for loop with the keyword for, and three items inside parentheses, followed by the body of the loop that you want executed multiple times. The first item inside the parentheses lets you initialize a loop index that keeps track of the number of times you execute the body of the loop. For example, for ($loopIndex = 0;...) sets the loop index variable named $loopIndex to 0 in preparation for the rest of the loop.

The second item inside the for loop's parentheses is the test condition that, when false, ends the loop. You typically use comparison operators here, together with the current value of the loop index. For example, for

($loopIndex = 0; $loopIndex < 5;...) means that you want to execute the loop when the condition $loopIndex < 5 remains true. When that condition is false, the loop ends.

The third item inside the for loop's parentheses is the increment expression, which you usually use to increment the value in the loop's index variable. For example, for ($loopIndex = 0; $loopIndex < 5; $loopIndex++) creates a for loop where the loop index is initialized to 0, keeps looping while the value in the loop index is less than 5, and increments the loop index at the end of each iteration of the loop.

The body of the for loop is enclosed inside curly braces, coming right after the section of the loop inside the parentheses. For example, for ($loopIndex = 0; $loopIndex < 5; $loopIndex++){ echo "PHP says hello five times!
"; } displays "PHP says hello five times!
" five times in a Web page.

Work with the for Loop

1 Set up a new for loop.

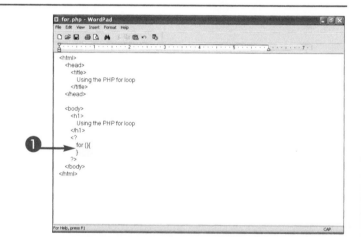

2 Place the control items inside the for loop's parentheses.

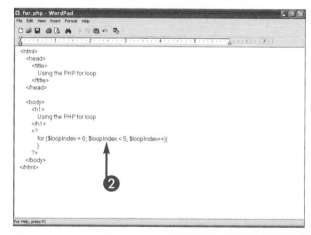

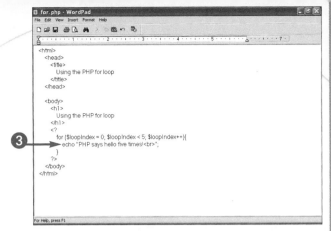

3 In the body of the `for` loop, echo a message to the Web browser.

4 Open the Web page in a browser.

The message "PHP says hello five times!" appears five times.

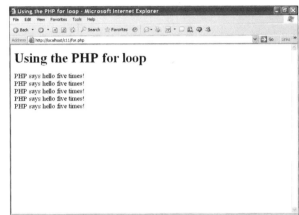

Apply It

You do not need to supply all three items inside the parentheses of a `for` loop. In fact, all three items are optional. Here is an example that omits the final item by incrementing the loop index variable in the body of the loop instead.

Example:
```
    <body>
  <h1>
    Using the PHP for loop
  </h1>
  <?
    for ($loopIndex = 0; $loopIndex < 5;){
      echo "PHP says hello five times!<br>";
        $loopIndex++
    }
  ?>
</body>
```

Work with the while Loop

You can use the while loop in PHP to keep executing a set of statements while a particular expression remains true. The while loop in PHP works just as the while loop in JavaScript does. You simply supply the condition to test, and the while loop continues to execute the body of the loop while that condition remains true.

To create a while loop, you use the keyword while, followed by a pair of parentheses, followed by the body of the loop. The body of the loop is enclosed in curly braces, { and }.

After the while keyword comes a pair of parentheses, and you place the test condition for the while loop inside those parentheses. You typically use a while loop to read from a file on the server, for example, and keep looping while there is more data to be read. You can also use

while loops with a loop index variable if you prefer; for example, starting a while loop this way: while ($loopIndex <= 5), means that you want to keep looping while the value in the variable $loopIndex is less than or equal to 5.

If you want to use a loop index in a while loop, initialize that loop index before entering the loop, like this: $loopIndex = 1; while ($loopIndex <= 5). And in the body of the loop, take care to increment the loop index variable yourself, as shown here: $loopIndex = 1; while ($loopIndex <= 5){ $loopIndex++; }.

In addition to handling the loop index, you can make this loop display the message "PHP says hello five times!
" this way: $loopIndex = 1; while ($loopIndex <= 5){ echo "PHP says hello five times!
"; $loopIndex++; }.

Work with the while Loop

① Create a new while loop.

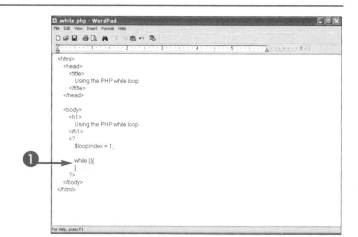

② Set the test condition of the while loop.

③ Add the body of the loop, making the loop display the message
`"PHP says hello five times!<br>"` five times.

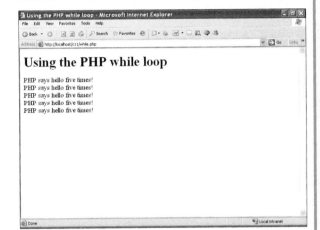

④ Open the PHP page in a browser.

The message "PHP says hello five times!" appears five times.

Apply It

There is also another form of the while loop that you can use — the do...while loop. With the do...while loop, you test the condition at the end of the loop, not the beginning, this way:

```
<body>
    <h1>
        Using the PHP while loop
    </h1>
    <?
        $loopIndex = 1;

        do {
            echo "PHP says hello five times!<br>";
            $loopIndex++;
        } while ($loopIndex <= 5);
    ?>
</body>
```

This is useful if the condition you want to test is not set until the body of the loop executes.

Work with the foreach Loop

You can use the PHP `foreach` loop to work with collections like arrays in PHP. Usually, when you want to loop over an array, you must supply the beginning and end conditions of the loop. If you work with a `for` loop, you must supply the initialization condition and the termination condition of the loop. If you work with a `while` loop, you must supply the test condition that makes the loop terminate. However, the `foreach` loop loops over collections without any need for a beginning or termination condition, which makes setting up such a loop far easier because you do not have to worry about being off by one when setting up a loop index, or getting test conditions wrong.

While you need to specify how many times `for` loops and `while` loops iterate, the `foreach` loop bases its operation purely on the number of items in the collection you are iterating over. For example, say you have an array with the elements `"Hello"`, `"from"`, and `"PHP."` in it, which you can create like this: `$data = array('Hello', 'from', 'PHP.')`. You can iterate over each element in that array easily using a `foreach` loop.

To use a `foreach` loop, you start with the `foreach` keyword, followed by specific instructions inside parentheses. For example, if you want to work with an array named `$data`, you begin your `foreach` loop this way: `foreach ($data as $value)`. This works with the `$data` array, and each time through the loop, the current value from the `$data` array will be assigned to the variable named `$value`. For example, if you want to display the values in the `$data` array in the Web browser, you can do something like this: `foreach ($data as $value) { echo $value, "<br>"; }`.

Work with the foreach Loop

1 Create a new array named `$data`.

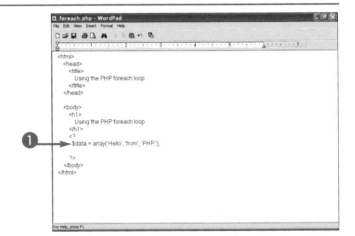

2 Create a `foreach` loop, naming the variable that holds the current element in the array each time through the loop `$value`.

③ Echo the current element in the array to the browser each time through the loop.

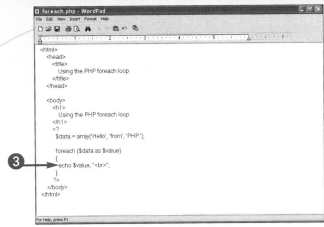

④ Open the PHP page.

The message "Hello from PHP" appears.

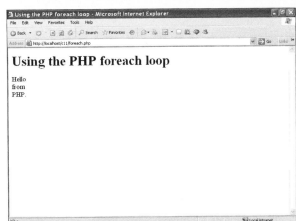

Apply It

There is another way to use the `foreach` loop in PHP. You can access both the key and the value of each element in an array if you specify `$key => $value`, not just `$value`, inside the `foreach` loop's parentheses. The following code displays `Allen, 58<br> Tina, 29<br>`, and `Mike, 98` in the browser.

Example:

```php
<?
    $scores = array();

    $scores["Allen"] = 56;
    $scores["Tina"] = 29;
    $scores["Mike"] = 98;

    foreach ($data as $key => $value)
    {
        echo $key, ", ", $value, "<br>";
    }

?>
```

Read Files on the Server

Y ou can use PHP to read from files on the server. That is one of the big advantages of working with server-side programming. You cannot read files from the hard drive using JavaScript, but using server-side scripting, you can read files on the server.

To read data from a file, you first must open that file, which you do with the fopen PHP function. For example, if you want to open a file named file.txt for reading, you can execute this statement: $fileHandle = fopen("file.txt", "r"). The file-opening process gives you a *file handle*, which corresponds to the open file, and which you use with all file operations from then on.

For example, to get a line of text from the open file, you can use the fgets PHP function, and you pass it the file handle corresponding to an open file. The fgets function

will return the data just read, and you can assign that return value to a variable this way: $data = fgets($fileHandle).

That statement, $data = fgets($fileHandle), reads a single line of text from an open text file. The next time you execute the same statement, fgets reads the next line of text from the file, and the next time, the next line of text from the file.

To determine when you have read to the end of the file, you can use the feof function, which returns true when you are at the end of the file. For example, feof($fileHandle) returns a value of true when you reach the end of the file from which you are reading. When you reach the end of the file, you can close the file with the fclose function like this: fclose($fileHandle).

Read Files on the Server

1 Open the file file.txt for reading.

File.txt contains the text "Hello from PHP" with each word on its own line.

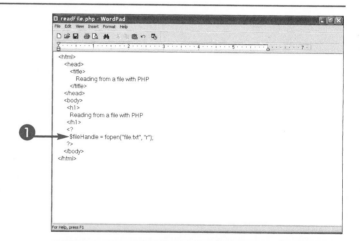

2 Read from the file and echo each line of text to the browser.

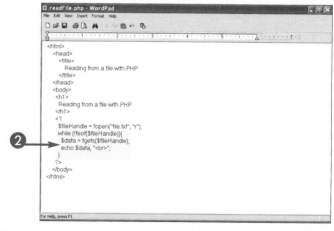

3 Close the open file.

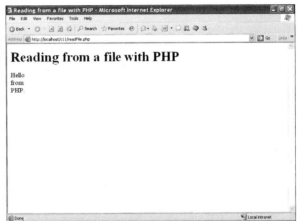

4 Open the PHP page in a browser.

The contents of the file are displayed.

Apply It

This code example opened a file for reading only, but if you open a file using `"r+"` instead of just `"r"`, you can both read and write to the file.

Example:
```
  <body>
<h1>
   Reading from a file with PHP
</h1>
<?
  $fileHandle = fopen("file.txt", "r+");

  while (!feof($fileHandle)){
    $data = fgets($fileHandle);
    echo $data, "<br>";
  }
  fclose($fileHandle);
?>
</body>
```

INDEX

INDEX

INDEX

INDEX